R. W. C. SHELFORD.

A NATURALIST IN BORNEO

BY THE LATE
ROBERT W. C. SHELFORD

OF EMMANUEL COLL. CAMBRIDGE, M.A.,
F.L.S., F.Z.S., F.E.S., LATE CURATOR
OF THE SARAWAK MUSEUM AND
ASSISTANT CURATOR OF THE
HOPE DEPARTMENT OF ZOOLOGY
OXFORD UNIVERSITY MUSEUM

EDITED WITH A BIOGRAPHICAL
INTRODUCTION BY
EDWARD B. POULTON

D.SC., LL.D., F.R.S., HOPE PROFESSOR
OF ZOOLOGY AND FELLOW OF
JESUS COLLEGE, OXFORD

SINGAPORE
OXFORD UNIVERSITY PRESS
OXFORD NEW YORK
1985

Oxford University Press

Oxford   New York   Toronto
Kuala Lumpur   Singapore   Hong Kong   Tokyo
Delhi   Bombay   Calcutta   Madras   Karachi
Nairobi   Dar es Salaam   Cape Town
Melbourne   Auckland

and associates in
Beirut   Berlin   Ibadan

OXFORD is a trademark of Oxford University Press

First published by T. Fisher Unwin Ltd., London, 1916
Second impression 1917
First issued in Oxford in Asia Paperbacks
and Oxford Paperbacks 1985

ISBN 0 19 582634 5

Printed in Malaysia by Peter Chong Printers Sdn. Bhd.
Published by Oxford University Press Pte. Ltd.,
10, New Industrial Road, Singapore 1953

To
MY WIFE

CONTENTS

ILLUSTRATIONS

The plates indicated by an asterisk have been wholly, those indicated by †
in part, reproduced, by kind consent of Dr. Charles Hose, from his and
the author's copyright photographs.

All plates of which the source is not indicated are from the author's
photographs or drawings.

ILLUSTRATIONS

xi

EDITOR'S INTRODUCTION—
BIOGRAPHICAL AND GENERAL

ROBERT WALTER CAMPBELL SHELFORD, the leading
authority on insects of the family *Blattidæ*, and a
naturalist of very broad interests, was born at Singapore on August 3, 1872—the son of a merchant who
was a member of the Legislative Council, and made
C.M.G. in recognition of his many public services.
There is no evidence that Shelford's strong taste for
natural history was inherited, and it did not appear in
any other member of his family. Prevented by a
tubercular hip-joint from taking part in the games and
ordinary outdoor pursuits of a boy and young man, his
active mind turned to observation, and he became a
naturalist. He was educated privately until he entered
King's College, London, and later Emmanuel College,
Cambridge. At this University, where he took a second
class in both parts of the Natural Science Tripos, he
received a solid foundation for the excellent zoological
and anthropological work of his mature years.

After taking his degree Shelford became, in 1895, a
Demonstrator in Biology, under Professor L. C. Miall,
F.R.S., at the Yorkshire College, Leeds. Two years
later he went to Borneo as Curator of the Sarawak
Museum, established by Rajah Brooke at Kuching.
During his seven years' tenure of this position he

availed himself to the full of the abundant opportunities for studying the animal life of the tropics, and of making observations in anthropology, a subject which always strongly attracted him. His fruitful labours in the increase and arrangement of the Sarawak Museum naturally led him to take a wide survey of the animal kingdom, and he soon began the study of mimicry, a subject which regards from one point of view a multitude of diverse forms, including insects of the most varied groups and their vertebrate enemies. He found Borneo a very rich and imperfectly explored field for the study of this subject, and before long he entered into a regular correspondence with me, sending large consignments of insects for investigation and determination. The result of his observations and work was the appearance in 1902 of an important paper in the *Proceedings of the Zoological Society of London* (p. 230). This valuable and interesting monograph is illustrated by five coloured plates showing Bornean mimetic insects of many widely separated groups. Our correspondence went on, and he continued to send the record of observations and specimens of great interest until his seven years' tenure of the Curatorship came to an end in 1905. Towards the close of this period he wrote to me saying that if it was impossible to provide a salary he must really come and work in the Hope Department at Oxford without one! Fortunately, at this moment, Magdalen College began to place an annual grant at the disposal of the University for the provision of extra assistance in the Departments, and it thus became possible to establish an Assistant-Curatorship, with a small income, augmented later on from the Common University Fund. Shelford accepted this position, and came to live at Oxford in the Autumn Term of 1905. After leaving Kuching, and before returning home by way of Japan, Vancouver, and the United States, he spent several weeks travelling in the Malay Archipelago, visiting many of the islands and making collections, which he presented to the Hope Department. Some of the specimens bear the record of interesting observations, throwing light on the difficult problems of adaptation and evolution in which he took so deep an interest.

On June 25, 1908, Shelford married Audrey Gurney, daughter of the Rev. Alfred Richardson, vicar of Combe Downe, Bath.

At Oxford Shelford worked with the greatest energy, at once beginning the study of the collection of Orthoptera in the Hope Department. He had always been especially interested in this order of insects, and was delighted when he found such an immense mass of material at Oxford, rich in types of the species described by the older authorities—Walker, Westwood, and Bates. He began with the *Blattidæ*, or Cockroaches. In the course of his work upon this group he worked through and named the species in all the great Continental collections, describing those that were new in a long series of valuable memoirs.

Numbers of duplicates were received, and, as a result of his labours, the Hope Department now contains by far the finest and best-arranged collection of *Blattidæ* in the world, including types or co-types of a large proportion of all the known species. Shelford then began to study other Orthopterous groups, especially the *Phasmidæ* and the *Mantidæ*. He was an indefatigable

worker, as will be realized by any naturalist who sees
what the Oxford *Blattidæ* became in four years from
the autumn of 1905 ; and it must be remembered that
all the time he was helping the Department in many
other ways, particularly in the arrangement and cata-
loguing of the library.

Of all the memoirs which he wrote Shelford was, I
think, most interested in that "On Mimicry amongst the
Blattidæ" (*P.Z.S.*, 1912, p. 358)—a subject on which he
had reflected and had been accumulating material for
some years ; one, moreover, which combines two departments of natural history—Systematics and Bionomics—
departments as wide apart as the poles, but affording
each other mutual support, and both equally dear to
him. It was also a special delight to him to show the
high interest and in many species the extreme beauty of
the universally despised cockroaches. It is a pathetic
circumstance that the publication of this long-looked-for
paper was nearly coincident with its author's death.

In addition to the researches on insects which formed
the main work of his life, Shelford was a keen and
enthusiastic student of Anthropology, as the concluding
chapters of this book will abundantly testify.

He was especially interested in Bornean Tatu, and
wrote, in conjunction with Dr. C. Hose, an important
memoir on the subject,[1] of which the greater part is
reproduced in Hose and McDougall's "Pagan Tribes of
Borneo," vol. ii. p. 245.

When three years old Shelford contracted tubercular

[1] *Journ. Anthrop. Inst.*, vol. XXXVI., n. Ser. IX (1906), pp. 60–91.

disease of the hip-joint as the result of a fall downstairs, and was condemned to spend many years on his back. A severe operation was performed when he was ten, and at thirteen he was able to leave home and reside with a tutor. He was left with a stiff joint, and from time to time suffered greatly from sciatica. During his residence in Sarawak a fall from a rickshaw produced an abscess, from which he entirely recovered. For the first four years in Oxford his leg seemed to give him no trouble except for occasional attacks of sciatica, and, in spite of his lameness, he used to find great pleasure in playing golf. He enjoyed life to the full, his interests were many-sided and keen, and he ran risks which, to one with his active, energetic temperament, were perhaps inevitable. An accidental slip, in April 1909, led to the recrudescence of the old disease, and to all the terrible suffering of his last illness. A too brief respite in its course enabled him to return for a time and carry on the old work for which he was always longing, and when he was compelled to give this up he still continued, until within a few months of the end, to help the Department in many ways. In a letter from Margate, where he had gone in the hope that the bracing air would restore his health, he wrote : " I am so pleased to think that I can do something at any rate, even if small, for the Hope Department." His death, on June 22, 1912, was mourned by a wide circle of friends interested in the most varied sides of natural history, all of whom felt not only a keen sense of personal loss, but also the loss to the science to which they had devoted their lives. We at Oxford retain grateful memories of pleasant years spent in hard work and constant friendly intercourse, and his efficient control of the Sarawak Museum and bright, attractive,

many-sided personality will be long remembered in
Borneo.[1]

This book was written by the author during his long
illness. Knowing the activity of his mind and his longing for work I suggested to him that the notes and
memories of seven years in Borneo would form the
foundation for a volume which, I was sure, would
interest many readers. So from time to time he worked
upon the manuscript, and it is pleasant to think of the
interest and brightness brought to weary hours by the
task. But the pain, which became worse and more
continuous towards the end, prevented him from completing his work, and the long delay in the appearance
of this volume is the direct result of the amount that had
still to be done before it was ready for publication. In
its preparation I have had much kind and efficient help
from several of the author's friends; but help that is to
be of any use is almost invariably help given by those
who have already too much to do and cannot render
it continuously. Delay has been inevitable. In the
somewhat arduous task I have received the greatest
encouragement and assistance from my friend Dr.
G. B. Longstaff, whose book, *Butterfly-hunting in Many
Lands*, had been carefully read in proof by Shelford—
another piece of work which brought interest and
pleasure to the hours of enforced idleness. Dr. Long
staff took the manuscript of the present volume with
him on a voyage to the Cape towards the end of 1913,
sending back the chapters as they were finished. Again,
in 1914 it accompanied me, on the memorable visit of

[1] This account of the author's life is founded on the present
writer's Obituary Notice in *The Zoologist* for July 1912.—E. B. P.

the British Association to Australia, by way of the Cape
and back by the Mediterranean. The manuscript has
also been read by Dr. Charles Hose and Mr. H. N.
Ridley, F.R.S., who, with their profound knowledge of
the East, have given me the greatest help. The proofs
have been carefully read, not only by these three, but
also by Mr. Henry Balfour, Dr. H. Eltringham, and
Commander J. J. Walker, all of whom have made sug-
gestions of great value and have helped in the detection
of printer's errors. Commander Walker also kindly
undertook the preparation of the index and Professor
Selwyn Image the design of the title-page. I have also
gratefully to acknowledge the assistance of friends, to
whom I have written for information on various doubtful
points—friends whose names will be found in footnotes
here and there throughout the book. Notes contributed
by any of the above-mentioned friends are indicated by
their initials.

The manuscript as I received it was very far from
ready for publication. Many references had been left
blank or incomplete, many names of species omitted.
In nearly all cases it has been possible to make good.
The author had written a list of chapters, with marks
indicating "rough draft" or "completed" or "almost
so." Chapters I (Mammals) and II (Birds) were marked
as rough drafts, III (Snakes) as completed, but all three
were carefully written in ink by Shelford himself, and he
had probably omitted to alter the sign for I and II.
Chapter IV, originally entitled "Other Reptiles and
Frogs," or alternatively, "Some other Reptiles and some
Amphibia," he had not marked at all, probably because
the frogs had been not even begun. The manuscript

was written at Shelford's dictation by his wife. I have altered the title to "Crocodiles, Turtles, and Tortoises," these being the actual reptiles treated of. Chapters V and VI, marked as completed, are in Shelford's handwriting. The original title of V was "Orthoptera," but as important sections of this order are omitted I have altered it to "Cockroaches, Mantises, and Stick-Insects." Chapter VI the author had called "Beetle Larvæ," but as there are also many observations on beetles themselves and their pupæ I have altered the title to "Beetles." Chapter VII is entirely, and VIII, except for a few pages, written in pencil, and both are marked as rough drafts. The title of VII was "Flies and Hymenoptera and Ants and Plants," but the manuscript treats only of the latter subject, which I have retained as the title. "Mimicry," the title of VIII, is unchanged. It should be borne in mind that this chapter, in its polemical style, was influenced by a controversy which had been going on at the time when it was written, a controversy in which the author was keenly interested. The dispute concerned the relative importance of two theories of mimicry. Their validity was not called in question—only the extent of ground which each was believed by its advocates to cover. The remaining chapters stand somewhat apart from the first eight, and the author had arranged them differently. Chapter IX was the "Natives of Borneo," which I have transferred to the end. It is marked as completed, and, like all the remaining chapters of this volume, written carefully in ink by the author himself. But it is a very brief account of a very large subject, and it is rendered still less complete by the entire omission of a chapter on "Their Arts and Crafts" which was to have followed it. I have therefore placed the author's Chapter IX at the end, leaving the other three, all concerned with expeditions, in the original order. The titles of IX and X are unchanged ; XI, without a title, I have called " Animal Life of the Shores : Visit to a Turtle Island." There is a little overlap at the beginning of Chapters X and XI, and it is possible that they were intended to form a single chapter, of which the opening paragraphs had been written twice. Allowing for the slight overlap I believe that the arrangement here adopted will be found convenient. The author's Introduction was never finished. The first sentence had been written by him carefully in ink, all the rest hurriedly in pencil, and the last page on both sides of the paper.

The illustrations were the chief difficulty. Only for Chapter I was there a full indication of what the author's intentions had been, and even as regards this the material for carrying them out was far from complete. I was confronted with a mass of drawings, finished and unfinished, named and unnamed, and with an immense number of negatives arranged in many series, but without numbers or any other indication by which to identify them with the names on their respective lists. However, by Dr. Hose's kind help, and by means of an album of Sarawak photographs, published in 1905 by him and the author, I was able to make out the subjects of a large number of the negatives. The unnamed drawings which had been prepared specially for the book were identified from internal evidence and by kind help which is acknowledged in the descriptions of the plates. In this way I have done my best to select suitable illustrations and to provide the descriptive legends. At the end of the volume I have added a selection of photographs of Kuching, the capital of Sarawak and the author's Bornean home, beginning with the Museum, the scene of his labours. These plates have been prepared from Shelford's negatives, and, indeed, the whole of the illustrations except the Frontispiece and Plate XIV have been selected from the material collected by him. Plate XIV, facing p. 169, has been very kindly lent by the South London Entomological and Natural History Society.

The slight changes that have been introduced are the direct result of the illness which prevented the author from completing his task. Allowing for this, I hope and believe that the book is what he would have wished it to be. The volume opens with the chapters on the natural history of the island. It will be realized by the reader that the author's knowledge of the living animals of Borneo was very wide and very intimate, and that these chapters contain the most significant contributions to learning that are to be found in the work. The concluding chapters are full of charm, breathing the spirit of living Nature and of man in the tropics, and revealing the author as the keen and loving observer of both.

E. B. P.

AUTHOR'S [UNFINISHED] INTRODUCTION

THIS book is the veriest hotch-potch of notes and observations plucked from my journals and my memory, together with a few extracts from scientific periodicals. I have striven to weld the mass into a continuous and symmetrical whole, but can hardly flatter myself that I have succeeded. It appears to me that there is a small but increasing section of the reading public that describes itself as taking an interest in Natural History, and it is to this section that I appeal for a verdict on the merits of the book. This public reads popular works on Natural History but not scientific journals, and yet in the volumes of the latter are concealed amid a mass of technical and arid detail facts and observations of the greatest interest to all lovers of Nature. I have not hesitated to disinter these facts whenever they relate to Bornean Natural History and to interpolate them in my own story, but I have been careful to acknowledge the sources from which they are drawn, and I trust that by dressing them up for popular consumption I have neither spoilt nor altered their flavour. A comprehensive work dealing with the realm of Nature in Borneo is not the labour of one man but of many, not the outcome of observation extending over seven years but over seventy times seven, and this book pretends to be little more than a presenta-

tion of the facts and of the observations gleaned by the
writer during a seven years' sojourn in Sarawak. If my
readers in their reading can taste one-tenth of the
pleasure which I experienced in making my observations
and in setting them forth, I shall feel well rewarded.

For seven years I occupied the post of Curator of the
Museum at Kuching, Sarawak, and I would fain pay a
small tribute to the delights of this appointment. The
pay was adequate ; I was granted abundant opportunities
to visit other parts of the State for making collections ;
there was an entire absence of tedious officialism and
red-tape, for all the Museum accounts were kept at
the Treasury. The Museum was well stocked, and yet
acquisitions to it were always welcome, as the collections
were by no means complete. The Rajah had wisely
ordered that the Museum should be confined to the
fauna, flora, and ethnography of Borneo, and as this rule
was strictly adhered to, the collections did not become
unwieldy, and there was no great difficulty in the determination of species. The officials of the Sarawak
Government vied with each other in presenting
specimens, so that a constant stream of material flowed
into the Museum. In fact there never was a museum
where the accessions were obtained at so small a cost,
and as the Museum staff was composed of a Chinese
clerk, Malay attendants, and Dayak hunters, the wages
bill was small. The Museum to-day contains the most
complete collections illustrating the fauna, flora, and
ethnography of Borneo, and its annual upkeep amounts
to under £750 [Note 1, p. 312]. A museum in the tropics
has a treble function : it provides for the inhabitants
of the country a constant source of interest ; it makes
possible an increase in the knowledge of the fauna, flora,

and ethnography of the country ; and it is a centre of
scientific research. In establishing and maintaining the
Museum at Kuching, H.H. the Rajah of Sarawak has
deserved well of science. Although foreign countries
have been quick in expressing gratitude for the services
he has rendered to naturalists visiting his country,
the debt has never been acknowledged by a single
English learned society.

Sarawak, as most people know, is a large tract of
territory in Borneo, owned and ruled by the Rajah,
Sir Charles Brooke, G.C.M.G., second of his line.
This independent State is quietly prosperous, and, since
it is very much off the track of the globe-trotting tourist,
it is never much in the public eye. The annual revenue
now amounts to over 1,000,000 Straits dollars, a
proportion of which is derived from a poll-tax of two
dollars levied on every adult male. The State of Sarawak
is parcelled out into districts, each of which is placed
under the charge of one or more English officers known
as Residents. At headquarters is a fort where the
Resident lives, with a force of Malay police or of Dayak
soldiers under his command. When the time for collecting the tax arrives the natives in the immediate vicinity
of the forts pay their dollars directly into the State coffers,
but visits must be paid to the outlying districts in order
to receive the sums due to the Government. The Rajah
believes—and believes justly—that the success of his rule
over the naturally turbulent and warlike tribes that make
up the bulk of the Sarawak population is due to the
personal influence exerted by himself and his officers.
The *force majeure* is rarely called into activity, because
the relations between rulers and ruled are for the most
part friendly and even cordial. Such results can only be

established by constant intercourse, and the annual tax-collecting visits are utilized as opportunities to cultivate friendly relations with new-comers to a district, to renew old friendships, and to inquire into grievances. It may seem strange to European minds that tax-collectors are welcome visitors, but the natives of Sarawak consider the blessings of peace and security as cheaply purchased for an annual poll-tax, whilst the coming of a white man to an inland village is an excitement that affords topics of conversation for weeks after his departure.

Nearly the whole of Sarawak is smothered in dense and luxuriant jungles, and as there are no roads beyond the purlieus of the towns and stations, the rivers serve as the highways. Unlike British North Borneo, Sarawak is blessed with rivers that are navigable for miles inland, and it is by the rivers that the Government officer journeys into the " back blocks " of his district. The lower reaches of these Bornean rivers are monotonous in the extreme ; mangroves and Nipa-palms fringe their sides for mile after mile, and the banks themselves at low tide are uninviting stretches of black viscid mud. Fortunate is that officer who has at his disposal a steam-launch to convey him swiftly regardless of tide over the first weary miles. Failing a launch, he must install himself in a long, narrow canoe roofed with a thatch of palm-leaf, and manned by a crew of twenty to thirty sturdy Malays : here he must stay for hour after hour, tying up to some riverside hut when the tide is against him, waking the drowsy crew in the middle of the night when it turns. And yet to one who has not to make the voyage too often there is a charm about this method of travel which is not to be found in the rapid transport of the modern steam-launch. The traveller lies at his ease on a mattress on the floor of his boat; before him are his crew, their backs swinging rhythmically and untiringly to the paddle-strokes. Framed in the opening to his covering of palm-leaf is the brilliant blue of the tropical sky, a kite or osprey perhaps soaring in the empyrean or sweeping in grand curves out of the field of vision : the brown turbid water slides past unceasingly, and the regular chunking of the paddles against the boat's gunwale and the splash of the water upon the blades has an indescribably soothing and even soporific effect. At intervals the bowman or steersman gives a shout, and the long, rhythmic swing is changed instantaneously into a short, digging stroke that makes the boat quiver from stem to stern and propels her with lifting jerks through the water, until gradually the spurt dies down and the old steady stroke is resumed.

THE PRINCIPAL CONTRACTIONS USED IN THE FOOTNOTES ARE AS FOLLOWS :—

Ann. Mag. Nat. Hist.—Annals and Magazine of Natural History.

Journ. Anthrop. Inst.—Journal of the [Royal] Anthropological Institute.

Journ. Roy. As. Soc. S. Br.—Journal of the Straits Branch of the Royal Asiatic Society.

Linn. Soc.—Linnean Society of London.

P.Z.S.—Proceedings of the Zoological Society of London.

Proc. Ent. Soc.—Proceedings of the Entomological Society of London.

Trans. Ent. Soc.—Transactions of the Entomological Society of London.

Other contractions can be made out from elements in the above, or are sufficiently obvious.

AUTHORSHIP OF THE NOTES.

Unsigned notes, or occasionally signed R. S., are by the author.

Notes signed H. B. are by H. Balfour.

Notes signed C. H. are by C. Hose.

Notes signed G. B. L. are by G. B. Longstaff.

Notes signed E. B. P. are by E. B. Poulton.

Notes signed H. N. R. are by H. N. Ridley.

A NATURALIST IN BORNEO

CHAPTER I

MAMMALS

THE most interesting mammal in the island of Borneo is, undoubtedly, the large Anthropoid Ape, *Simia satyrus*,[1] for both in anatomy and habits it shows so many resemblances to the highest type of creation, man himself, that we are justified in believing both man and ape to have sprung from a common stock in "dim ages past." The trivial names whereby this ape is known to European zoologists, Orang, Orang-Utan and Orang Utang or Outang, are rather unfortunate, for the first is Malay for "man," the second means "man of

[1] Changes of the scientific names of animals, especially mammals, have been so frequent and numerous during the past ten years, that only specialists are able to recognize the species under their new names. The practice reached the height of absurdity when *Simia satyrus* was solemnly re-named *Pongo pygmæus*. By this ridiculous application of a Bantu negro name for the Chimpanzee to a Malayan ape a storm of long-suppressed protest was raised, and a committee of zoologists is now deciding what names of animals are to remain unaltered. It was high time that such a step should be taken, for who knows if Dr. Smellfungus and Professor Dryasdust will not proclaim that the name *Homo sapiens* should be altered? But perhaps *sapiens is* a misnomer when applied to these pedants.

2

the woods," and the third means "debtor." Malays never think of applying any of these names to the ape; they have their own name for it—Maias, and by this name the animal will be styled in this chapter.

The Maias is fortunately still abundant in Sarawak, but it is very local in its distribution, being found only up the Simunjan, Batang Lupar, and Rejang Rivers. A specimen was once recorded from the upper waters of the Sarawak River, but it had evidently strayed from its usual "beat," and soon disappeared. Some years ago an American naturalist visited the Simunjan River and slaughtered so many Maias that the Rajah of Sarawak wisely issued an order in which the number of specimens that could be killed by one collector was strictly limited. The species at present is confined to Borneo and Sumatra, but there are traditions in the Malay Peninsula, where it is known as Mawas, of its occurrence there in times past.

When I left England for Sarawak a distinguished anthropologist of my acquaintance asked me to investigate the habits of the Maias. "I want to know how many wives he keeps," said my friend, "and how he treats them." With the best will in the world I was unable to settle these knotty points. The Maias is essentially an arboreal creature, rarely coming down to the ground except to drink, and its haunts are situated, for the most part, in swampy and marshy land, through which the eager investigator can only laboriously make his way, whilst the object of his search progresses at a fair pace in the tree-tops: moreover, considering its size, the Maias is remarkably inconspicuous in its natural surroundings. Until men can acquire arboreal habits it seems likely that the

Nest (indicated by arrow) of the Maias, on the Asan River, Rejang District, Sarawak. (From a photograph taken about 1904 by Dr. C. Hose.)

Plate II.

To face p. 3.

domestic arrangements of the ape will remain undiscovered.

The Maias is a great traveller, and I have never heard
of one haunting a small area for any length of time.
As they are fruit-eaters it is necessary for them to cover
a good deal of ground in order to find suitable and
sufficient food, and consequently unlike less dainty
animals they are continually on the move.

At night they make a kind of nest by pulling and
bending down small branches to form a little platform
in the fork of a bough. The platform is remarkably
small, often not much bigger than a rook's nest and
never exceeding 4½ feet in diameter; it is constructed
in comparatively small trees.

When the Maias goes to rest, it lies flat on its back
on its nest and holds like grim death with hands and
feet to the branches in the fork of which the nest lies;
and so it passes the night, half supported by the frail
platform, half suspended by the hands and feet, whose
grip is secure even in the deepest slumber. A young
Maias that I kept as a pet for many months always
slept in an empty room in my house : the only article
of furniture in this room was an iron bedstead, and on
to the steel laths of this the ape would solemnly climb
every evening at about 6.30 ; he invariably sprawled on
the flat of his back, pulled over his head and chest a
piece of sacking with which he was provided, and with
hands and feet got a good grip on the posts or frame
of the bed. In a few minutes he would be asleep, and
his snoring was so loud that it could be heard nearly
all over house.

If, in the daytime, this young ape desired to rest in
a tree, he would construct a rough attempt at a platform,

and lie on this, hanging to the branches with hands and feet and swinging in the breeze for an hour or so at a time. It is easy now to account for the fact that the Maias makes its sleeping quarters amongst slender branches in the tree-tops; if the nest were made in the fork of some huge bough the ape would have nothing to grasp when asleep; moreover, in the lower levels of the tree there would be a dearth of branches suitable for the construction of a sleeping platform, and these would have to be carried from elsewhere. The Maias evidently dislikes sleeping at too great a height above the ground, for the nests are never found in the tops of lofty forest giants, but in trees of quite a moderate size and height, say 30 to 40 feet high. The natives assert that the female Maias, when about to give birth to a young one, makes a very large platform amongst big branches and stays on it for several days; but I cannot vouch for the truth of this statement.

The Maias is a very harmless creature as a rule, but it has been known to attack man when enraged. Wallace, in his *Malay Archipelago*, cites an instance, and more recently there was an account in the *Sarawak Gazette* of one of these apes descending from a Durian-tree, where it was feasting on the fruit, and making a furious onslaught on a Dayak who was trying to drive it away from its plunder. As the Maias is endowed with colossal strength, the unfortunate native was seriously injured, and would have been killed if his friends had not come to the rescue and beaten off his assailant.

As a pet a young Maias is unrivalled; it is cleanly, affectionate, extremely intelligent and amusing. One that I kept for some months used to throw itself about and scream like a naughty child if it was teased, and

A young Maias from Sadong, near Kuching. (Photographed in an orange-tree by Dr. C. Hose, at Marudi, Baram District, Sarawak, about 1900.)

Plate III.

To face p. 4.

if it was left out in the rain would yell until it was brought under shelter; but as a rule the Maias is a very silent animal, only grunting a little in a fretful manner occasionally. They are very sedate and deliberate in their movements, even when feeding. If presented with a fruit or some other article of food that is new to its experience, the Maias will carefully scrutinize and smell the morsel, a small bite will be taken, and the fragment of food will be rolled round and round inside the mouth; then the lower lip will be shot out to its utmost extent with the piece of food on it, and the ape will squint down his nose in the most ludicrous manner, as if to see how the food is getting on during the process of mastication.

The simian characteristics of the human baby have been remarked frequently enough; one little point has, however, escaped notice. The young Maias when it picks up a very small object, such as a pea or pellet of bread, does so, not with the tips of the thumb and first finger, but pushes the object with the ball of the thumb against the side of the proximal phalanx of the first finger, all the fingers being flexed, and, so holding it, lifts it up. A young baby nearly always acts in the same way when trying to pick up a small object.

The young Maias is quite unable to swim, and if thrown into deep water, flounders about in the most helpless manner and soon sinks below the surface; I doubt if the adults are any more adept at swimming than their young.

The other anthropoid ape of Borneo is the Gibbon. There seems to be some doubt as to whether the different varieties in the island are to be regarded as distinct species or merely as local races, but the following remarks apply to a uniformly grey form, known as *Hylobates mülleri*, which is common throughout the greater part of Sarawak. The Gibbons go about in large herds; their cry is extremely musical, and in the early morning the jungle fairly rings with it. I know no more joyous sound in nature than the delightful bubbling shouts of these creatures, and he must be indeed a confirmed slug-a-bed who can resist their call to be up and doing in the most delicious hours of the tropical day. The Malay and Kayan names for the Gibbon—Wa-wa and Wok—are onomatopœic in that they represent two notes of the series of whistles and hoots that the animals utter. Forbes, in his *Naturalist's Wanderings in the Eastern Archipelago*, has endeavoured to represent graphically the cry of the Gibbon, but I know of no instrument on which the cry can be well imitated except a simple thing made by the Kayans out of a bamboo-joint and known as Buloh Wok; with this the cries can be imitated with such great exactitude that the apes are often decoyed within a few yards of the performer.

Gibbons make excellent pets, and are kept by natives as well as by Europeans. The manner in which they can swing from rafter to rafter in a native house gives some idea of their perfect adaptation to an arboreal life—a life for which they are much better adapted than are the larger and heavier Maias, Chimpanzee, and Gorilla. On the ground the Gibbon can progress in an erect posture, but the arms are always carried aloft, apparently to maintain the balance, and the gait is rather staggering and uncertain. In intelligence the Gibbon ranks far below the other anthropoids, and its gymnastic proclivities make it a very disturbing captive in a European's house.

A careful examination of the hand of a Gibbon shows that in every way it is beautifully adapted for gripping the branches of trees. It is very long in comparison to its width, owing to the great development of the metacarpals and phalanges. The thumb is very short and is scarcely opposable, in fact not nearly to the same extent as is the big toe.[1] Nearly all the creases or lines, as a palmistry expert would call them, are for the most part straight up and down, or transverse, whereas these lines in the human palm are more or less oblique. In the human hand the thumb can be placed in opposition to each of the fingers, and the movements of both thumbs and fingers are very complex, but in the Gibbon the fingers are modified almost entirely for gripping, and can do little but bend and unbend. The fingers of the Gibbon on their palmar aspect are very flat, and a long deep crease runs down the middle of each. All the fine lines of the human palm and fingers are much coarser in the ape, so that a better grip is maintained with this roughened surface, and on the fingers these coarse lines are arranged in a chevron-like way converging on the middle crease, not unlike the chevron lines on the driving wheels of traction engines ; such lines are expressly designed to prevent slipping, an object which is not attained so well if the lines are directly transverse. Although an examination of the Gibbon's hand shows that it is wonderfully adapted for gripping, we also learn from it how much man owes his position at the very summit of the animal kingdom to the adaptation of his hand

[1] Cf. Fitzwilliams, *Ann. Mag. Nat. Hist.* (7 *Ser.*), XX. (1907), p. 155

to all sorts of purposes. The great anatomist, Goodsir, has pointed out that while the hand of an ape is well fitted to grasp a cylindrical object like the branch of a tree, it is unable to grasp a spherical object properly.

I found it very interesting to compare the methods of drinking adopted by the Maias, the Gibbon, and the common Macaque of Borneo. The first, if offered drink in a bowl placed on the ground before it, will generally bend down and drink out of the bowl without handling it. The Macaque lifts the bowl up, if not too heavy, with both hands and drinks out of it very much as a man would drink. The Gibbon dips one hand into the bowl and then, throwing the head back, sucks the moisture off the hair on the back of the hand ; it is a very characteristic action, and it is repeated again and again until the thirst is satisfied.

There are two common Macaques in Borneo, and one rare species, *Macacus arctoides*, which I have never seen either alive or dead. *Macacus nemestrinus*, the pig-tailed Macaque, or Brok of the Malays, is a highly intelligent animal, and Malays train them to pick coconuts. The modus operandi is as follows :—A cord is fastened round the monkey's waist, and it is led to a coconut palm which it rapidly climbs, it then lays hold of a nut, and if the.owner judges the nut to be ripe for plucking he shouts to the monkey, which then twists the nut round and round till the stalk is broken and lets it fall to the ground ; if the monkey catches hold of an unripe nut, the owner tugs the cord and the monkey tries another. I have seen a Brok act as a very efficient fruit-picker, although the use of the cord was dispensed with altogether, the monkey being guided by the tones and inflections of his master's voice.

The males of this species are very savage, and a
friend of mine, who hunted all sorts and conditions of
jungle animals with a pack of mongrel dogs, told me
that the male Brok was the most dangerous of all to
tackle ; when at bay they stand with their backs to a
tree, and seizing the dogs with hands or feet slash and
tear them with their terrible canine teeth, sometimes
almost disembowelling them. The Brok goes about in
droves, a big male leading ; but often solitary males are
to be found, and these, I expect, have been driven from
the leadership of their droves by younger and more
powerful rivals. It must be these solitary males only,
or " Brok tunggal " as the Malays call them, which can
be hunted by dogs, for I do not suppose that any pack
could deal with a drove.

M. nemestrinus exhibits a peculiarity in the fine lines
on the palmar aspect of the finger-tips which I have not
observed in any other species ; the lines, which are
arranged in simple loops and not in the complicated
patterns characteristic of the human finger, are connected here and there by little transverse bridges.

As a pet the Brok is distinctly amusing, but it must
be kept in a cage, or chained up, for if allowed full
liberty it is, with its congerer, *M. cynomolgus*, the most
wantonly destructive animal of my acquaintance. It
lives very well in captivity, but will not breed with
females of its own species, though hybrids between
the Brok and *M. cynomolgus* have been produced in
menageries more than once. A captive, Brok spends a
great deal of time in making most hideous grimaces, and
in adopting ludicrous attitudes ; it does this apparently
for its own amusement. Mr. H. N. Ridley [1] relates of

[1] *Journ. Roy. As. Soc. S. Br.*, No. 46 (1906), p. 143.

one in the zoological collection at the Botanic Gardens in Singapore, that it would put one hind-leg over its neck and beat it on the ground, pretending that it could not get it back again to the normal position. Another, that I kept in captivity for many months, would stand on one leg, seize this leg just above the knee with both hands and the disengaged foot, and then bend the body up and down, "mopping and mowing" all the time like an old witch.

The Crab-eating Macaque, *M. cynomolgus*, is undoubtedly the commonest monkey in Borneo ; it is smaller, noisier, and more active than the Brok, and has a long tail. The native name, Kra, is onomatopœic, and represents fairly well · the grating cry that the monkey utters when alarmed or defiant. This species has, as a matter of fact, quite an extensive vocabulary, including a shrill squeal of terror, a querulous sort of sound really indicative of pleasure, a smacking of the lips also showing pleasure, and a grunt of anger. Mr. Ridley asserts that it is actually possible to distinguish between the alarm note of this monkey for a tiger and that for a man.

The trivial English name of the species is derived from its habit of hunting for crabs on river-banks and even on the sea-shore ; I have often seen them so engaged at the mouth of the Sarawak River at low-tide in some numbers hunting for little crabs of the genus *Sesarma*, and occasionally diving into the water. They fall frequently victims to the watchful crocodile. The Crab-eating Macaques are almost omnivorous, and their tastes in insect-food are catholic, as I found when experimenting on some with the intention of finding out the relative palatability of certain insects.

According to Mr. Ridley [1] this species goes about in
groups consisting of two or more adult males, some
younger males and several females; these family groups
are very jealous, and a new member is not admitted
without a severe fight. "The leading monkey having
established his position, takes his food first, and has his
selection of the females first. The other males he drives
away should they presume to attempt to usurp his rights.
In processions from one place to the other he always
comes last, but if one of the younger monkeys gets into
a dangerous position or is attacked he always runs to
its rescue, and drives off the enemy, and the other big
males often assist him if necessary. The wild monkeys
always sleep in particular trees, those with bare branches
and very lofty, and towards evening they may be seen
slowly moving along, stopping here and there to eat,
till they reach the sleeping place about sundown, they
then settle down for the night, sitting usually in pairs
or singly on the bare boughs. The same tree is occupied
every evening for weeks at a time, and whereever they
are in the evening they make for the same spot. They
never sleep in a bushy tree, probably for fear of being
surprised at night by snakes. Young monkeys are
always born in the early hours of the morning before
daylight, as almost if not all mammals are, and are born
in the boughs, or if in a cage on the perch; never I
believe on the ground. In cases of difficult parturition
at least, the other females act as accoucheuses, with
sometimes disastrous results to the baby. . . . The K'ra
breeds very easily in captivity, the females producing one
at a time about once a year. The young one when born
has black hair which gets lighter colored with age."

[1] *Journ. Roy. As. Soc. S. Br.*, No. 46 (1906), p. 142.

All the other monkeys of Borneo belong to the *Semnopithecinæ*, and fall into two genera—*Nasalis* and *Semnopithecus*.[1] Of the former genus only one species has been found, *Nasalis larvatus*, and it is not known to occur elsewhere. The adult male has a large fleshy nose, which droops at the end almost over the mouth, but in the young male and in the female the nose is smaller and is distinctly *retroussé*. This is not the only monkey in the world with a well-marked nose, for there are two species of *Rhinopithecus* from China with sharply upturned noses. The Malay name for *Nasalis* is "Orang Blanda," or "Dutchman," a poor compliment to our friends across the water. "Blanda" is, however, certainly used by Malays very often as an adjective signifying inferiority or coarseness, in the same way as we prefix the word "horse" to certain words. Just as we talk of "horse-chestnuts" and "horse-radish" so do the Malays call the "Soursop" *Anona muricata* [Note 2, p. 312], which is rather like, but much inferior to, the true Durian, "Durian Blanda." [2]

The *Nasalis* lives in small troops in trees growing in swampy lands, and it feeds almost entirely on the fruit and young shoots of the "Pedada," *Sonneratia lanceolata*. As it is well known that all the *Semnopithecinæ* have complex ruminating stomachs, and are purely herbivorous in their diet, I was surprised to see, in the Field

[1] Now known, I believe, as *Presbytes*.
[2] The word "blanda" certainly means "foreign," being simply a corruption of "Hollander." I should suggest that the long-nosed ape is called "Orang Blanda" directly from its nose being like that of a Dutchman (or European foreigner). In Timor Laut the native, when he wants to carve a Dutchman, gives him a peaked hat and a very sharp-pointed nose, the latter being a distinctive character of the carving.—H. N. R.

Columbian Museum at Chicago some years ago, a mounted group of *Nasalis*, shown as robbing a wood-pecker's nest and tearing the mother-bird to pieces; it is to be hoped that this "zoological inexactitude" has by now been rectified. The animal does not flourish in captivity, as it is difficult to obtain the proper food in sufficient quantity. Captain Stanley Flower, Director of the Ghizeh Zoological Gardens at Cairo managed to keep a young male alive for some months, but even this moderate success has not been repeated [Note 3, p. 312]. The cry of the adult male is a sort of snorting bark, and in the production of it the large fleshy nose undoubtedly plays a part.

The species of *Semnopithecus* are all timid, gentle creatures, very unlike the boisterous and easily tamed Macaques. They are much more arboreal than the Macaques, and they feed entirely on leaves, fruits, and flowers. A specimen of *S. cristatus* that I kept for some time as a pet throve fairly well on a diet of *Hibiscus* flowers; this is a pretty grey species with the native onomatopoeic name of Bigit. *S. femoralis*, a black species, and *S. rubicundus*, a russet-coloured species, are fairly common, and go about in small troops of seven or eight. There are several other species, but attention need only be called to *S. hosei*, a handsome black-and-white monkey, from which are obtained the bezoar stones or gall-concretions so highly prized by the Chinese for their medicinal qualities.

The Lemurs are represented in Borneo by two species—*Nycticebus tardigradus* and *Tarsius spectrum*. The former of these, the Slow Loris, is a small arboreal animal with no tail and large eyes. In disposition they are very surly, and I never succeeded in taming them, though I have kept many in captivity. They spend the greater part of the day huddled up in a ball with the head bent down between the thighs and covered by the arms; if roused from slumber the head is slowly raised, a querulous grunt uttered, and the somnolent attitude is again resumed. All their movements during the day-time are very slow and deliberate, but at night they wake up, and then can move at a fairly rapid rate. They feed very largely on insects, but thrive well in captivity on fruit with a little raw meat. They must be handled with caution, for they are very fierce, and the bite of a newly captured specimen, which has been living mainly on an insect diet, is very poisonous, producing a nasty suppurating wound.

On account of its very peculiar appearance the Slow Loris is considered by the Malays to possess magical properties, and they have many quaint recipes for employing various parts of its body for medicinal and magical purposes.[1] A few of these may be quoted here.

"The right eye dried and ground to powder and mixed with human or goat's milk and some sweet oil may be used as an eye-ointment which will make dim sight bright by the will of God. The left eye ground fine and mixed with rose water, honey and camphor (*Sumatran*) can be used as an eye ointment or eaten with 'sirih' leaf, the nerves of which meet together causes all who look on us to love us, and if given to a wild beast it will become tame. . . . If its backbone is buried beneath the door of the house we can prevent thieves from entering. If the bone of its left leg be kept in the mouth during a conversation with a rajah,

[1] H. N. Ridley, *Journ. Roy. As. Soc. S. Br.*, No. 34 (1900), pp. 31-34.

The Bornean Lemur, the Tarsier, *Tarsius spectrum*. (Photographed from life by the author, at Kuching.)

Plate IV.

To face p. 15.

it will prevent his doing any acts of tyranny to us,
and if we cook it with oil of snake or tiger or olive
oil and rub it on the feet of a weak person, it will
strengthen him. . . . If the liver be dried and a piece
taken and rubbed up and given to a woman to eat it will
produce in her feelings of love towards us." Its tears,
when applied to human eyeballs, are supposed to impart
such clearness of sight that ghosts become visible. Its
tears can be induced to flow by taking the Loris amongst
a herd of cows, whereupon it will weep copiously;
another plan, which sounds more reasonable, is to
wrap the animal in a cloth and throw pepper in its
eyes.

Singular in appearance as is the Slow Loris, it is
less remarkable than the other Bornean Lemur, *Tarsius
spectrum.* The Tarsier is the most curious little ghoul
of an animal imaginable, and as no specimen has ever
reached a European menagerie, the naturalist, when he
first encounters the animal in its native land cannot
fail to be fascinated by its quaintly unfamiliar aspect.
The body, which is clothed in a soft brown fur, is
about $5\frac{1}{2}$ inches long; the tail is 6 inches in length
and is quite naked except for a tuft of sparse hairs at
the extremity. The head is almost globular and the eyes
are enormous. The large ears stand well out from the
head and are very mobile and sensitive; in repose the
ear-conchs are wrinkled and partly contracted in transverse folds, but on the slightest noise they are pricked
forward and all traces of wrinkles disappear. The muzzle
is quite short, and the lips are rather thick and fleshy,
giving the animal a ludicrously smug expression, which
is intensified during moments of content and well-being.
I have occasionally been asked by friends to admire

the "smile" of a favourite horse or dog, but after a considerable experience of animals I can safely say that none can smile like the Tarsier.

In proportion to the body the hind-legs are very long, and consequently the Tarsier is able to make prodigious leaps. But perhaps the most remarkable features in its anatomy are the hands and feet; these are naked except for a little down on the back of the metacarpals and metatarsals; both fingers and toes are extremely long and slender, terminating in large flattened discs like the suctorial discs of a tree-frog. The animal exhibits another froglike feature in the great length of the ankle-joint. As in the Amphibia, the astragalus and calcaneum (the two ankle-bones which articulate with the shin-bones) are slender and produced. By means of its sucking discs the Tarsier can cling quite well to vertical surfaces, if they are not too smooth. The nails of all the fingers and of all the toes, except the second and third, are very small, somewhat triangular in shape, and embedded in the fleshy discs, but on the second and third toes the nails are erect claws. The big toe is opposable, but the thumb is not. If the under surfaces of the finger- and toe-discs are examined with a lens, it will be seen that they are traversed by fine longitudinal and parallel lines; similar lines, curiously enough, are present on the upper surface of the discs, but here they are con-centrically arranged. The skin covering the palmar surface of the fingers and toes is broken up by deep creases into numerous little blocks, more or less cubical in shape, and each of these blocks has its own system of fine lines, oblique, longitudinal, or transverse. This arrangement is, I think, an adaptation enabling the

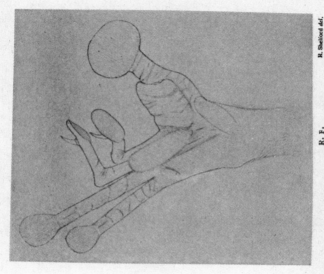

L. H.

D.

R. F.

Right foot (R. F.), and left hand (L. H.), of the Tarsier, *Tarsius spectrum*, showing the clinging discs, with the fine lines on them, as well as on the sole and palm, which enable the animal to grasp its prey. Also the upper surface of a disc (D.) with its concentric lines and the small triangular nail, seen from above. (From the author's drawings.)

Plate V.

Tarsier to hold securely the insects on which it feeds, for the palmar surface is roughened by its division into innumerable little prominences, and the prominences themselves are grooved by the lines which, as I have said, run in all directions, on one prominence transversely, on another obliquely, and so on.

I used to feed a captive Tarsier on cockroaches and grasshoppers, and I observed that almost invariably the little beast would spring on to its prey, grab it in one or both hands, crunching it badly in the process, and would then bite off all the parts of the insect that protruded from its fist. Even the slipperiest cockroach could not make its escape once seized in those long, slender fingers. On the palms of the hands and soles of the feet occur large pads, the position of which is shown in the figures; the surface of these pads is grooved with lines, which I expect play a useful part in grasping and clinging actions. The tail is not prehensile, but its under surface is distinctly sticky, and no doubt this helps the animal to cling to vertical surfaces. Down the back of the thigh runs a strip of skin devoid of fur, looking strangely like the apterium of a bird.

The Dayaks assert of the Tarsier that it can turn its head right round in a complete circle; this is an exaggerated statement of the fact that the animal can turn its head through half a circle; that is to say, if it is clinging to a vertical surface it can, without moving its position, look straight into the face of an observer standing directly behind it.

During the day the Tarsier rests almost motionless, clinging to some support, the knees drawn up almost to the face, the eyes half closed, with their pupils con-

tracted to mere slits. But in the evening it wakes up
and commences its hunt for food, which consists
entirely of insects. One was seen hunting for insects
in the pitchers of Nepenthes, fishing out and devouring with evident gusto the drowned beetles and flies
which had fallen into the water that always accumulates
in these curious vegetable insect traps.

The only sound that I have ever heard the Tarsier
utter is a little plaintive squeak. The creatures do not
flourish in captivity, and it always was a source of
annoyance to me that while the surly, cross-grained,
and comparatively uninteresting *Nycticebus* would
support captivity for months or even years, the docile
and highly interesting Tarsier would die in a few weeks
in spite of every care taken to secure a varied and
ample diet. The animal has a very characteristic odour,
which I can only describe as being a pleasant mouse-
like smell, if such an apparent contradiction in terms
can be realized. Both *Nycticebus* and *Tarsius* bear but
a single young one at a time; the latter has been seen
carrying her baby in her mouth, just as a cat carries
her kitten.

The Bats are represented in Borneo by forty-six
species belonging to twenty genera, but it cannot be
said that the habits of any single species are well
known.

The big Fruit-Bats, *Pteropus edulis*, are as familiar a
feature of a Bornean landscape at evening as are in
England the rooks winging their way home to roost;
the bats, however, are on their way to some fruit-trees
where they will feed all night, yelling and wrangling
the while like all the cats of Kilkenny. During the
day they hang in numbers from the branches of trees,

often at a considerable distance from the last feeding-place, and they look like bunches of some grotesque fruit. In Java these bats are such a pest that most of the cultivated fruit is plucked before it is properly ripe in order to save it from their attacks. They bite very fiercely, but though they have a disagreeable odour the flesh is white and quite palatable. The lesser Fruit-Bats of the genus *Cynopterus* are also common, and are even more voracious than *Pteropus*; a single bat will think nothing of devouring far more than its own weight in bananas in one night.

The external parasites of bats are very remarkable, and quite unlike those which infest other mammals. Fleas are rarely, if ever, found on bats, but their place is taken by those strange apterous flies, the *Nycteribiidæ* and the *Streblidæ*. The pupæ of some fly, not belonging to either of these families, have been found embedded in the wing membranes of a species of *Hipposiderus*, one of the Indo-Malayan insectivorous genera. But most remarkable of all is the strange earwig *Arixenia esau* which lives in the brood-pouches of a large Bornean bat, *Cheiromeles torquatus*.

The bat itself is a peculiar-looking creature, almost entirely devoid of hair and with thick, leathery wings, the membrane of which is attached in such a way to the sides of the body, upper arm, and thigh, that a big pouch is formed under the armpits extending to the back of the shoulders and sides of the chest. In these pouches, which are present in both sexes, the young are carried, and in the female the teats are situated here, close to the armpits. It has been suggested that when the female gives birth to twins, one of the off-spring is carried about by the father, but I do not think

that any observations supporting this belief have been
made, and there is no reason why the female should
not carry both her young, as, of course, there is a
brood-pouch on each side of the body. On the other
hand, if the male never carries about the young, of
what use are the pouches to him ?

It is not known exactly how the parasitic *Arixenia*
lives ; fragments of chitin and part of the leg of a fly
have been found in the intestines of one of these earwigs, from which it may be concluded that the parasite
at times leaves its host in search of living insects.   If
living insects are the sole source of the earwig's food-
supply, it is not a parasite in the strictest sense of the
word ; the relations between bat and earwig would
then be better described as symbiotic. Parasites are
so rare amongst the Orthoptera that only one other
example is known, namely, *Hemimerus talpoides*, a
curious ·little insect, remotely connected with the earwigs, which lives on an African rat of the genus
Cricetomys. *Hemimerus* is a true parasite, for it feeds on
the scurf and skin of its host.

In addition to the brood-pouches, both sexes of
Cheiromeles are furnished with a pouch across the base
of the neck. These pouches receive the openings of
glands that secrete a fluid with a most offensive odour,
which Dr. C. Hose compares to the smell of burning
leather. In spite of their odour, Dayaks will readily
eat these bats. *Cheiromeles* form small colonies in hollow
trees [usually the Tapang, *Abauria*—C. H.], but apparently
not in caves, in which, however, are found hosts of
other bats, such as *Pipistrellus*, *Myotis*, and *Vespertilio*.

Galeopithecus volans, the so-called Flying Lemur, occupies a very isolated position amongst the Mammalia.

Originally placed amongst the Lemurs, it was then transferred to that dumping-ground for so many anomalous creatures, the order Insectivora. Undoubtedly it does show some affinities with the latter, but so remote that it is now regarded as the sole representative of a distinct order, the Dermoptera.

Galeopithecus is nocturnal and arboreal in its habits; during the daytime it hides amongst the leaves and branches of trees, and, owing to the greenish-brown mottled fur with which it is clothed, harmonizes very closely with its surroundings.[1] Occasionally a beautiful rufous variety is seen, the hair in some lights being almost golden.

Extending along each side of the body, and attached anteriorly along the outer border of the fore-limbs, and posteriorly along the inner border of the hind-limbs, is a fold of skin, the parachute-membrane, which, when the limbs are stretched out, becomes taut, but when the animal is at rest lies in folds along the sides of the body. The short tail is enclosed in a similar fold extending between the hind-limbs, and other folds extend from the sides of the neck to the inner border of the fore-legs. By means of this parachute *Galeopithecus* is enabled to take flying leaps from one tree to another; the direction of the flight is, of course, not strictly horizontal, for the animal has no powers of propulsion once it is in the air, but terminates at a much lower level than the point of departure. The parachute can only serve to delay its fall and to diminish the force of impact on landing, but in con-

[1] Dr. C. Hose informs me that *Galeopithecus* often clings to the trunk of a dead tree—a situation in which it is nearly invisible.— E. B. P.

sequence of this equipment *Galeopithecus* is enabled to
traverse a greater space than could an animal without
any apparatus to buoy it up. Dr. H. Gadow, in his
delightful book *Through Southern Mexico* (1908), draws
attention to the fact that in the tropical American forests
a striking characteristic of the arboreal animals is the
prehensile tail, whereas amongst Malayan forest animals,
instead of the prehensile tail, all sorts of contrivances
for securing a parachute flight are developed. In subsequent pages of this book attention will be called to
some of these contrivances.

On the ground or any flat surface *Galeopithecus* is
very helpless ; the limbs are weak and the animal
cannot stand on all-fours, but rests on the fore-arms
and shins ; it can scramble along in a shuffling sort
of way, but cannot be said to walk, the parachute
membrane appearing to hinder the free movements of
the limbs considerably. The claws are sickle-shaped
and very sharp, admirably adapted for sticking into
the bark of trees, and when the animal is placed on
the trunk of a tree far too large for it to embrace with
its arms, it can nevertheless "swarm" up the trunk
at a good pace, the sharp claws acting like climbing-
irons. The animal can also hang back downwards for
long periods of time ; in fact, when the female is
carrying about her single young one, the normal position of rest appears to be this pendulous attitude ; the
young one clinging to the breast of the mother is
then almost as completely shrouded and protected as
if it were lying at the bottom of a bag. The mother
carries her young one about with her until another is
almost ready to be born.[1]

[1] I have twice found *Galeopithecus* resting by day clinging flat to

In its diet the Flying Lemur is a strict vegetarian,
feeding chiefly on fruit, but also on leaves and shoots,
as I found by an examination of the stomach-contents
of a specimen which I shot. The incisors are peculiar comb-like teeth, and Dr. Annandale suggests that
they function as a strainer through which the pulp of
fruit is sucked into the mouth, stones and fibrous
matter being rejected. I doubt if this is a sufficient
explanation of the function of these teeth, for *Galeopithecus* is provided with a full set of molars for grind-
ing and munching its food, and, as I have said, it
feeds on leaves as well as on fruit; if it fed purely
on fruit pulp a marked reduction in the molar denti-
tion would surely be noticeable.

The animal has a peculiar smell, due to the secretion of an open gland at the root of the tail, coloured
orange in the male. The eyes are very large, in adaptation to nocturnal habits, and as the iris is very dark
the eye appears to be all pupil, like the eyes of deer;
the native name of Kubang Plandok for *Galeopithecus*
is indicative of this feature, for Plandok is the native
name for the Mouse-Deer *Tragulus*. These Flying
Lemurs are extraordinarily tenacious of life, not only
enduring long periods of starvation, but resisting all
but the most violent methods of killing; none the less
they do not endure captivity well.

Ptilocercus lowi, the Pen-tailed Shrew, was first found
in Borneo, and was for long regarded as peculiar
to that island; it has, however, turned up recently

a tree, holding the young one between it and the trunk, when,
owing to its speckled green-grey colouring, it was very difficult
to see. All I have opened had the stomach full of chewed-up
leaves, but I fed one on bananas, which it ate readily.—H. N. R.

in Bali and the Malay Peninsula. It is a little grey
Tree-Shrew with a long, slender tail, naked except for
some stiff white hairs at the end, arranged like the
vane of a feather. It is a rare animal, and I . was
never fortunate enough to see it alive. It lives in
hollow trees, but stray specimens find their way into
houses; the first specimen ever found was taken in
Sir Hugh Low's bungalow at Labuan, and a friend of
mine brought me one that had jumped out of a cup-
board in his house at Seyu, in Sarawak. The latter
specimen was seized by a dog, which, however, almost
immediately dropped the Shrew and shook his head
violently, as if to rid himself of a disagreeable odour
or taste. It is probable that all of the Shrew tribe are
distasteful creatures. There are several species of little
Ground-Shrews of the genus *Crocidura* found in Borneo,
and, like the English Shrew, their dead bodies are often
found lying on paths and roads. Natives, who are close
enough observers of nature, but are not good at finding
the causes of things, assert that it is death to a Shrew to
cross a road. The true explanation is that predatory
animals [including the small Owls (*Scops*)—C. H.] kill
Shrews but do not devour them; those that are left in
the scrub or jungle are never found, but those that
are dropped on paths are easily seen.

The commonest Insectivores in Borneo are the Tree-
Shrews of the genus *Tupaia*, which have long excited
interest on account of the great resemblance that some
of the species bear, in their colouring [and movements—C. H.], to certain species of Squirrels.

The following table shows in a succinct manner the
general similarity in coloration between the principal
species of Bornean Tree-Shrews and some Squirrels ;—

Tupaia ferruginea ⎫ Unicolorous above, rufous-yellow below.
Sciurus notatus ⎭   Low country.

Tupaia minor ⎫ Unicolorous above, underside pale, tails long
Sciurus jentinki ⎭   and thin. Low country.

Tupaia gracilis ⎫
Sciurus tenuis ⎬ A similar pair to the above. Low country.

Tupaia montana ⎫ Unicolorous, rufous-brown above, paler below.
Sciurus everetti ⎭   Mountains.

Funambulus laticaudatus is very similar in colour though a little
   paler ventrally ; the snout is markedly elongate, and so somewhat resembles that of a *Tupaia.*

Tupaia tana   ⎫ Striped dorsally.
Funambulus insignis diversus ⎭

Tupaia picta and *T. dorsalis* also have dorsal stripes, but in none
   of the Tree-Shrews is the striping so well marked as in the
   squirrel.

The local correspondence in these resemblances is
especially noteworthy. Thus, on Mt. Penrisen *Sciurus
everetti* replaces the common low-country species *S.
notatus,* and the very similar *Tupaia montana* is found
there instead of *T. ferruginea* of the lowlands.

This segregation in given localities of similarly coloured
species, belonging to two very different orders of mammals, is evidence enough that the resemblances are not
fortuitous, but it is by no means easy to explain them
satisfactorily It has been suggested that these facts
must be classed under the heading, Aggressive Mimicry,
it being supposed that the insectivorous Tree-Shrews, by
their mimicry of the harmless vegetarian Squirrels, are
enabled to approach more easily their unsuspecting prey.
There are a great many difficulties in the way of accept-
ing this view. In the first place it is by no means
certain that the species of *Tupaia* feed very largely on

insects; they certainly feed to some extent on fruit. Mr. H. N. Ridley[1] has seen in Singapore a *Tupaia ferruginea* capture and drag off into the jungle a large Bull-Frog, *Callula pulchra*; presumably the Shrew captured the frog in order to eat it, and this in spite of the fact that *Callula pulchra* exudes a sticky substance from the back when irritated. Even if insects were the staple form of the Tree-Shrew's diet, there is no reason to suppose that any insects are endowed with sufficient intelligence to appreciate the differences or resemblances existing between any two groups of mammals; the mere approach of *any* mammal, bird or reptile, is enough to scare away a palatable insect from its resting-place, a fruit-eating Squirrel acting quite as efficiently in this respect as a *Tupaia*. In other words, the disguise of the *Tupaia*—if disguise it be—has not been gained for the purpose of deceiving creatures so low in the scale of creation as insects. For my own part, I believe that if we are to regard these resemblances as mimetic, the advantages of the mimetic association are on the side of the Squirrels; that is to say, it is the Squirrel which mimics the *Tupaia*, not the *Tupaia* the Squirrel. A Squirrel is a toothsome morsel, as any one can find out for himself: a *Tupaia* is just the opposite, as I and one or two other naturalists have found out by actual experiment. If the tastes of the animals which prey on such small deer as Squirrels at all coincide with those of man, I can well imagine that an animal which had once killed and eaten a *Tupaia* would not desire to repeat the experiment unless hard-pressed by hunger, and if a few Squirrels out of some hundreds escape on account of their resemblance to Tree-Shrews

[1] *Journ. Roy. As. Soc. S. Br.*, No. 45 (1906), p. 279.

the object of the mimicry is attained. The Squirrels
are much more abundant than the Tree-Shrews, and
this complicates the problem still further, for in mimetic
associations it is almost invariably found that the distasteful, or so-called protected form, is very much more
abundant than the mimicking form.

The distastefulness of the Insectivora reaches its
culminating point in *Gymnura rafflesii*, an animal of
about the size of a rabbit, but resembling more than anything else a big white rat with a long, pointed snout.
The body is clothed with a scanty white fur, but the tail
is nearly naked : some varieties are blotched with black.
It is a somewhat repulsive-looking creature, and it
possesses a most disagreeable acrid odour, which makes
it an unpleasant captive to keep anywhere near a house.
The conspicuous appearance of the animal—and there
is nothing more conspicuous in the jungle than dead
white—is correlated with the distasteful odour. This
is a pretty general rule in the animal kingdom, and
many other examples of it will be noticed in the course
of this work. It can readily be understood that if an
animal is possessed of an odour or taste disagreeable
to its possible enemies, it is of the utmost importance
that these properties should be sufficiently advertised,
otherwise there is grave danger that the foe will not
discover them until their possessor has fallen a victim
to the onslaught. The suitable name of " warning
colours " has therefore been applied to the various
devices whereby certain animals attract attention to
their dangerous or distasteful properties.

The *Felidæ* are represented in Borneo by six species.
The largest of these is the Clouded Leopard, *Felis
nebulosa*. Its beautiful skin and the canine teeth are

so much in demand by Dayaks, Kayans, and other tribes that few specimens ever find their way into museums. The skin is made up into war-coats and the teeth are worn in the ears by chiefs, a large hole being punched in the upper part of the conch for the reception of these remarkable ornaments. The Clouded Leopard spends much of its life in trees, and, unlike its congeners the Tiger and Panther of the Malay Peninsula, is somewhat timid and retiring, and has never been known to attack man.

Owing to the absence of ferocious Carnivores, camping out in Borneo is not attended with the anxiety about their attacks which travellers in the Malay Peninsula or Sumatra must feel. In the Land-Dayak village of Singgi, Upper Sarawak, a Tiger's skull is preserved in the chief's house, and is regarded as a very potent charm, ensuring the prosperity of the village. The late Mr. A. H. Everett, the naturalist who did so much to make known the fauna of Borneo, tried very hard to examine this skull more closely, but he was not allowed to do so. The skull is of an unknown antiquity; there is, however, no evidence to show that it once belonged to a Tiger indigenous in Borneo.

Felis bengalensis is the commonest Cat in Sarawak, and it wreaks havoc amongst native hen-coops; the kittens are the most beautiful little creatures imaginable, with their fluffy fur and bright blue eyes; there are usually four young ones at a birth. Of *F. planiceps* Dr. C. Hose records[1] that "it is very fond of fruit, and has constantly been known to dig up and eat the potatoes which are grown by the natives of Borneo"; certainly a very remarkable habit for one of the cat

[1] *Mammals of Borneo*, London, 1893, p. 20.

family. *F. badia* is a very rare species of a handsome chestnut-red colour ; it is peculiar to the island.

It may be mentioned here that the domestic Cat of the Malays is quite a distinct variety, which, however, on account of its ugliness, is never likely to become as popular in cat-fancier circles as the beautiful Siamese breed. It is a very small tabby with large ears and a body so short and hind-legs so long that it altogether lacks the sinuous grace which even the most mongrel English Grimalkin exhibits. The tail is either an absurd twisted knot or else very short and terminating in a knob ; this knotting of the tail is caused by a natural dislocation of the vertebræ so that they join on to each other at all sorts of angles. A cross between the Malay breed and an English Cat produces a hybrid with a tail that has a slight kink in it, just two of the vertebræ, perhaps, joining at an angle, and the kink in the tail is one of the most important "points" of the Siamese Cat—in fact, I doubt if a Siamese Cat with a perfectly straight tail would take a first prize at a Crystal Palace Show.[1]

The Musteline Carnivora are represented in Borneo by a fair number of species. Mr. R. I. Pocock has recently[2] published a very interesting memoir on the coloration of these animals, and has shown in the most convincing way that certain forms are protected by nauseous odours or other distasteful properties,

---

[1] H. O. Forbes, I think, exhibited a kink-tailed Malay Cat [Note 4, p. 312], showing the cause of the phenomenon to be the development of wedge-shaped cartilages between the vertebræ of the tail. It is said that these Cats are common in Portugal, whence perhaps they were introduced into Malaya. A pure-bred Siamese Cat has a straight tail ; a kink shows crossing with a Malay Cat.—H. N. R.

[2] *P.Z.S.*, 1908, pp. 944-59.

which are advertised by conspicuous markings. The most familiar example is the Skunk of North America, which advertises from afar its appalling odour by its large white tail borne aloft like a banner. Rivals of the Skunk in malodorous properties are the species of *Mydaus*, a Malayan genus. *M. meliceps*, the Bornean representative, is very rare, but its congener, *M. javanensis*, is quite common in Java, and another form is not uncommon in the Natuna Islands. Mr. E. Hose, who collected in the Natunas, told me that his native hunters flatly refused to skin the specimens that he shot, on account of the revolting odour, and Mr. Hose was therefore obliged to skin the animals himself, but he had to pay for his zeal with much nausea and vomiting.

The Bornean, Javan, and Natuna Islands forms of *Mydaus* are all darkly coloured animals, striped or otherwise conspicuously marked on the back or head with white—a type of coloration which Mr. Pocock shows to be highly characteristic of distasteful Mustelines. In Java *Mydaus* is mimicked by a non-distasteful Musteline, *Helictis orientalis*, which is striped with white just like its repulsive model. In Borneo, however, the only species of *Helictis* occurring in the island, *H. everetti*, is a cryptically coloured animal, that does not mimic the *Mydaus* at all. For some reason which can only be guessed at, the Bornean *Mydaus* is exceedingly rare, whereas the Javan species is fairly abundant. It is quite obvious that if a distasteful species is not dominant, a mimic of it is less likely to acquire immunity from attack than the mimic of an abundant species, and it is also plain that if a distasteful warningly coloured species becomes extinct its mimic runs grave danger of becoming extinct too; for its conspicuous livery is now a signal of palatable qualities instead of being associated in the minds of its enemies with the nauseous properties of the extinct model. It is therefore in the highest degree probable that the rarity of *Mydaus meliceps* accounts for the fact that it is not mimicked by the *Helictis*, as is *M. javanensis*. Evidently *Mydaus meliceps* has a great struggle to maintain its position, if it is not actually on the verge of extinction, and on account of its rarity its conspicuous colouring cannot be a very familiar object to the creatures that prey on small Carnivora—in fact, to put it crudely, the *Mydaus* in Borneo is a poor model to copy. The fact that a highly distasteful form is extremely rare in one island and is comparatively abundant in another is very instructive, for it shows that unpalatability is not necessarily a complete protection. The numbers of the Bornean *Mydaus* may perhaps be kept down by parasitic worms, or it may be peculiarly susceptible to certain bacterial diseases from which the Javan form is free.[1] These are mere speculations, but it is well to realize that an animal, which naturalists call "protected" by nauseous properties, may have hosts of enemies entirely indifferent to these properties.

The Bornean Stoat, *Putorius nudipes*, is rusty-red

[1] Dr. Hose writes: "*Mydaus* is found in Borneo where the land has been cultivated, and but seldom in the dense forest. It makes burrows in the earth and feeds to a great extent upon worms. It would be impossible for it to get worms in the net-work of roots in the forest. In the hilly cultivated districts of the interior where the old jungle has been completely cleared it is not uncommon."—E. B. P.

in colour with a white head; it is, like its European relatives, a ferocious little creature.

There are two species of Mongoose in Borneo, but neither of them is as docile as the Indian species, and weeks of captivity do not soften their naturally savage disposition. A number of native stories have collected round the Malayan Mongoose, but all of them are quite unfit for publication.

Cynogale bennetti is a most peculiar mammal, superficially resembling an Otter. It is clothed in a thick brown fur, grizzled on the head and fore-quarters; long stout whiskers spring from the lips and cheeks, and the muzzle is broad and heavy. The tail is short and the feet are webbed. It is found in swampy places, and on the banks of rivers; it can swim well, but, according to Dr. Hose, will climb trees when pursued. On account of its peculiar odour, resembling that of newly cut rice ears, the Malays name it "Padi bharu" ("new rice").

Nearly all the Viverrine Carnivora of Borneo make good pets, for they are practically omnivorous and flourish well in captivity on a diet of fruit. All the species are arboreal, and their dexterity in climbing is very wonderful, seeing that they are not endowed with fully prehensile tails nor, as a rule, with grasping feet. *Arctictis binturong*, the Bear-Cat or Binturong, does, however, possess a prehensile tail: this animal and the Scaly Manis enjoy the proud distinction of being the only non-Marsupial mammals in the Old World that are thus fully endowed [Note 5, p. 313]. The Binturong is black in colour grizzled with rufous-grey, the ears are tufted and the tail is very long. When the animal is young the grip of the tail is sufficiently powerful to sustain the weight of the suspended body, but with advancing years and increase of weight the Binturong cannot remain long suspended by the tail alone. Another adaptation for tree-climbing is exhibited by the hind-feet; these are capable of such freedom of movement at the ankle-joint that their soles can be turned inwards until they face each other. When a Binturong descends a branch of a tree, it does so head foremost, firmly gripping the branch with the widely spread hind-legs, the soles of the feet closely pressed to the bark: it can rest quite comfortably in this attitude, and even raise the fore-part of the body away from the branch. In walking along more slender boughs great use is made of the tail, which is wound round the support. Two young are brought forth in some hollow tree, and the little creatures when weaned make the most delightful pets, playing together like kittens, and uttering all the time the most absurd querulous squeaks.

Of the two Bornean Palm-Civets or Munsang [in Dayak, Musang in Malay—C. H., H. N. R.], one, *Paradoxurus leucomystax*, is rather uncommon; the other, *P. hermaphroditus*, is extremely abundant and is a great nuisance to fruit-growers and keepers of poultry. Both Macaques and Munsangs are very fond of ripe coffee-berries and do much damage in plantations. The planter, however, gets a bit of his own back, for the animals cannot digest more than the soft pulp surrounding the hard kernel or " berry " of the coffee-fruit; consequently the berries are passed entire and uninjured, and are carefully collected. As only the ripest and best fruit is selected by the monkeys and Munsangs for their meal, the *dejecta* are regarded as of first-rate quality and fetch a good price in the market—a fact which is mercifully concealed from the British consumer. Though without the prehensile tail, the Munsang is an adept at climbing and moving about in trees. A captive specimen of mine could walk along a stout wire stretched between two posts, turn round in the middle and walk back to the starting-point; in this balancing feat the tail was waved from side to side and served to maintain the equilibrium. Both species of *Paradoxurus* have at times rather a disagreeable odour, proceeding from the secretion of glands under the tail.

Closely allied to the Munsangs is *Hemigale hardwickei*; it is fawn-coloured with broad transverse bands of chestnut-brown, which give the animal a conspicuous appearance when removed from its natural haunts. In its own surroundings, however, the alternate dark and light bands serve to break up the outline of the body and so render it almost invisible; the striping of the zebra has exactly the same effect.

I have no personal acquaintance with any other of the *Viverridæ*, and will therefore pass on to the little Malayan Honey-Bear, *Ursus malayanus*. This is one of the smallest members of the bear-tribe; when standing upright on its hind-legs it does not attain five feet in height. The hair is short and sleek, black in colour except for a large cream-coloured patch like a torque on the throat. The torque is hidden when the Bear walks on all-fours, but is very conspicuous in the erect attitude which he adopts when at bay, and Mr. Pocock has suggested that this patch of colour is of the nature of a warning signal to foes; this is a bold attempt to account for a very peculiar type of marking that undoubtedly must have some significance. When driven

to bay by dogs, the Bear becomes very bewildered and
backs up against the trunk of a tree, shielding its head
and neck with the fore-paws, and occasionally striking
out at its enemies : then woe betide the dog that is
within reach, for one slash with the powerful hooked
claws will disembowel it.

The Bear feeds very largely on the honey of wild bees.
There are three species of *Apis* in Borneo, and all of
them construct single combs which are suspended from'
the branches of trees, and these must afford a succulent
feast for Bruin. Far more abundant, however, are the
little stingless bees of the genus *Melipona*, which make
their nests in hollow trees. The combs in which the
dark and rather bitter honey is stored are not made up
of beautifully symmetrical hexagonal cells like those of
the honey-bee, nor are they in the form of flat sheets,
but they are irregular masses of little urn-like cells
adhering to the walls of the nest or rising in shapeless
piles from its base. The entrance to such a nest, or
hive, is often a mere slit in the hollow trunk, and if the
slit or passage is too large the bees partially close it up
with a resinous sort of wax, and frequently build out
in addition a porch or even a tunnel of the same
substance, in order to prevent rain from entering. The
Bear can, of course, easily pull to pieces the fragile
defences built by the bees, and if the slit in the tree-
trunk is wide enough to admit a paw, the contents of
the hive are soon scooped out and devoured. But
sometimes the entrance is too narrow, and the grooves
scored in the wood and bark around it show that Bruin
has been frustrated in his attempts at stealing a meal.

Dr. Hose tells me that the Malayan Bear also feeds
on Termites ; the strong claws are certainly very suitable

for pulling the nests to pieces, but otherwise the creature shows no modification of structure adapted to this diet, as do the Ant-Eaters and the Scaly Manis. Perhaps it is the enormously distended queen Termite which is the dainty sought by the Bear. In captivity this animal flourishes on fruit, and no doubt in a wild state this is also a regular item in a very catholic menu. When young, Malayan Bears are amusing and docile pets, but as they grow older they are apt to grow vicious and, on account of their strength, dangerous. When irritated the adult utters a loud bark.

The great order *Rodentia* is well represented in Borneo by sixteen species of Squirrels, twelve species of Rats, and three species of Porcupines.

The beautiful Flying Squirrels of the genera *Petaurista* and *Sciuropterus* are not very common; the most abundant species is *Petaurista nitida*. It measures about 18 inches in body-length and the tail is equally long; the colour of the fur is a rich maroon-chestnut above, becoming almost black on the spine and paler on the belly. In *Petaurista* a flap of skin extends from the outer border of each fore-limb along the sides of the body on to the hind-limbs; the flaps are somewhat triangular in shape, being broader in front than behind. From the outermost wrist-bones springs a stout, curved, cartilaginous spur, which is embedded in the front edge of the parachute skin-flap and serves to stiffen it; the bones of the arm are long and very slender. The cartilaginous spur is capable of a certain amount of movement, for when the Squirrel is not taking a parachute flight it lies almost in a line with the bones of the fore-arm, but when the parachute is spread it projects at almost a right angle to the wrist, thus drawing the

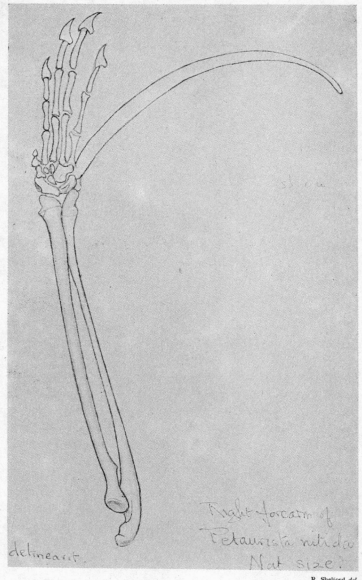

R. Shelford *del.*

Skeleton of right fore-arm of the Flying Squirrel, *Petaurista nitida,*
showing the curved cartilaginous spur which supports the front
edge of the parachute-like skin-flap. Natural size.

Plate VI.

To face p. 36.

membrane taut and giving it a considerable outward
extension and support. There is no membrane between
the hind-legs, so that the tail is quite free, nor is there
any skin-flap extending from the sides of the neck on
to the inner border of the fore-legs. This animal is
quite as good a flyer as *Galeopithecus*, but I have not
seen the little *Sciuropteri* fly at all, though they have all
the apparatus for so doing. The tail in *Sciuropterus* is
very broad, owing to the long hairs standing out on
each side of the vertebræ at a right angle, and the tail
looks rather like a beautiful soft feather. When these
little Squirrels go to sleep they roll up like a Dormouse,
and the broad feathery tail curls up over the face and
top of the head as far as the nape of the neck.

Rhithrosciurus macrotis is a magnificent species found
only in Borneo ; it is chestnut-brown in colour with
an enormous bushy grey tail and long pencils of hair
springing from the tips of the ears. The Dwarf Squirrels
of the genus *Nannosciurus* are pretty little creatures.
Mr. H. N. Ridley has seen *N. exilis*, a species which
occurs both in Borneo and Singapore, catching and
eating winged Termites as they emerged from the nest
to take their nuptial flight ; surely a very curious habit
for an animal belonging to a family regarded as strictly
frugivorous.[1]

All but two of the Bornean Rats belong to the world-
wide genus *Mus*. One of the commonest species about
Kuching is *Mus ephippium* ; it rarely comes into houses,
but lives in burrows in clay banks or else frequents
undergrowths and bushes. The common house Rat is

---

[1] The flight of the winged Termites is a great event in the animal
year. I have in Ceylon seen a dog eating them greedily, and am
told that cats do the same.—G. B. L.

Mus neglectus, a form of the widely distributed *Mus rattus.*

Mus sabanus is a large rufous Rat with white belly ; it is generally found in caves, especially such as are formed in limestone cliffs and are frequented by the Swift, *Collocalia*, which constructs the edible nests so beloved by the Chinese.

The common Porcupine of the country is *Hystrix crassispinis*. It does considerable damage in pine-apple plantations, and specimens which have fed on this luscious fruit are remarkably good to eat. The Porcupine is easily tamed and thrives in captivity. A pet specimen of mine escaped from its cage one brilliant moonlight night, and strolled in a leisurely manner across the lawn in front of my house ; my two dogs, on catching sight of the animal, hastened out with the intention of worrying it, but the Porcupine proved to be quite capable of taking care of itself, and the subsequent proceedings were amusing to watch. The Porcupine would run full tilt for several yards with the dogs in hot pursuit, then it would halt suddenly and run backwards, elevating all its quills and producing a loud rattling noise with its tail. Sundry yelps from the dogs showed that they found the Porcupine a very awkward customer to tackle ; they could not seize it by the throat, for it was always too quick for them, either turning the hind part of the body towards its assailants or else dashing away at full speed. Eventually I drove the dogs off and rescued the Porcupine from the encounter, which, however, it seemed to enjoy as much as the dogs.

The rattling noise which the Porcupine makes is produced by means of a very simple mechanism

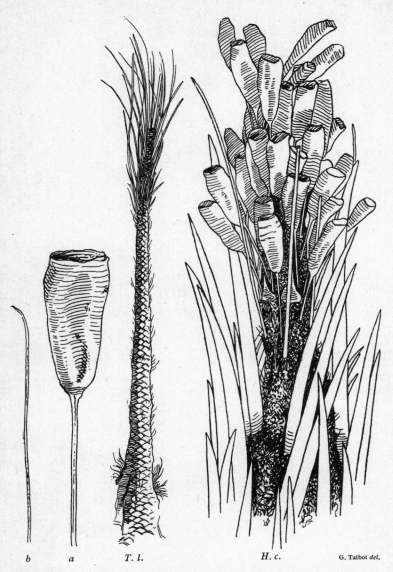

b *a* *T. l.* *H. c.* G. Talbot *del.*

The tail *H. c.*) of the common Bornean Porcupine, *Hystrix crassispinis*, showing the modified quills, enlarged at *a*, which make the rattling noise.
Tail (*T. l.*) of quill-less Porcupine, *Trichys lipura*, showing the scaly covering
and the fine terminal quills, enlarged at *b*.

Plate VII.

To face p. 39.

Amongst the ordinary sharply pointed, stiff quills on the tail are a number of peculiarly modified quills ; their stalks are very slender, but they expand at the apex into a thin-walled and hollow cylinder open at the top. When the tail is violently agitated these hollow cylinders wag to and fro on their slender stalks, and bang against each other and against the stiff tail quills, thus producing a loud rattling noise. The well-known black and white quills, that cover the Porcupine's body, serve to make the animal very conspicuous, and as the quills are really quite formidable weapons, being sharp and strong and capable of penetrating the skin of an enemy such as a carnivore, it seems likely that both the colouring of the Porcupine and the rattling noise produced by the tail are warning signals, comparable with the white bushy tail of the Skunk and the rattle of the Rattle-Snake. In the embryo Porcupine the developing quills are arranged in longitudinal rows, so that a striped appearance is produced—a character, be it noted, of the young of many mammals.

The curious quill-less Porcupine, *Trichys lipura*, is peculiar to Borneo. The following account of this animal is quoted from Hose's *Mammals of Borneo* (p. 61) : " All the upper and lateral parts of the body are densely covered with flat flexible bristles of moderate length, grooved on the upper as well as the lower surface. Underfur very scantily represented by fine woolly hairs ; and on the rump some long hair-like bristles project beyond the flat ones. . . . The general tint of the upper parts of the animal is brown, each spine being white at the base, and brown towards the point. On the sides the brown colour gradually passes into the white of the lower parts." An adult measures in body-length

from 15 to 17 inches and the tail is about 8 inches
long. At the extreme base the tail is furnished with
spines, but throughout nearly "the whole of its
length it is covered with rhombic scales of relatively
large size, and arranged regularly in oblique series or
rings. A short fine hair . . . starts from the base of
each scale and lies closely adpressed to its median line,
giving to the scale the appearance of being keeled (like
the scale of a snake). Towards the end of the tail the
hairs become longer, and the terminal quills are much
elongated, 2–3 inches long, and compressed with a
shallow groove, like blades of grass, only much narrower,
and form a thin bundle. The majority are truncate at
their extremity and hollow." These quills may be
regarded as homologous with the peculiarly modified
caudal quills of other Porcupines, but their structure
shows that no rattling noise can be produced by them
when the tail is shaken. Curiously enough, adult specimens are sometimes found without any tail at all, and
for some time it was supposed that there were two
species of *Trichys* in Borneo, a tailed species and a
tailless one. Dr. Hose, however, procured a tailless
female accompanied by her young one, which was
furnished with a fully developed and normal tail. This
proved beyond reasonable doubt that there was only one
species of *Trichys* in Borneo, but what has never yet
been satisfactorily explained is the reason of the disappearance of the tail in certain individuals.[1] Can this
Porcupine shed its tail, when seized by that appendage,
as do so many lizards ? This question has yet to be

[1] Dr. Hose writes : " The tailless specimens of *Trichys* I have
noticed in nearly every case are females, and I am inclined to think
that the tails are often bitten off when chased by the males."—E. B. P.

settled. The loss of the tail may be related to the very remarkable thinness and delicacy of the skin of the body. In dead specimens the skin tears almost as easily as tissue paper, and it is not easy to prepare good museum specimens. The *Trichys* lives in burrows, and is largely a nocturnal animal.

The *Ungulata* are but poorly represented in Borneo and the noblest of them all, the Elephant, occurs in British North Borneo only, and there in very small numbers. These are probably the descendants of a small herd presented long ago to the Sultan of Brunei by a Sultan of some Malay State. Tradition has it that the Sultan of Brunei soon tired of his expensive present, and turned all the animals adrift into the jungle. That the Elephant was once truly indigenous in Borneo is, however, proved by the discovery in a limestone cave at Bau, in Upper Sarawak, of a semi-fossilized fragment of an Elephant's molar, but it must have been long since this species ceased to range the Bornean jungles, for not one of the native tribes have any word in their language for Elephant other than the Malay name Gajah, nor is there any tradition of such animals having existed in Sarawak.

The Rhinoceros, *R. sumatrensis*,[1] is still extant, but it seems to be confined to the mountainous regions in the far interior of the island, and I do not suppose that more than half a dozen specimens have been sent to European museums. The horn is much prized by the Chinese for medicinal purposes, but the other parts of the animal, having no commercial value, are not brought down by the inland natives to the bazaars

[1] Common in British North Borneo. I passed four in one trip.—H. N. R.

of the river towns and Government stations. In many books it is stated that *R. sondaicus* also occurs in Borneo, but I do not know what authority there is for this statement.

Three species of Wild Boar are now distinguished from Borneo ; the commonest is *Sus barbatus,* and so far as I know the habits of all the species are very similar. The gregarious instinct of the Wild Boar is well marked. At times great droves of them pass from one part of the country to another ; hundreds may be seen for a day or two trotting through the jungle, and when they come to a river they plunge into it without hesitation and swim across to the other side.[1] The non-Islamic tribes of Borneo hail with joy these migrations, and slaughter the beasts wholesale. Driving them on to some point of land projecting into the river, the hunters spear or shoot the Boars as they emerge from the jungle and plunge into the water. The cause of these migrations is obscure ; perhaps they are due to a failure of food-supply in certain tracts of the country, but it has also been suggested that an outbreak of swine-fever or some allied epidemic drives the animals to seek in haste some non-infected area. That wild swine are

---

[1] It has been asserted, though with how much truth I cannot say, that the domestic pig, when forced to take to the water, cuts its throat in the act of swimming, the hoofs of the fore-legs slashing the fat jowl until some large blood-vessel is severed. If this be true of the domestic pig, it is certainly not true of the wild species, for they swim admirably.—R. S.

The statement is certainly not true of the domestic pig, as I know from experience. The mistake was corrected by A. R. Wallace in *Geographical Distribution of Animals,* 1876, vol. I., p. 13. —H. N. R.

subject to periodic devastating epidemics is a fact
that becomes patent to any one who has occasion to
travel about much in the country; moreover, such
epidemics are frequently communicated to the domestic
pigs belonging to native tribes.

The following incident, illustrating the gregarious
instinct of wild swine, is vouched for by one of the
most trustworthy naturalists of my acquaintance, Mr.
Ernest Hose, who was an actual eye-witness of the
scene. Hearing one day in the jungle, close to his
house at Santubong, a tremendous noise of wild pigs
grunting, snorting, and squealing, he ran out to see
what was the reason of it, and presently came on a
large Python that had seized a young pig and was endea-
vouring to crush it. The snake was surrounded by
a number of full-grown swine, which were goring it
with their tusks and trampling on it; so resolute was
their attack that the Python was compelled to relin-
quish its hold of the loudly protesting young pig,
when the herd, catching sight of Mr. Hose, hastily
made off, the young one, apparently little the worse
for its adventure, trotting away with its companions.
Mr. Hose examined the snake, and found it to be so
slashed and mangled that it was unable to crawl away
from the scene of battle.

In old jungle not uncommonly may be found areas
in which the ground appears trampled and the undergrowth broken and tossed on one side; these are
the resting-grounds of Wild Boars or places where a
sow has given birth to her young. The unwary
traveller who sits down in one of these spots has
soon plentiful occasion to rue his lack of experience,
for they literally swarm with ticks and other parasites

of the swine. The dancing-grounds of the Argus Pheasant present a very similar appearance, but are a good deal smaller.

The young of *Sus verrucosus* are striped with rusty-red, but the stripes disappear as soon as the young are old enough to look after themselves. In the young pig the upper lip on each side is deeply notched to accommodate the tushes which, however, have not yet made their appearance. This is an interesting point, for we must suppose that the notching of the lip was originally brought about by the hypertrophy of the tushes, whereas the notches now antedate their original cause by several months. An argument more favourable to Lamarckism could not well be found.

The Mouse-Deer, or Plandok, of which there are two species in Borneo, *Tragulus napu* and *T. javanicus*, is the hero of many native beast stories which bear the closest resemblance to the " Brer Rabbit" tales of the American negro. Just as Brer Rabbit outwits animals stronger than himself, such as the Wolf and Fox, but in turn is outwitted by animals weaker than himself, such as the Tortoise, so does the Plandok gull the Deer, the Pig, and the Bear, and is deceived by the Tortoise and the Hermit-crab. Anthropologists can quote scores of such parallels in folk-lore, existing amongst widely sundered races, and attention will be called to one or two in a later chapter of this book. Of the instance quoted above only this need be said : The Brer Rabbit stories originated in West Africa, where there is an indigenous species of Hare; through the channel of slavery the stories were carried to North America, and the characters, though not the

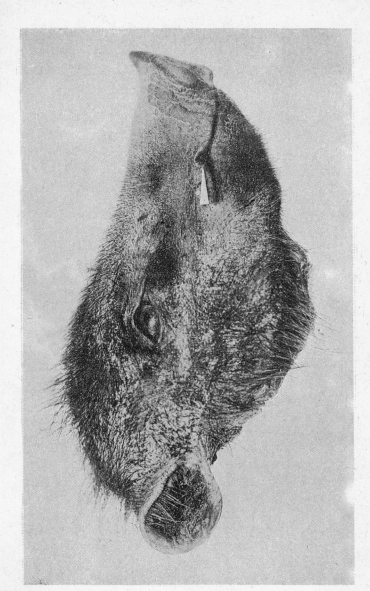

Plate VIII.

Head of young Wild Boar, showing the notch in the upper lip ready for the tush, which has not yet made its appearance. (From the author's photograph.)

To face p. 44.

motif, of the stories became somewhat altered to suit the change in the fauna.[1] The Malayan stories undoubtedly owe nothing to the West African negro, for there can be no community of descent in the two races ; they must have been independently evolved. It is legitimate to suppose that the two sets of native races, the West African and the Malayan, impressed by the fact that such defenceless creatures as the Hare and the Mouse-Deer could flourish amidst far more powerful animals, sought to account for it by attributing to the weaklings a superior intelligence and cunning, and their belief has been enshrined in these folk-tales. It is true that the upper canine teeth of the male Plandok are long and sharp, and severe cuts can be inflicted by them, the head being moved rapidly with a curious sideways action, but on the whole the Plandok is a very defenceless creature, and trusts to its remarkable speed to elude its enemies rather than stand on its defence.

The other Deer of the island are the Barking Deer, or Kijang, *Cervulus muntjac*, and the Rusa, *Cervus equinus*. The antlers of the Rusa are rather small, and make but poor trophies when compared with those of the Sam-

[1] It is interesting to note that one of the Brer Rabbit stories has been transplanted to Europe, and in the process has become greatly changed to suit, not a difference of fauna, but a different moral code. The Hare and Tortoise story has been told to many an English child in order to inculcate the maxim "Slow and sure wins the day." The Hare, too confident of victory, lies down to sleep after running a short distance, and the plodding Tortoise arrives first at the winning-post. Readers of the incomparable "Uncle Remus" need not be told that the tortoise defeats Brer Rabbit by pure guile and deceit, and the story is the reverse of moral according to English ideas. The Hermit-crab employs exactly the same deceit against the Plandok.

bur and Red Deer; they have only six points. A very
curious abnormality of the antlers has twice been found
in Borneo. The tines are expanded into curious spatulate processes and the shafts are much thickened. A
specimen now in the British Museum of Natural History, was picked up in the jungle by a native. It
would be interesting to know if this remarkable variation is correlated with abnormality of the sexual
organs.

The tear-pits of the Deer are called "night-eyes" by
the Malays, who believe that the animals see with them
in the dark. The young Deer are sometimes, but not
invariably, spotted, and a melanic variety is also known
to occur in the damp forests of Mt. Dulit, in the
Baram district of Sarawak.

The Wild Ox, or Tembadau, elsewhere known as the
Banteng, *Bibos sondaicus*, is not abundant; it is found
in the north and in the interior of the island. The
well-known Water-Buffalo, *Bos bubalus*, has been
domesticated by the inhabitants of the northern parts
of Borneo, and is quite a familiar object of the
country-side. Two or three herds have run wild at
the mouth of the Baram River, and have afforded
exciting sport to not a few of the Sarawak Government officials.

Dugongs, Porpoises, and even Whales have been
found in Sarawak waters. Of the three or four species
of Porpoise, the most remarkable is *Sotalia borneensis*,
known only from three specimens, all taken close to
the mouth of the Sarawak River. In life this is a beautiful creature about 7 feet long, with a pure white
glossy skin marbled with grey spots on the back.
When the skin is bruised it turns red, and when dried

changes to a dark mahogany colour. On the forehead
is a large globular swelling, cartilaginous in its framework, with fat or blubber in the interstices.

A large Rorqual, or Fin-back Whale, apparently to
be identified with *Balænoptera schlegelii*,[1] was once
stranded on the Sarawak coast near Lundu. It was
over 60 feet in length, and its vast putrefying carcase
supplied food to Dayaks, wild pigs, Crocodiles, and
Monitor Lizards for some weeks. The gathering together
of the bones, their transport, and the subsequent
mounting of the skeleton, taxed the resources of the
Museum and the ingenuity of its curator to the uttermost, but *finis coronat opus*, and the mounted skeleton
is still displayed in the grounds of the Sarawak
Museum, a never-failing source of wonder to up-country
natives.

The Edentates have but a single representative in
Borneo, namely the Scaly Ant-Eater, *Manis javanica*,
the Tengiling of the Malays. The body and tail above
are covered with large imbricated scales, and the tail
is prehensile. With its strong claws the Manis can
excavate and rip to pieces the nests of Termites, on
which insects, together with ants, it feeds. As in the
Ant-Eaters of South America, the jaws, mouth, and
tongue are all highly modified for this particular diet.
The Manis makes a docile pet, but it is difficult to
obtain sufficient suitable food. In proportion to its
size, the strength of the animal is prodigious; a live
specimen was brought to me late one evening, and I
placed it temporarily in a small packing-case with a
large slab of stone as lid, but in the course of the

[1] Generally considered now to be a mere variety of, if not actually
identical with, *Balænoptera physalus*.

night my prisoner succeeded in prising off the stone
and escaped. When the animal is molested it curls
itself up into a tight ball in order to protect the scale-
less and vulnerable under-surface of the body, and it
is well-nigh impossible to pull it out straight, so great
is its muscular strength. If imprisoned in a space
sufficiently confined to hinder it from curling up, the
Manis strongly arches its back and exerts such a pressure on the roof of its prison that this, if not most
strongly secured, bursts open. More than one observer
has seen this species "swarm" up tree-trunks, the
strong claws getting a good hold of the bark. My
Chinese assistant in Sarawak saw a Manis hurl itself
from a tree and, curled up in a semicircle, fall on its
back; it seemed to be none the worse for its fall, and,
rolling on to its feet, walked off.

This chapter may close with a pleasing Malay story
of the ingenuity of this animal. When the Manis can
find no ants' or Termites' nests, it lies down in the
jungle curled up and pretends to be dead. Those
universal scavengers the ants flock in hundreds to feast
on the supposed corpse, and as the edges of the
Manis's scales are slightly raised owing to its curled-
up position, the ants swarm underneath them in order
to attack the soft skin. When the Manis considers
that it has collected sufficient numbers of the ants, the
corpse comes to life again, straightens itself out, and
in so doing shuts down the scales and imprisons the
ants. It then trots off to the nearest pool of water
or stream, into which it plunges and arches its back,
thus raising the scales again. The ants float off on to
the surface of the water and are licked up with the
long slender tongue.

CHAPTER II

BIRD-NOTES

IT is popularly supposed in England that nearly all the birds of the tropical regions are brilliantly coloured and either most unmelodious in their cries or else entirely silent. It is certainly true that during the heat of the day the jungle is a silent place, and it is equally certain that the harsh shrieking of the gorgeous Macaw and the metallic note of the brightly coloured Barbet are anything but pleasing to the human ear. However, it is never safe to generalize from insufficient evidence, and further inquiry reveals the fact that in any tropical area the number of dull-coloured, soberly clad birds exceeds the number of brilliant species, while every tropical land can boast its songsters which rival, if they do not excel, those of the temperate regions.

In Borneo the Dayak omen-bird, Nandak, *Cittocincla suavis*, is a frequently heard and a most melodious song-bird ; the Magpie-Robin, *Copsychus saularis*, also sings sweetly ; the melody of the Bulbuls is far-famed. The song of the Crested Bulbul, *Trachycomus cristatus*, a species occurring in gardens and along the river-banks of Sarawak, is, in my humble opinion, quite unrivalled ; it is a richly bubbling, gurgling melody,

5

poured out in an almost unceasing flow for several
minutes; instinct with a gladsome vitality, it infects the
sympathetic listener and vividly suggests the luxuriant
wealth of tropical life.

Copsychus saularis is one of the commonest Bornean
birds; it frequents the lawns and shrubberies of gardens, and is as familiar to the English exile as the
House-Sparrow is to his stay-at-home fellow country-
man. It is a black-and-white species, about as large
as a Blackbird, to which it is more nearly related than
it is to the Robin. In the evening this bird used to
assemble in small numbers on the gravel path outside
my house, and the males would indulge in what I can
only call singing contests. One or two would begin
the performance by spreading out the wings and tail
and depressing them, so that they touched the ground;
the head was raised and thrown back, and in this posture the birds would scuttle about the path singing
loudly all the time; then they would stop and two or
three others would repeat the manœuvre. I never saw
any hen-birds in these assemblages of males, which
apparently indulge in the contests out of sheer exuber-
ance of spirits, and not with the idea of attracting the
females.

Mr. F. M. Chapman, in his *Camps and Cruises of an
Ornithologist*, records of the Prairie-Cock of Nebraska
displays and fights of the male birds which are un-
witnessed by the hens, and, if my memory serves me,
Mr. Edmund Selous has observed much the same thing
of the European Blackcock. Mr. Chapman writes:
" Probably we may regard these exhibitions as the
uncontrollable manifestations of that physical energy
which in animals reaches its extreme development

during the mating season," and this, I believe, is the correct explanation. No doubt the birds will behave in the same way when actually courting the females— in fact, Mr. H. N. Ridley's description [1] of the courting performances of *Copsychus saularis* tallies pretty closely with the above account of the males' singing contests— but it is clear that the presence of the female is not the only stimulus required to call forth these "manifestations of physical energy." Mr. Ridley remarks (pp. 83, 84) further of *C. saularis* that it is "a most useful insect-destroyer, attacking and devouring even large caterpillars. I once saw one pecking at an unfortunate young mouse, which had apparently been somehow washed out of its nest by a heavy storm of rain. On another occasion I saw one furiously attack a squirrel (*Nanosciurus exilis*) which was climbing on a tree and knock it off the branch to the ground. Again the squirrel attempted to climb up, and again it was struck to the ground; even then the *Murai* pursued it till it fled to refuge in the bushes, still pursued by the bird."

Another bird, whose note soon became familiar to me, was the common Night-Jar of the country, *Caprimulgus macrurus*. On bright moonlight nights these birds love to settle on roads and paths and utter their single monotonous note, "tok, tok, tok"; the sound may aptly be compared to the noise made by a stone skipping along a sheet of ice, and this comparison by some strange reflex saved me from the irritability which so many Europeans display when on some stifling tropical night the bird strikes up its monotone within their hearing; to me the sound recalled cold days at home, the ring of skates on ice, frost-bound earth and water, and

[1] *Journ. Roy. As. Soc. S. Br.*, No. 31 (1898), p. 84.

the mere thought of such things was soothing. I never heard this species utter the jarring "churr" of the English Night-Jar.[1] It is singular that in many parts of the world sinister habits are attributed to the Night-Jar. In England the bird has been accused of sucking the udders of cattle and goats, as its alternative name, the Goat-Sucker, signifies. The more Rabelaisian fancy of the Malay charges the bird with attacks on human beings, which for modesty's sake I dare not specify further.

That curious bird, the Frog-Mouth, *Batrachostomus auritus*, is also a member of the Night-Jar family, but is much more uncommon than *Caprimulgus macrurus*, and is never seen near towns or human habitations. The nest is a curious structure, being a thick circular pad of fine down closely matted together and firmly attached to the slender branch of some shrub or small tree ; a single egg is laid. The egg by its weight soon forms a small depression in the pad of down, but at first there is no such depression, and it is never deep enough to hold the egg securely. It is difficult to understand how the egg is kept in position ; the slightest oscillation of the branch on which the nest is made would suffice to throw the egg to the ground, if the mother-bird were not incubating it. I am inclined to suppose that a very small quantity of some albuminous or glutinous substance may help to hold the egg in its precarious position. This may seem a far-fetched suggestion, but it is quite certain that the down composing the nest is felted together with some glutinous substance secreted by the bird, and the under-surface of the nest is stuck fast to the bough on which it is

[1] It does do so in the breeding season for a short time.—H. N. R.

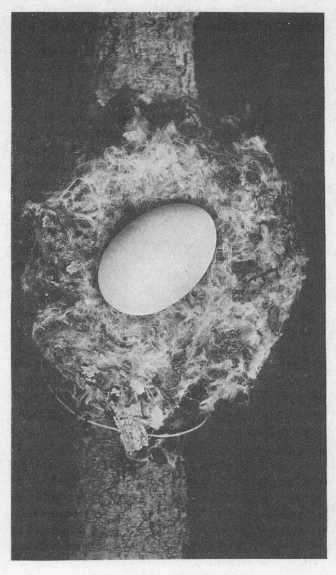

Nest and egg of the Bornean Frog-Mouth, *Batrachostomus auritus.*
(From a photograph taken by J. C. Moulton in the Sarawak
Museum, Kuching.)

Plate IX.

built up by the same secretion ; a slight excess of the
secretion would serve very well to fasten the egg to
the upper layer of down [Note 6, p. 314].

The Frog-Mouth, when incubating her egg, rests in
the characteristic Night-Jar attitude, along and not across
the branch bearing the nest. It is interesting to note
that *Caprimulgi* are closely related to the Swifts, one
species of which, the Edible-nest Swift, *Collocalia
fuciphaga*, constructs its white nest entirely of a mucilaginous substance secreted by the salivary glands.
Some of the nests contain a few embedded feathers,
whilst in others (e.g. *Collocalia lowi*) the proportion is
so great that the nests are useless from a gastronomic
point of view [Note 7, p. 314].

The nest of the Crested Swift, *Macropteryx comatus*,
is a tiny cup of feathers and down closely cemented
together with mucin, and the single pure white egg,
which measures 20 millimeters by 15, fits accurately
into it. The nest itself is attached to some slender
twig at the top of a lofty tree, and in a stiff breeze it
must be jerked to and fro to a considerable extent,
exposing the egg to not a little danger when the
mother is not actually protecting it with her body.
Here again I would venture to suggest that the egg
is partially secured in position by an excess of the
mucilaginous matter with which the substance of the
nest is cemented together.

In the bird-realm there are few more remarkable nests
than that made by *Arachnothera longirostris*, a member
of the Sunbird family. The species of this genus have
long and slender bills, and they live on spiders and
insects which they extract from flowers, crevices in the
bark of trees, and other hiding-places ; the bill un-

doubtedly plays no small part in the construction of
the nest. I have seen but two examples of the nest of
A. longirostris, and both of them are in the Sarawak
Museum; the curator of the Museum, my friend Mr.
J. C. Moulton, kindly lent me one of the specimens, from
which Mr. Edwin Wilson made the two beautiful drawings shown on the opposite Plate. The nest is attached
to the under surface of a large leaf,[1] and at first sight
appears to be composed entirely of skeleton leaves, but
a closer examination shows that these are merely the
covering of the nest proper, which is a hemispherical
cup of interwoven fibres, apparently the mid-ribs of
leaves; it is slung by silken threads to the leaf which
supports it, there being a space of less than an inch
between the rim of the nest and the under surface of
the leaf, just room enough to let the bird creep in.
These suspensory threads, which are taken from a
spider's web, are passed through holes made in the leaf
by the bird's bill and the ends twisted up into knots
to prevent slipping. The nest proper is covered over
with skeleton leaves, the covering extending much
beyond the confines of the nest, so that the whole
structure appears to be a roughly oval mass. These
skeleton leaves are also secured by transverse lashings
of spider silk passing through the supporting leaf and
knotted at each end. At one end and at the sides of
the structure the skeleton leaves are lashed down tightly,
but at the other end their attachment is looser, and this
marks the entrance to the nest; the mother-bird here
can creep under the protective covering of skeleton
leaves and so into the nest proper. On the upper surface

---

[1] The other specimen in the Sarawak Museum is attached to
the under side of a banana-leaf.

The nest of *Arachnothera longirostris*, one of the Sunbirds, seen from the under side. The entrance is at the upper end of the figure. On the left hand is seen the upper surface of the leaf from which the nest is hung, showing the knotted ends of the suspensory threads. (From a drawing by Edwin Wilson of a specimen from the Sarawak Museum. The figure is about ⅔ of the natural size.)

Plate X.

To face p. 54.

of the supporting leaf are visible in a double row the knotted ends of the silk threads which sling the nest and serve to keep in position the skeleton leaves. A nest such as this is not only pretty secure from observation but is well protected from snakes, those inveterate destroyers of birds' eggs; moreover, the protective covering of skeleton leaves keeps the nest from swinging about, and there is no danger of the eggs being thrown out, however violently the leaf to which the nest is attached may wave in the breeze.

Mr. Ridley (*loc. cit.*, p. 87) describes the nest of another Sunbird, *Arachnothera modesta,* as "made of skeletons of leaves and fibres and bast, apparently from the lining of a squirrel's nest, and bark, between two leaves of these plants [*Heliconia*], which had been pegged together by bits of stick, by some person." I have little doubt in my own mind that the "person" who pegged the leaves together was the bird which built the nest.

Mr. Ridley also describes (p. 86) the nest of another Sunbird, *Anthothreptes malaccensis*: "It makes a hanging nest on the end of a bough, about six inches long, of bark fibres and nests of caterpillars, and lined with feathers. The nest is pear-shaped with a hole at the side, and a kind of little eave is thrown out over it to keep the rain from getting into the nest." I do not exactly know what "caterpillars' nests"[1] are, unless by this term the writer means the large communal cocoons woven of silk and attached to tree-trunks by the larvæ of a Noctuid moth belonging to the genus *Hyblæa*; there is also a Pyralid moth which has

[1] They were large communal webs like those of *Clisiocampa* made over bushes.—H. N. R.

much the same habit, and as these cocoons do not contain any of the urticating hairs which render the cocoons of some moths most unpleasant, if not dangerous, to handle, they might doubtless prove extremely suitable for nest-building.

To Mr. Ridley we are also indebted for an interesting observation on the habits of the Racket-Tailed Drongo, *Dissemurus platyurus*.[1] This bird has often been seen in some numbers accompanying a troop of the common Macaque, *Macacus cynomolgus*, as it wends its way through the tree-tops in the jungle. So familiar is the sight to Malays that they have nicknamed the bird "the slave of the K'ra." The reason of the habit is this : the monkeys as they move through the trees disturb all sorts of insects, such as grasshoppers, mantises, and moths, and the Drongos snap them up as they fly into the air away from the monkeys. It is therefore the monkeys which serve the Drongos by flushing the insects, and it is not the Drongos who slave for the monkeys.[2] The Drongo is mimicked by a cuckoo, *Surniculus lugubris*, which deposits its egg in the nest of its model. It need not be supposed that the sole object of this mimicry is to enable the cuckoo to approach unnoticed the nest of the Drongo ; it is far more probable that the

[1] *Journ. Roy. As. Soc. S. Br.*, No. 35 (1901), p. 105.

[2] The Malay is a good observer of Nature, but he generally comes to grief when attempting to give reasons for the phenomena which he has witnessed. The relations existing between the Drongos and monkeys is a case in point ; another may be quoted here. The habit which certain fossorial wasps exhibit of storing their nests with caterpillars is well known to the Malay, but he accounts for it by naïvely supposing that the wasps, being childless, steal and adopt the children of more fortunate insects,

cuckoo, on account of its resemblance to a bold, gregarious bird, escapes the attacks of hawks and other birds of prey. Drongos are quite capable of looking after themselves, and will mob a hawk without the slightest fear or hesitation.

That very remarkable Passerine bird, *Pityriasis gymnocephala*, is found in Borneo alone. Unfortunately very little is known about its habits, and, in spite of the efforts of the three men who, more than any one else, have made known to science the avifauna of Borneo, viz., the late Alfred Everett, the late John Whitehead, and Dr. Charles Hose, the nest of this species still remains undiscovered. My predecessor at the Sarawak Museum, the late Edward Bartlett, by a lucky accident discovered what the egg was like ; he shot a female, whose oviduct contained all ready to be laid a large, pale blue egg, spotted with brown ; the shattered fragment is still preserved in the Sarawak Museum, and is the only " document " relating to the breeding habits of the bird that we possess. That *Pityriasis* has more or less gregarious habits is shown by the fact that the call of a wounded individual attracts all the others that are anywhere within hearing, and the distressed bird is soon surrounded by a flock of his friends, uttering their harsh cries and fluttering their wings in anger at the enemy.

The bird, which is about the size of a Jackdaw, owes both its generic and specific names to the peculiar head-covering, or lack of covering, of the adult. The head is bald save for a clothing of peculiar yellow scurf-like scales ; so much does the head look as if it was affected by a skin-disease, that the name of one, *Pityriasis*, has been employed for the generic term. The plumage is black, except for a red ruff round the neck ; the sexes are similar. The fully fledged young birds differ from the adults in having the crown of the head covered with red feathers like those round the neck, but after the first year these are shed and replaced by the scurfy scales.

Bald-headedness in birds is uncommon and most difficult to explain. The naked head and neck of the Vulture are adaptations to a scavenger's life ; we may even stretch a point and similarly account for the bald cranium of the Adjutant Bird, though one might have supposed that the long beak would keep the head out of reach of the sullying offal on which this bird feeds. But why should the insectivorous or frugivorous *Pityriasis* and *Allocotops calvus*, one of the Mountain-Babblers of Borneo, be bald ? The latter species has no feathers, not even scurf on the top of its head ; the bare skin is dull yellow in colour and the female is as bald as the male. Sexual adornment, though it would be strange to apply the term adornment to baldness and scurfiness, evidently cannot be invoked, and the phenomenon remains a mystery. The hypothesis that baldness in these birds is now a normal condition, originally derived from a pathological condition, is so wildly fascinating that it must be repulsed as one of the wiles of the Evil One.

The exact systematic position of *Pityriasis* amongst the Passeres is very uncertain. Some ornithologists have regarded it as a sort of Shrike, others, as related to the Starlings, whilst I always thought that it had a very Crow-like appearance. Mr. Pycraft, however, our greatest authority on bird-anatomy, places it amongst the Shrikes, in the Family *Gymnathidæ*.[1]

The nesting habits of the Hornbills are very remarkable, and though they have been studied by more than one naturalist, there is much that still remains to be discovered. The nest is always built in a hollow tree, and it is essential that the cavity should communicate with the exterior by means of a slit or hole. Very often the hollows in trees are the result of the ravages of Termites, and it is no uncommon thing to find a Hornbill's nest built on the top of a Termites' nest. If the slit, whereby the hollow communicates with the outer world, is not at exactly the right elevation—and this must happen very often—the hollow has to be filled up from the bottom with sticks and other vegetable detritus until the pile reaches such a height that the hen-bird· when sitting on it can thrust her bill through the slit. On the top of the pile of decayed wood and sticks is a thin stratum of feathers, evidently plucked from her own body by the hen-bird.

The next stage in the building process is the walling-up of the hen-bird by the male. The sides of the orifice leading into the hollow of the tree are plastered with a peculiar substance, apparently secreted by the bird, until merely a long and very narrow slit is left, up and down which the beak of the imprisoned female can move. I have examined some of the material used by *Buceros rhinoceros* to seal up the opening to the nest ; it was quite hard, but rather friable on the surface, and was made up of woody particles in a matrix

[1] See Dr. Hose's note on this species in *The Ibis* (6 Ser.), V. (1893), pp. 393–94.—E. B. P.

which dissolved after a prolonged soaking. It looks as if the Hornbills swallowed fragments of wood, and then regurgitated them in a comminuted condition, together with a copious secretion of either salivary or proventricular glands; but this is a point that requires further investigation.

Until the nestlings are from two to three weeks old the female is kept a close prisoner, and is fed by the male with fruit, seeds, insects, and parts of frogs and lizards; each portion of food is enclosed in a membrane of rubber-like consistency, a product of the proventricular glands; from this it is clear that the male, when foraging for his mate, swallows the food destined for her and regurgitates it in the form of these membrane-enclosed pellets. While feeding the female, the male clings to the bark of the tree, or sits on a branch if conveniently near, and jerks the pellets into the gaping beak of the hen as it protrudes from the slit; two to four pellets are said to form a meal. When the female is biting the food some fragments of it are apt to fall to the ground; any seeds which these fragments may contain take root, germinate, and sprout, and expert natives can approximately judge, not only the date of incubation by the age of the seedlings, but also the number of years during which the Hornbills have nested in the same tree. Generally when the nestlings are two to three weeks old, but perhaps later, the hen-bird leaves the nest, breaking down with her beak the woody plaster until she can effect her exit, after which the orifice is closed up as before, and both parents now devote themselves to feeding their young, until they are old enough to be released. This sealing-up of the mother and young affords splendid protection against the attacks of snakes, monkeys, and predaceous arboreal Carnivora, such as *Arctogale, Hemigale, Paradoxurus*, etc.

One pair of Hornbills will use the same tree as a nesting-place for many years in succession, and, seeing what difficulty there must be in finding a suitable site, and what labour goes to the perfecting of it, this constancy to locality is no matter for surprise. One, two, or three eggs are laid ; the egg of *Buceros rhinoceros* is white, closely mottled with brown, giving it a pepper-and-salt appearance; that of *Anthracoceros malayanus* is pure white. The young nestlings are hideous, naked squabs with protuberant abdomens and loose, wrinkled skin. The pygidium, which is that part of a bird's anatomy known colloquially as the "Pope's nose," is turned upwards and forwards, thus concealing the oil-gland. The feet are relatively very large ; their soles and the prominent "heels" (junction of tibia and metatarsus) are densely covered with granular scales. It is chiefly on the heels that the young nestling rests, and not on the plantar surface of the feet, as erroneously shown in Wallace's *Malay Archipelago*.[1] Even in a six weeks' old nestling the feathers merely show as small points just pushing through the skin, and it is not till the ninth or tenth week after hatching that the nestlings present a decently clad appearance.

In spite of their repulsive appearance, Dayaks will eat the young nestlings raw. The native method of catching the female during incubation is ingenious, though decidedly brutal. The tree is scaled, the entrance to the nest is broken open, and the frightened

[1] Vol. I., p. 212 of the original (1869) edition.

bird flutters up the hollow trunk of the tree, but is igno-
miniously brought down by means of a thorny stick,
which is thrust after her and twisted about until a
firm grip in her plumage and flesh is obtained.

Dr. Hose witnessed an interesting incident in Hornbill life on Mt. Dulit, and I retail it here in his own
words : "Espying on a tree the external signs of a
Hornbill's nest, and a male *Buceros rhinoceros* perched
close by, I shot the male, and while waiting for my
Dyak collectors to make a ladder up the tree to secure
the female, I observed several young male birds fly to
the nest and assiduously ply the bereaved widow with
food, a fact which seems to indicate a competition . . . as
severe as that among human beings." [1]

Hornbills are interesting and amusing pets, for they
become exceedingly tame, and will follow their owner
about like a dog.   They are extraordinarily adept at
catching food thrown to them, and Mr. Ridley[2] records
of a captive *Anthracoceros convexus* that it would catch
the sparrows which flew through its cage, and, after
crushing them in its powerful beak, it would throw
them up into the air, catch them again, and swallow
them whole.   In all except one species, *Rhinoplax vigil*,
the casques on the bills of these birds are hollow,
or rather partially filled with cancellated tissue, so
that they are quite light.   In *Buceros rhinoceros* the
casque is brightly coloured, being orange and red ;
the pigment is situated in a layer of horny tissue
lying immediately under a thin outer transparent layer.
It has been observed that this species frequently
polishes up its beak by rubbing it against the oil-gland

[1] *The Ibis* (7 Ser.), V. (1899), p. 549.
[2] *Journ. Roy. As. Soc. S. Br.*, No. 31 (1898), p. 78.

situated at the base of the pygidium, and after this operation the colours of the beak appear brighter than ever. This is simply due to the fact that the oiling of the beak makes the outer layer more transparent, and consequently the underlying pigment shows through more distinctly. If the bird is not in a good state of health, the oil-gland does not secrete properly, and the colours of the beak become much duller. Some time after death the outer horny layer becomes quite opaque and the beak turns to a dirty white, but much of its pristine beauty can be restored by the application of a little vaseline or salad oil. *Rhinoplax vigil* has a small but perfectly solid casque, and the beak of this species is therefore a rather formidable weapon. The use or purpose of the casque in the Hornbills is quite obscure: as it is present in both males and females, it is not a sexual adornment comparable with the tail of the Peacock, and it does not add to the effectiveness of the beak as a weapon or tool, owing to its extreme lightness, *R. vigil* of course being an exception.[1]

The Cuckoos are represented in Borneo by a number of species, all but two of which are parasitic, laying their eggs in the nests of other birds. The two species which make their own nests are *Carpococcyx radiatus* and *Centropus sinensis*. Nothing much appears to be known of the habits[2] or nest of the former species,

[1] Dr. Hose kindly sends me the following note : " The casque of *Buceros rhinoceros* is hollow except for a fine network inside, and it has occurred to me that it might possibly affect in some way the call of the bird, which makes a deep note resounding through the jungle. Hornbills make holes in trees sometimes, and the heavy bill with a casque attached would, it seems to me, be of some use in so doing."—E. B. P.

[2] Dr. Hose informs me that *Carpococcyx*, like *Centropus*, frequents

which is distinctly rare, but the latter is one of the commonest birds in the country. It is a large black and rusty-brown coloured bird which frequents gardens and any land that has been cleared of forest.

The native name for this Cuckoo, Bubut, is onomatopœic, and the monotonous call is very often heard in the places which the bird frequents—scrub and waste land overgrown with long grass and *Lantana* bushes. It feeds on all sorts of insects, even the most obnoxious species, such as the " woolly bear " caterpillars of Lasiocampid moths, the hair of which will produce sores on the human skin. Dayaks assert that the excrement of the bird will remove the skin from the hand, and even if this is an exaggeration it is quite evident that *Centropus* must be blessed with an intestinal canal of " triple brass."

There is an amusing folk-tale concerning this ˙bird and the Argus Pheasant, which runs as follows: Once upon a time the Ruai (Argus Pheasant) and the Bubut met together in the jungle and agreed to disguise themselves with tatu marks, as their enemies were over-plentiful and vigilant. The Bubut tatued the Ruai in a very effective way, as the plumage of the bird bears witness to this day, but the Ruai was lazy and could not be bothered to tatu his friend in return ; so, crying out that his enemies were approaching, he picked up the vessel containing the tatu-pigment, poured it over the Bubut's head, and then hastily decamped ; to this base treatment the Bubut owes its peculiar colouring.

The nest is a large, untidy structure, of loosely open spaces of cleared land, and is seldom met with in the forest.—E. B. P.

woven "lalang" grass (*Imperata cylindrica*); it is
placed on the ground, and is well hidden amongst the
tall rank grass which furnishes the bird with its building material. The embryos, when nearly ready for
hatching out, and the young nestlings present a most
peculiar appearance, for they are clothed on the dorsal
surface with a mane of long white hairs which affords
a striking contrast to the inky-black skin ; the ventral
surface is naked, and on the chin and belly the skin
is whitish. These hairs in reality are the immensely
prolonged tips of the feather-sheaths, the feathers being
still incompletely developed and quite hidden under
the skin. Since these structures are not true hairs it
is better to apply to them the name of "trichoptiles."
In the nearly ripe embryo the trichoptiles are very
long and are directed backwards in a flowing mane,
but a few days after hatching out the mane becomes
very rumpled, and the tips of the trichoptiles are
broken off, no doubt as a result of the movements
of the young birds in their nest and of the brooding
of the mother-bird. The bodies of adult birds are not
uniformly clothed with feathers, even though at first
sight they may appear to be, but the feathers grow
in certain tracts, known as "pterylæ," and the bare
unclothed spaces are known as "apteria." The shape
and arrangement of the pterylæ and apteria are of
great importance for purposes of classification. Seeing
that the trichoptiles are merely the elongated tips of
the sheaths which enclose the definitive feathers, it
might be supposed that their distribution over the
body of the embryo and nestling would be strictly
prophetic of the arrangement of the feathers of the
adult bird; but this is not so, for the trichoptiles are

6

absent from the ventral surface of embryos and nest-lings, and these parts are covered with feathers in the adult. It is clear therefore that the ventral feather-sheaths of the adult are not produced into trichoptiles, and this is probably due to mechanical reasons. The embryo lies in the egg in a curled-up position, the head being bent over to cover the belly in part, and consequently there is no room for a dense mane of trichoptiles to develop, as on the back. Moreover, the young nestling squirms about on its belly and chest, and a trichoptilar covering of these parts would quickly be worn off; as it is, the dorsal mane soon becomes sadly rumpled and abraded. It is reasonable to suppose that ventral trichoptiles are not developed, because if so they would be worn away on, or soon after, their first appearance. As the nestling grows older the horny feather-sheaths push through the skin; those on the dorsal surface are rufous with black bands, while the ventral ones are cream-coloured; the trichoptiles are now very short, and before long they entirely disappear. When finally the feather-sheaths are shed the young Bubut appears in a livery of yellowish red, banded with black, and it is a year before the adult colours are assumed. The significance and purpose of the trichoptiles is quite unknown to me; they do not serve to render the nestlings inconspicuous, quite the reverse; the nestlings, being buried in a deep nest hidden in dense grass, are presumably independent of adventitious aids to concealment; and the fact that the trichoptiles are far better developed in the embryo than in the nestling seems to dispose of the suggestion that their purpose is to aid the mother-bird in deter-mining the exact position of her young, shrouded in the obscurity of the nest.

The monotonous notes of the Cuckoos are quite a family characteristic. There is one species, *Cacomantis merulinus*, which is suitably known as the Brain-Fever Bird. It has the maddening habit of perching at night in some tree or shrub close to a house, and there, for hour after hour, at more or less irregular intervals, it will whistle its monotonous call. This call is a descending chromatic scale, and if this scale were always of the same number of notes the monotony could possibly be endured; but it varies, sometimes being of only three notes, sometimes of six or seven. He who is trying to woo the sleep that is so elusive on a hot, still night is compelled against his will to listen and to count the varying notes of these oft-repeated scales until he is driven to a frenzy, which may culminate in a volley of boots and household articles in the direction of the bush in which the maddening songster is concealed.

Two other species, *Hierococcyx fugax* and the closely similar *H. nanus*,[1] frequenters of old jungle, whistle in the twilight four notes, which Malays interpret as " Abang Kantong," i.e. " elder brother Kantong." The story goes that a cruel elder brother cut off the bird's

The author had not written the name of the Cuckoo he was referring to. The following note by Dr. Hose makes it clear that two species are involved, and I have altered the text in this sense (E. B. P.) : " I know these birds by the native name Kong-ka-put and Kapa-kapang, names which have been given from the note of the bird. It is supposed to foretell a good fruit year. The fact is that it feeds on insects on the blossoms and keeps up its monotonous note while engaged in searching for its food. *Hierococcyx fugax* is the species he probably means, and is the most common ; but *H. nanus* is so like *H. fugax* that it is hardly possible to see any difference. Their notes cannot be distinguished.—C. H."

leg, and ever since it has haunted the jungle calling
to its brother to restore the limb. I asked the Malay
who told me this tale if all these Cuckoos were one-
legged, to which he diplomatically replied that if his
story was true, then had the birds but one leg apiece.

Another familiar night-sound is the whistling hoot,
usually of two notes only, of the little Scops Owls;
these pretty little creatures have been known to fly
into houses to catch the geckos which run about on
walls and ceilings in numbers. Malays consider the
appearance of one of these birds in the house as an
omen of approaching death.

For nearly three years I kept in captivity a specimen
of the owl, *Photodilus badius*. When first the bird came
into my possession the contour-feathers were white,
narrowly barred with brown, but as time went on its
plumage became darker and darker until the feathers
were all dark brown with narrow bands of reddish
brown. This change of colour was not effected by
moulting, that is to say, by new feathers replacing old
ones, but simply by the spreading of pigment along
the barbules of the original feathers, so that the narrow
dark bands of the young bird gradually encroached
on the white parts of the feathers. This Owl had at
least three distinct cries: a harsh scream, uttered when
the bird was hungry; a sort of chuckling sound when
the food offered was seized, or when the bird was
tickled behind the ear; and a noise like the loud
crack of a whip, made in moments of fright. I could
never discover how this cracking noise was produced;
the beak was moved slightly but not sufficiently to
cause of itself the sound; probably the tongue played
some part in the performance, but its action could not

The Bornean Owl, *Photodilus badius*. (Photographed from life by the author, at Kuching.)

Plate XI.

To face p. 69.

be seen. The power that the bird had of discerning the approach of an enemy on the darkest of nights was very remarkable, and I tested it frequently. At this time I had also in captivity a young Palm-Civet, and if I carried this pet in my arms towards the end of the verandah of my house, where the Owl lived, no matter how dark the night, I would hear the loud cracking noise and great flutterings of wings, betokening violent efforts to escape, long before I could see the bird myself. If I approached alone, the Owl, being extremely tame, would show no signs of terror at all. I feel sure that the Owl was actually able to see the Palm-Civet, that it was not indebted only to its sense of smell for the power of distinguishing its enemy in the darkness, because if after handling the Civet-Cat I went near the Owl the bird was quite at its ease, though my hands and clothing must still have borne distinct traces of the effluvium which these mammals emit.

It interested me greatly to note the very important part which the tongue of *Photodilus badius* plays in the deglutition of food, and I have little doubt that other birds of prey, both Hawks and Owls, put it to the same use when swallowing their meal. The tongue of *Photodilus badius* may be roughly described as shaped like an arrow-head, the tip of the arrow pointing forwards, the barbs pointing backwards. This arrow-head is borne on a thick muscular stalk, the attachment being midway between the barbs and the point. The arrow-head is rather horny, and its upper surface is roughened : it may be sensory, but I doubt it.

No predatory bird munches or chews its food. If

the prey is small, it is bolted whole; if large, pieces are torn off it and swallowed. My Owl was fed mainly on the carcases of birds, the skins of which went to enrich the collections of the Sarawak Museum, and I watched the way in which the food was devoured many scores of times. If the food offered to the Owl was the carcase of some small Passerine, it would be held in the grasp of one foot while the Owl, bending its head down, would peck at the food in a tentative way; then all of a sudden the carcase would be seized in the beak, and the Owl, throwing its head up, would jerk the food well back into the gape of the mandibles. The pointed tip of the shell-pink tongue could now be seen pushing out from under the carcase, and finally, as the food was shaken further and further back into the gape, the whole arrow-head part of the tongue would appear projecting beyond the carcase. As soon as this point in the proceedings was reached, the tip of the arrow-head would be depressed and the barbs would correspondingly rise, then with a powerful muscular contraction of the tongue-stalk the whole tongue would be withdrawn, carrying with it the mass of food, against which the elevated arrow-barbs strongly pressed. In fact, a tongue of this type is nothing but an apparatus for hauling bulky masses of food from the mouth down the throat. I expect it will be found that this type of tongue is almost universal amongst raptorial birds.

The end of my pet was a sad one. I had occasion to be absent from Kuching for over a month, and during this time the Owl was fed on lumps of meat and bullock's liver. On my return the diet of small birds' carcases was resumed, but with fatal results, for

I found by autopsy that the gizzard had become—as a result of an unnatural food—so soft and flaccid that a bone of one of the ingested carcases had penetrated its wall, and peritonitis had ensued. This case is parallel with the classic one of John Hunter's Sea-Gull.

The Adjutant Bird is by no means so common in Borneo as it is in some parts of India, where it serves the useful purpose of general scavenger. The bird has a very raffish and dissipated look, and one that lived in captivity—or perhaps I should say under surveillance—in the Museum compound was always alluded to by a friend of mine as "that bird of yours which looks like a drunken parson." The black and white plumage, the bald head with sparse hair-like feathers on the back of the neck and the fishy eye suggested the resemblance, and when the bird stalked about the lawns in front of my house, it bore certainly a comical resemblance to a stooping old gentleman in a black tail-coat and white shirt-front with his hands behind his back.

The Adjutant is a most voracious feeder and is practically omnivorous. One day a Malay brought me for the Museum collections a snake about 5 feet long, but as there was already an abundance of examples of this species in the Museum, I cut the newly acquired specimen in two and gave one half to my Adjutant Bird, the other to a Sea-Eagle which was at that time a guest of mine. The Adjutant, after a few preliminary pecks at the snake, seized one end of it, and, with a little shaking of the head and prodigious gulpings, bolted it whole; the Sea-Eagle was still tearing at his moiety of the snake twelve hours later. Adjutants soon attach themselves to their human friends, and become so tame that there is no need to confine them in any way. My specimen spent much time stalking over the large grounds which surrounded the Museum, looking for frogs, lizards, and such-like small deer. One day an amusing rencontre between my Adjutant and a small Malay boy was witnessed. A broad gravel path leads across the Museum grounds, and along this at noon was walking a Malay urchin, a string of fish recently purchased for his parents' dinner dangling from his hand. The Adjutant Bird spied these tasty morsels and soon was alongside the little boy, making vicious dabs with his huge, powerful beak at the fish ; the urchin hastily plucked a fish from the string, threw it from him as far as he could, and took to his heels. It was the work of but a few moments for the Adjutant to retrieve the jettisoned fish and take up the pursuit again. Once more a fish was sacrificed, and with the same result as before, and finally, when their number was reduced to a scanty few, the unfortunate infant flung all to his insatiable pursuer and burst into tears. When the Adjutant Bird expects food to be thrown to it, it squats down so that the entire length of the metatarsi rests on the ground and then nods its head up and down, uttering the while a continuous harsh grating sound like a rusty saw cutting through wood ; at other times it is a very silent bird.

Few birds exhibit a more remarkable adaptation of structure to a specialized way of catching prey than the Indian Darter, *Plotus melanogaster.* This species was very common in North-East Sarawak at the mouths of the Trusan and Limbang Rivers. The birds could be seen perched in trees on the river-banks, with the wings widely spread out and the long neck bent near its base at an angle. The Darter feeds on fish, which it captures by diving into the water and bayoneting them with its long sharp beak. The edges of the mandibles are finely serrated, so that the struggling fish, after it has been freed from the "spear-point," can be securely held. The head is very small, not exceeding in circumference the thinnest part of the neck, which tapers from the base. The "kink" in the neck is due to a peculiar arrangement of the vertebræ; the eighth vertebra is articulated at right angles with the seventh and almost at right angles with the ninth. Powerful muscles pulling on the vertebræ can temporarily increase or decrease the angles at which this eighth vertebra is set in relation to those in front of and behind it, and as the Darter swims through the water in pursuit of a fish, the head and neck are constantly being jerked backwards and forwards, in a manner which has aptly been compared to the action of a man poising a spear preparatory to hurling it. When the Darter is sufficiently close to its prey, the head is driven forwards with great rapidity and the fish is impaled on the beak. The large webbed feet enable the Darter to rush through the water at a high rate of speed, and as the entire plumage is very oily, the bird when in the water is clothed with a pellicle of air shining like silver. The feathers on the neck are quite minute and set very closely together, so that they more resemble a furry covering than anything else.

CHAPTER III

SNAKES

BORNEO, like other tropical countries, is a land abounding in reptiles, and a newcomer is apt to scrutinize with care the odd nooks and corners in his house which he thinks likely places for the harbouring of venomous serpents, or to tread delicately when first he ventures into the jungle, lest he. disturb some monster Python or vicious Cobra. But a few months' experience will soon teach him that his fears are groundless. Snakes are not creatures that obtrude themselves on the notice of mankind, and the idea that a poisonous snake savagely attacks its human enemies or even stands boldly on its own defence is for the most part quite erroneous. Moreover, in a densely forested country like Borneo snakes have innumerable hiding-places and are never easy to find ; as will be seen later on, many species spend much of their lives in trees, and to this fact may be attributed the great rarity of cases of snake-bite in the Malayan region. During a seven years' residence in Borneo not half a dozen came under my notice. In India, with its dense population, cases are common enough, but I believe that a scrutiny of statistics would reveal the fact that the majority of snake-bites occur in those parts of the Empire in which there is comparatively little dense forest.

The great majority of Bornean snakes are harmless to man. Excluding the Sea-Snakes, which are all extremely poisonous, there are, out of a total of 113, only 11 poisonous species; or, including the Sea-Snakes, 24 out of a grand total of 125. The knowledge that only a small proportion of snakes in any given locality is poisonous affords small comfort to most people. In some the mere sight of a snake inspires terror, in others a Berserk desire to kill the noxious object, all investigation of its dangerous or harmless properties being postponed till the creature is dead. There can be little doubt that this horror of snakes manifested by all men is instinctive, and it is interesting to learn from some experiments conducted in the Zoological Society's Gardens by Dr. P. Chalmers Mitchell and Mr. R. I. Pocock[1] that our nearest relatives in the animal kingdom, the Primates, also show extreme terror when confronted by snakes, even though these may not be poisonous species. These observers, writing of the panic shown by two Orangs, state : " Both . . . are usually extremely slow and deliberate in their movement, but as soon as they got sight of a snake and long before it was near them, they fled silently but with the utmost rapidity, climbing as far out of reach as possible with a ludicrous celerity." Chimpanzees, on seeing the snakes brought near their cage, " fled backwards, uttering a low note sounding like ' huh, huh.' They soon got more excited and began to scream." Of all the Anthropoid Apes the Gibbon showed the least alarm, and it is suggested that these animals, being arboreal in their

[1] *P.Z.S.*, 1907, pp. 792–4.

habits, are brought less into contact with snakes, so that
their natural fear has been lost; but it may be pointed
out that the Orang is almost as arboreal in its habits as
the Gibbon. Furthermore, a very large number of snakes
in the Malayan region are tree-dwellers. Baboons,
Macaques, Langurs, Spider-Monkeys, all showed extreme fear at the sight of snakes, but Lemurs, the next
order to Primates, exhibited no fear at all, but instead,
interest and curiosity. Other animals, such as rodents,
ruminants, and birds, were quite indifferent to the
presence of snakes. Mr. H. N. Ridley,[1] however,
obtained rather different results in some similar experiments conducted on animals kept in captivity in the
Botanic Gardens, Singapore. He found the Orang
indifferent to snakes, but I believe that the specimen
was very young, and its horror perhaps had not
developed. "Common monkeys [i.e. Macaques] are
usually very excited, crowding together to look at it,
and chattering loudly. . . . The binturong, on bringing
a cobra near it, turned its face away as if in horror, but
really no doubt recognizing that its most vulnerable
portion was its face. The Water Mungoose, *Herpestes
brachyurus*, like the Indian Mungoose, bristles up its
fur and attacks and devours the snake. Some deer,
when a large python was brought past their paddock,
though at some distance, crowded together at the bars,
gazing at it and stamping their feet, evidently recognizing
it as a dangerous enemy." To these experiments I may
add that a small workshop attached to the Sarawak
Museum was freed in a day or two of a veritable plague
of Rats by a small Python that had found its way into
this happy hunting ground. The Python unfortunately

did so much damage amongst the glassware stored in the workshop that it had to be removed, and the Rats soon made their reappearance. A stuffed specimen of a large Python was then substituted for the living one, and for a long time proved very effectual as a "scarecrow," but eventually the Rats overcame their terror of this dummy and resumed possession of their old quarters.

A certain number of Bornean snakes have burrowing habits; such are the species belonging to the genera *Typhlops*, *Cylindrophis*, *Xenopeltis* and *Calamaria*. These snakes, though belonging to different families, yet present a general similarity that is brought about by the burrowing habit. The head is blunt, the eyes small, the body is shining and quite smooth, thus offering little resistance to the soil as the snakes bore their way underground; they are, moreover, of almost equal diameter throughout, so that without careful examination it is difficult to tell where the body ends and the tail begins. The species of *Typhlops* are the most modified for burrowing; they are little, worm-like snakes that spend nearly all their life underground or under stones, and nothing seems to be known of their habits. *Cylindrophis rufus* is a very common species; it is black with a few white spots, an orange collar, and the tip of the tail is marked with red and is pointed; the ventral surface is banded with black and white. This snake is extraordinarily flexible; when handled it assumes every sort of shape from cylindrical to nearly flat and ribbon-like, and this power of altering its form enables it to squeeze through extremely narrow clefts. A specimen that I kept alive in a box half filled with clay and covered with a bell-jar pressed down into the clay until the rim touched the bottom of the box, burrowed into the clay and

eventually escaped by squeezing itself under the rim
of the bell-jar. When the snake is teased it assumes a
very characteristic attitude; the head is more or less
concealed under coils of the body, but the tip of the
tail is raised in a threatening manner and bears a
rough resemblance to a head.[1] In this attitude the
red colouring of the tail is displayed to the best advantage and, with the resemblance to a head, serves
no doubt to intimidate prospective enemies. The natives
of Sarawak aver that the snake has a head at each end
of the body and that a bite from either head is very
deadly; I once demonstrated to a Malay the innocuous
character of this creature by opening its mouth and
forcing it to bite my finger, and showing him the tiny
teeth too small to inflict a wound on a moderately
thick skin, but I only drew from him the comment
that white men were certainly wonderful beings, for
they were immune to serpents' venom! This species
does not, like *Typhlops*, live entirely underground, but
occasionally takes to water; one specimen I found in
an old well, and its stomach contained an eel almost
as large as itself; another example in the Sarawak
Museum was taken in the act of swallowing a Water-
Snake, *Fordonia leucobalia*. Another species of the same
genus, *Cylindrophis lineatus*, is very rare; only three specimens have been discovered, one in Singapore and two in
Sarawak; it is characterized by two broad red lines
running along the back, and by a red head and tail-
tip. *Xenopeltis unicolor* is a beautiful iridescent snake;
an adult specimen observed by Captain S. S. Flower[2]
used to twist itself, when annoyed, into an "irregular

[1] Flower, *P.Z.S.*, 1899, p. 656.
  Ibid., p. 657.

pile of tight coils, except the tail, which was held on
one side, raised from the ground, and the tip kept
vibrating at a great speed."

Since the trees in the Bornean forests are even more
densely crowded with animal life than the floor of the
jungle itself, it is not surprising to find that some
snakes are driven to search for their prey in surroundings that we are not accustomed to associate with
limbless animals. Snakes can easily climb trees by
working their way up the trunks, their ventral scales
getting a good hold on the asperities in the bark, or
they insinuate themselves between the twisting stems of
the creepers which festoon most of the jungle trees,
forming rope ladders, of which they readily avail themselves. No doubt most kinds descend by the way up
which they climb, but three species have the power
of making a sort of parachute flight from a lofty elevation to a lower level. These three are *Chrysopelea ornata*,
C. chrysochlora, and *Dendrophis pictus*. To assert that
snakes can " fly " is bound to challenge criticism, if
not to provoke vigorous protests against wilful perver-
sion of the truth ; it will be well then to give in
some detail an account of the "flying" habit manifested by *Chrysopelea ornata*. When I first arrived in
Sarawak I was entertained by some of the Kuching
residents with stories of the strange and wonderful
habits of the animals of the jungle ; many of the
stories were palpably manufactured with intent to
deceive the guileless newcomer, and the story of the
flying snakes was one that I inwardly put into this
category. When the Dayak hunter attached to the
Sarawak Museum brought in one day a dead specimen
of *Chrysopelea ornata* and remarked that he had seen

it fly out of a tree I paid little serious attention to
his statement. However, some weeks later the same
man brought in a specimen of *Chrysopelea chrysochlora*
and said that he had seen this also fly out of a tree.
On cross-examination I found that by "flying" he
meant to say that the snake shot out at an angle from
a tree and descended in an oblique line to the ground
with its body held quite straight. The matter seemed
now to be worthy of serious investigation, and I gave
instructions that the next specimen captured was to
be brought to me alive, and eventually a living
example of *C. ornata* was found. As soon as I
handled the snake I gained some idea of the means
whereby it could "fly." The scales along the belly

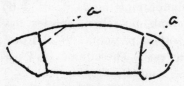

in snakes are broad plate-like structures, and in *C.
ornata* and also in *C. chrysochlora* each scale has a
hinge-line on either side, marked *a* in the adjoining
diagram. As the snake writhed about in my hands
I could feel that every now and then the ventral scales
by a forcible muscular contraction were drawn inwards, so that the snake became deeply concave along
all its under-surface. The scales moved inward on
their hinge-lines, and at the same time there was a
slight spreading out of the ribs. When the muscles
working the scales relaxed, the snake re-assumed its
ordinary cylindrical shape. The snake, in fact, may
be compared, when at rest, to a cylindrical piece of
bamboo; when restive, to a cylinder of bamboo bisected

along its length, convex on one side, concave on the opposite side. Now if a cylinder of bamboo and a split length of bamboo of equal weight be dropped from a height, the former will reach the ground before the latter, provided that the latter be dropped with the concave surface directed downwards, for by virtue of its concave surface it will be buoyed up to a certain extent; now, it seemed to me that the same might be the case with the "flying" snake. So I took the snake up to the verandah of the Museum and threw it into the air, but I was disappointed to see it fall in writhing coils to the ground, which it hit with a distinct thud. Then I allowed the snake merely to fall from my hands to the ground, and after one or two false starts eventually I felt it glide rapidly through my hands, straightening itself out, and hollowing-in its ventral surface as it moved; this time it fell not in a direct line to the ground but at an angle, the body being kept rigid all the time. The height from which the snake descended was not great enough for it to be possible to determine with any accuracy whether the snake fell more slowly than when it tumbled in irregular coils, but this certainly appeared to be the case, and there can be little doubt that the hinged ventral scales of these snakes, enabling them to draw the belly inwards, are a modification of structure rendering a parachute flight possible. Some years later I gained an indirect confirmation of the "flight" of snakes, for another Dayak hunter brought me a specimen of *Dendrophis pictus*, and asserted that he had seen it "fly" down from a tree. On examining the snake I found that this species also possessed hinged ventral scales, and that it too had the power of hollowing-in

7

its ventral surface so as to become very concave. It is interesting to find confirmation of the "flying" habit in snakes from other observers. Captain Flower [1] reports having seen a small specimen of *Chrysopelea ornata* "take a flying leap, from an upstairs window, downward and outward on to a branch of a tree and then crawl away among the foliage. The distance it had jumped was measured and found to be nearly 8 feet." Mahon Daly,[2] writing from Siam, says that he and a Kareen interpreter "saw a snake, about $2\frac{1}{2}$ feet long, sail from a very high tree on one side of the road to a lower one the opposite side."

Chrysopelea ornata has a wide distribution, ranging from India to the Malay Archipelago and Southern China, and Mr. G. A. Boulenger, F.R.S., informs me that more than once he has received specimens at the British Museum from various parts of its range with the note that the specimens had the reputation of being able to "fly." More than one writer waxes very enthusiastic over the agility and activity of this snake, and it certainly is a very beautiful creature. It is variable in colour, but the commonest variety is black above, each scale with a round greenish-yellow spot and a series of coral-red spots along the back—each of these spots like a tiny four-petalled flower in shape; the ventral scales are green, edged with black. Its congener, *C. chrysochlora*, is also a handsome species.

These snakes prey for the most part on tree-haunting lizards, but one has been reported to have eaten a bat.

Green is a colour that, as might be expected, is characteristic of tree-haunting snakes, and three

[1] *P.Z.S.*, 1899, p. 684.
[2] *Journ. Bombay N.H. Soc.*, XII. (1898–99), p. 589.

common Sarawak species are of a very vivid green. These are *Coluber oxycephalus*; *Dryophis prasinus,* the Whip-Snake ; and *Lachesis wagleri,* the Tree-Viper. The first two of these belong to the great family *Colubridæ,* but to different sections of that family. The *Colubridæ* are divided into three sections—the *Aglypha,* the *Opisthoglypha,* and the *Proteroglypha.* The *Aglypha* are not poisonous, and all the teeth are solid ; the *Opisthoglypha* have the hinder teeth situated on that part of the upper jaw known as the maxilla ; these teeth are grooved, and some of the species are poisonous, though their poison has seldom much effect on man. The *Proteroglypha* are provided with a deadly poison, and have the front teeth or fangs on the maxilla grooved or perforated ; the ducts of the poison glands lead to these fangs. *Coluber oxycephalus* is one of the *Aglypha, Dryophis prasinus* one of the *Opisthoglypha,* or suspected Colubrines, as the snakes belonging to this section are sometimes called : the Cobra is an example of a Proteroglyphous snake. *Coluber oxycephalus* is found amongst herbage, in bushes, or in trees. The body is bright grass-green, but the tail is of a peculiar brownish colour, and as there is no gradation from the one colour to the other at the point of junction of tail and body, the snake has a rather curious appearance. The Malays calls this species " ular ikor mati," or the snake with the dead tail ; the Sea-Dayaks say of it that if a man be bitten by it when the moon is full he will take little or no harm, but if bitten when the moon is new, then he will certainly die. One specimen I found amongst scrub growing on the sandy foreshore at the mouth of the Trusan River in Northern Sarawak. In adaptation to its surroundings this specimen was bright ochreous except the tail, which was of the usual brown colour. On bottling the specimen in formalin I was surprised to see that the ochreous colour very soon turned into the bright grass-green of the tree- and shrub-haunting form. From this observation it is quite obvious that this species has considerable powers of altering its colour to suit its surroundings ; its usual habitat is arboreal, and the green colour is the more primitive. In response to a change of environment the snake can alter its colouring, but sudden death destroys the mechanism whereby this change is brought about, and the snake in death reverts to the primitive colouring of the species [Note 8, p. 314].

Another species of the same genus, *Coluber tæniurus*, is found in limestone districts amongst rocks, and its mottled colouring harmonizes wonderfully well with the limestone and the lights and shadows produced by overhanging foliage. Mr. H. N. Ridley obtained specimens inside quite dark caves in the Malay Peninsula, and found them very much paler than specimens caught outside the caves—in fact, almost white. These cave-dwellers lived on the bats that thronged about them. The two last-named species are then characteristic protectively coloured snakes, but their congener, *C. melanurus*, though not a very conspicuous species, does not rely so much on its resemblance to its surroundings to protect it as on a very aggressive attitude that it adopts when irritated. It is rather a savage snake ; when it is teased it raises the front third of the body just slightly off the ground, throws this part into a series of **S**-shaped curves, and hisses threateningly. In this attitude the front part, at least, of the animal, which has a series of prominent black markings on the sides of the neck, looks very much larger than it really is, and presenting a sort of dim resemblance to the dilated hood of a Cobra, is sufficiently alarming. Another Malayan species—though not occurring in Borneo—*C. radiatus*, has the neck, according to Captain Flower, "apparently dilatable," but this observer does not state whether this species sits up like a Cobra when teased.

Dryophis prasinus is the most beautiful and graceful creature imaginable; it is quite gentle, and is one of the few snakes which Malays and Dayaks acknowledge to be harmless, and they have little or no objection to handling it. To see one of these snakes gliding amongst foliage is to realize the meaning of the phrase "poetry of motion." Often they may be seen with the tail and part of the body twisted round a branch, whilst the front third of the body is held out almost straight, the head and neck slowly turning from side to side; and the sinuous grace of this posture reveals the wonderful perfection of a serpent's muscular development. The commonest variety of this snake is grass-green in colour, but I have also met with salmon-pink, pale brown, and speckled grey forms. I do not know if these varieties are constant, or if one form is capable of turning into another, as in the case of *Coluber oxycephalus*. A nearly allied species of *Dryophis,*—*D. mycterizans,* from India, has the reputation of being rather savage, and the Tamils and Singhalese apply to it names which signify that it strikes at the eyes of persons and cattle. Curiously enough, this idea has received support from a European observer who, when handling some specimens, was

bitten by one which darted at his eye;[1] two punctures were made by the snake on his eyelids, and a
tooth of the snake was found in one of the wounds.
Capt. F. Wall,[2] a leading authority on the snakes of
India, relates that an Indian native bitten by a *Dryophis mycterizans* had his hand and forearm greatly
swollen, and though there was no pain they felt
numb, and the swelling did not subside for about two
days; so there can be no doubt that the secretion of
the salivary glands of this species possesses toxic properties. I have never known *D. prasinus* to bite, so
cannot say if it resembles its congener in the degree
of potency of its salivary secretion, but it is probable
that all the *Opisthoglypha* secrete poison which is
sufficient to paralyse their prey.

The third arboreal green species is the Tree-Viper,
Lachesis wagleri, a snake with a head like the ace of
spades in shape, a short tail, and a covering of small
scales. All the *Viperidæ* are venomous, but *L. wagleri*
is not dangerous to man, and though the fangs are
rather formidable-looking the poison-gland is small.
Whilst in Sarawak I heard of one or two cases of
Viper-bite, but in no case was the bite followed by
death, or even by much pain and inconvenience.
Some varieties of the green Tree-Viper are ornamented
with narrow red bands, and the young (which are
brought forth alive) are always red-banded, yet these
red bands do not in the lights and shades of the forest
render the snakes conspicuous, but serve rather to
break up its outlines, cause the animal to merge into
its background.

[1] *Journ. As. Soc. Bengal*, LXVII., Pt. II. (1898), pp. 66-7.
[2] *Journ. Bombay N.H. Soc.*, XVI. (1904-5), p. 549.

The two Bornean Pythons, *Python reticulatus*, above, and *P. curtus*, below.
(Photographed from life by the author, at Kuching.)

Plate XII.

To face p. 87.

Lachesis borneensis is a brown species, and is found on the ground amongst decaying vegetation. A young specimen that I captured was coiled up, and so closely resembled a fungus that I nearly placed my hand on it before I realized its true nature. All the Bornean vipers are sluggish creatures, and trust to their protective coloration and to immobility to elude the observation of their enemies rather than to hasty flight. They lie in wait for their prey ; and here again their colouring plays an important part, for their victims are as easily misled as are their enemies.

The snake which perhaps is more feared than any other is the Python. There are two species in Borneo —*Python reticulatus,* which is common and sometimes attains enormous proportions, and *Python curtus,* a much rarer form and considerably smaller. Tales of the prodigious strength of these crushing snakes are told by native and European alike, but a good discount must generally be allowed for exaggeration. Fables, too, have grown round these monsters, such as the belief of the Dayaks that if the terminal bone of the vertebral column be planted in the ground a new snake will grow from it. Much virtue is attached by the Chinese to the fat of the Python, which is regarded as a cure for rheumatism ; the excrement [solid urine] also, which is dry and bright primrose-yellow in colour, is considered to be a very efficacious remedy for many complaints. The popular belief that the Pythons and also the Boa-Constrictors of the New World, after crushing their prey into a shapeless mass, plentifully beslaver it with their saliva in order to make swallowing easier, is quite erroneous. The prey is seized with a violent bite, and if it is small the snake makes no attempt to surround it with coils of its body, but if the prey is of large size, or if it struggles violently, then it may be embraced in one or more coils. When the victim is suffocated the Python [1] "passes its head all round the prey, playing over it with its forked tongue, and by some means other than that of sight, as the choice is made equally in the dark, perhaps by the sense of touch in the muzzle or lips, selects the head of the carcase to begin the process of swallowing." The amount that a Python of over 20 feet long can swallow is something astounding. Mr. Ridley states that a specimen measuring 22 feet in length that was brought to him at the Botanic Gardens in Singapore contained the remains of a deer, and I have seen a specimen of 18 feet in length which had just swallowed a large pig; in this example the middle of the body was enormously distended, so that the skin was stretched almost to bursting-point, and the scales, instead of lying side by side and almost overlapping, were situated quite far apart, and between them it was possible to see the hairs of the pig through the skin and stomach-wall of the snake. This power that snakes have, of swallowing very large masses, is, as is well known, due to the loose attachment of the various bones by which the jaw apparatus is slung on to the skull, permitting a wide gape to be made; the mandibles, or lower jaws, also are not fused in front but the two halves are merely joined by elastic tissue. The process whereby a Python swallows its meal has been described as follows: [2] "It gives a huge gulp

[1] Mitchell and Pocock, *P.Z.S.*, 1907, p. 786.
[2] *Ibid.*, p. 787.

and fixes its teeth as far back over the body [of its prey] as is possible, and then slowly, in big wrinkles, pushes a portion of its mouth and gullet forwards; then with another gulp gets its teeth fixed still a little further on to the prey and repeats the forward bringing up of the body, the general appearance of the motion being similar to that of the progression of an earthworm." The colouring of *Python reticulatus* strikes a visitor to a museum as highly conspicuous, but as a matter of fact the snake in its natural haunts in jungle is difficult to see; it is occasionally found coiled up amongst the roots of some forest giant, but when on the look-out for a meal is said to hang head downwards along the trunk of a tree with its tail coiled round a branch; from this position it can make a grab at any passing animal. Only two authentic cases of men having been attacked by a Python have ever come to my notice. One of these was a Land-Dayak who was seized by the calf of the leg as he was passing a tree down whose trunk hung a Python; a companion who was walking behind him chopped off the head of the snake, but the man still bore the scars of the Python's bite some years after.

The following is quoted from the *Sarawak Gazette* of April 1891, p. 52 :—

"At Judan, a village some six miles from Muka, a man and his son, aged from 10 to 12 years, were sleeping in their house, inside a mosquito curtain. They were on the floor near the wall. In the middle of the night the father was awakened by his son calling out, the lamp was out and the father passed his hand over his son but found nothing amiss, so he turned over and went to sleep again, thinking the boy was dreaming. Shortly afterwards the child again called out saying that a crocodile was taking him. This time the father, thoroughly aroused, felt again and found that a snake had closed his jaws on the boy's head; he then prized open the reptile's mouth and released the head of his son, but the beast drew the whole of his body into the house and encircled the body of the father; he was rescued by the neighbours who were attracted by the cries for help of the terrified couple. The snake when killed was found to be about 15 feet long. The head and forehead of the boy are encircled with punctured wounds produced by the python's teeth."

A third instance of a Python attacking a man appeared at the time to be authentic, but since my return to England I have had reasons to doubt it. The story is this: Two Malays who had been trading amongst the Dayaks of the Samarahan River reported to head-quarters in Kuching that, one evening whilst camping on the river-bank, a companion went down to the river to bathe; shortly afterwards they heard his shrieks for assistance, and running to the rescue, found him in the coils of a huge Python; they attacked the Python with their chopping knives and eventually succeeded in freeing their friend, but the snake escaped and its victim, all his ribs and one arm being broken, shortly expired; in a tropical climate a corpse cannot be kept for long, so they buried him. Their story was accepted in good faith by the authorities. The late Colonel Bingham, a well-known naturalist who had had a wide experience as a forest officer in Burma, to whom I retailed this story, told me that two similar reports were made to district magistrates in Burma to account for the disappearance of two natives. In each case the magistrates, suspecting foul play, caused the bodies to be exhumed, and it was found that the unfortunate men had been murdered; their bodies had been entwined with coils of rattan which were hauled tighter and tighter by the murderers until life was extinct. The murderers, contemplating an investigation into their crime, had chosen this method of committing it in the erroneous belief that the weals and bruises made by the rattan thongs simulated the marks made by a crushing snake, and that consequently the authorities could be gulled into believing that the murdered men had met their death in encounters with Pythons. With this gruesome evidence before one, it is permissible to regard the Sarawak Malays' story with considerable doubt.

The poisonous land-snakes of Borneo are represented by six *Proteroglypha* of the sub-family *Elapinæ*, and by five Vipers. The *Elapinæ* include two very venomous "Kraits," as they are called in India—the Banded Krait, *Bungarus fasciatus*, and the Red-Headed Krait, *B. flaviceps*, known to the Sea-Dayaks as Kendawan. The former is broadly banded with cream-colour and black; the latter varies in colour on the back from uniform olive-brown to deep black with brownish head; below it is grey or bluish black; lips, chin, and throat are bright yellow. My friend Mr. H. N. Ridley informs me that *B. fasciatus* when irritated thumps its tail loudly on the ground; this action may be interpreted as a warning signal, for if the snake is surprised in the jungle the beating of the tail against the dead leaves strewing the ground makes a considerable rattling noise that can be heard for some little distance. In India the Kraits are responsible for a great many of the deaths attributed to snake-bite, and from experiments conducted on animals it appears that the common Indian Krait, *B. candidus*, is even more deadly than the Cobra. Both the Cobra, *Naia tripudians,* and the King-Cobra, or Hamadryad, *N. bungarus,* occur commonly in Sarawak, but I cannot say that I ever heard of any one being bitten by either of them. Both species have the habit, when irritated, of rearing up the head and front part of the body, and expanding the skin of the neck—the so-called hood. The Indian Cobra is much paler than the Malayan form, and the hood is ornamented at the back with the well-known spectacle-marks, which make it very conspicuous. The Bornean Cobra and the Hamadryad are dark-brown snakes, but the skin on the neck between the scales is yellow, and when the hood is spread out this yellow skin shows up very distinctly between the scales. There can be no reasonable doubt that this hood-dilating habit is a danger signal, and we will discuss later on the reason why poisonous snakes display these signals whenever they are excited. The Malayan Cobra, in addition to rearing up its body and dilating its hood, has the habit of squirting out its saliva for a considerable distance and of uttering a peculiar snorting noise. Mr. Ridley[1] states that he was once struck in the face by the saliva, at a distance of 8 feet; the saliva causes only a very slight irritation of the skin, but if it enters the eye much inflammation is set up. The same spitting habit has recently been recorded for a West African Viper [see Note, p. 104]. The Hamadryad sometimes attains a very large size; the biggest that I have seen measured 14 feet 1½ inches. It was found in a dying condition in a ditch, and fell an easy prey to two Tamil coolies, who brought it in triumph to the Sarawak Museum. A few days before, this Museum

[1] *Journ. Roy. As. Soc. S. Br.,* No. 32 (1899), p. 201.

had received a specimen of 9½ feet in length, which
had made its appearance inside a house in Kuching,
and another of over 10 feet. This species is a snake-
eater, and I am inclined to think that snakes form
its sole article of diet. Mr. Ridley has seen a
Hamadryad holding a small Python in its mouth ;
the Python was not dead, but expired very shortly
after its enemy had been driven off. A Malay reported
to my predecessor at the Sarawak Museum, the late
Mr. Edward Bartlett, that he had seen a Python and
a Hamadryad fighting, but he killed both snakes whilst
the issue of the combat was still in doubt. Capt. F.
Wall [1] gives a list of snakes that have been recorded as
victims of the Hamadryad : these are the Banded Krait,
the Cobra, the Hamadryad itself, and the Indian Python.
Mr. L. Wray records *Adeniophis* (*Doliophis*) *bivirgatus*,
the Banded Krait, and two non-poisonous Colubrines
as having been taken from the stomachs of Hamadryads captured in the Malay Peninsula.[2] It is quite
evident that snakes are not immune to the poison
of other snakes, even to that of their own species,
and in a combat between two poisonous species he
must be four times armed who " gets his blow in
fust."

The next species on our list of poisonous snakes are
Doliophis bivirgatus and *D. intestinalis*, two small and
very brightly coloured species. The natives of the
Malay Peninsula assert that both species progress
with their tails held up in the air, thus exhibiting
to best advantage the red colouring of the under side
and warning their enemies of their poisonous properties ;

[1] *Journ. Bombay N.H. Soc.*, XVII. (1906–07), p. 393.
[2] *Journ. Fed. Malay States Mus.*, II. (1907), p. 64. Signed L. W.

but the statement needs confirmation.[1] Mr. Ridley [2] states that *D. intestinalis* [referred to as *Callophis*—E. B. P.] beats its tail upon the ground when annoyed, like *Bungarus fasciatus*. Both species of *Doliophis* are remarkable for the enormous development of the poison glands, which extend down the anterior third of the body, displacing backwards the heart and other internal organs ; but though these snakes must have a bigger supply of poison than other Colubrines they are by no means vicious, and there is no record of men having ever been bitten by either of them.

The Vipers are represented in Borneo by five species of the genus *Lachesis*, but only two of these, *L. wagleri* and *L. borneensis*, are at all common. Museum specimens of *L. sumatranus*, one of the rarer species, are brightly coloured, but I am not acquainted with it in a state of nature, and would not be surprised to learn that in its natural surroundings it is as inconspicuous as its congeners. The Vipers differ from the poisonous Colubrines not only in important anatomical details, and in their sluggish habits, but also in the character of their poison. If an animal be bitten by a Cobra the first symptom that manifests itself is a pronounced lethargy, then the hind-quarters became paralysed, the paralysis spreads slowly over the body, there is great difficulty in breathing, and finally death ensues through the paralysis of the respiratory centre in the brain. The heart, however, is not affected, and is found to be still beating in animals that have recently succumbed to the action of the poison. An examination of the blood of such

[1] Annandale, *Fasciculi Malayenses, Zoology*, Pt. I. (1903), p. 169.
[2] *Journ. Roy. As. Soc. S. Br.*, No. 32 (1899), p. 195.

an animal shows that the red blood corpuscles have
been broken up, and the clotting of the blood when
drawn off into a vessel is much retarded. In the case
of man, death from a Cobra bite ensues in three to six
hours, but it is even more rapid in the case of small
mammals such as rabbits. The symptoms of Viper-
poisoning are very different ; in cases where a very
venomous species, such as the Daboia Viper of India,
has injected a lethal dose, the power of equilibrium
of the stricken animal is upset, but there is no paralysis ;
violent convulsions ensue and terminate in death in
ten to fifteen minutes ; examination of the blood shows
that extensive clotting has taken place in the veins
and arteries, causing suspension of the heart's action.
Less powerful doses of the poison bring about fainting
fits, and the animal may live for many hours, or even
recover ; in these cases there is no intravascular
clotting, but the blood corpuscles are broken up, and
the walls of the small blood-vessels and capillaries
are injured, so that there is much extravasation of
blood from the various organs of the body. When
Dr. Calmette discovered an antidote for Cobra poison,
" anti-venin " as it is termed, it was hoped that this
would be efficacious in all cases of snake-bite, but
now that we know how different is the action of Viper
poison and Colubrine poison, it is not very surprising
to learn that it is of no avail in cases of Viper-bites.
It is, however, certainly surprising that the anti-venin
of Cobra is inefficacious in cases of poisoning from
Kraits, which in their symptoms are very like Cobra-
poisoning ; yet such is indeed the case, and it is now
certain that these anti-venins, many of which have
been prepared, are specific in their action, so that

a man bitten by a Krait can only be cured by the Krait anti-venin, and one bitten by a Cobra can only be cured by the Cobra anti-venin.

The Sea-Snakes, constituting the sub-family *Hydrophiinæ* of the *Colubridæ-Proteroglypha*, have a wide distribution, ranging throughout the Indian Ocean so far south as the Cape of Good Hope and throughout the Western South Pacific. All the species, with one exception, are truly aquatic, spending their life in the sea or in tidal rivers, though I have taken one of the marine forms, *Distira cyanocincta*, on land at some distance from water. *Platurus* is a somewhat anomalous genus connecting the *Hydrophiinæ* with the *Elapinæ*; one species is frequently found on land, and one specimen has been taken on a rocky island of the Philippine group at a considerable elevation above sea-level. This species, though provided with the formidable poison-apparatus characteristic of the Sea-Snakes, is very gentle, and allows itself to be handled without attempting to bite.[1] All the Bornean Sea-Snakes, of which there are thirteen, are very poisonous and vicious. One of the commonest species is *Enhydrina valakadien*, and I have seen great numbers of it in the sea between Singapore and Sarawak, and have admired the graceful way in which they swam. The species are generally banded in two colours, black and yellow, grey and white, or some other combination, and are consequently very conspicuous. The tail is flattened from side to side, and forms a very effective paddle for swimming. I have taken specimens that have been much infested by small barnacles of the genus *Dichelaspis* attached to the scales. A friend once caught a specimen of *Enhyd-*

[1] Boulenger, *Natural Science*, I. (1892), p. 44.

rina valakadien in rather peculiar circumstances : we were fishing with a seine net in very shallow water at the mouth of the Trusan River, and after one haul I noticed the head and neck of a Sea-Snake protruding through the mesh of the net ; since the mesh was fairly wide, I could not understand how so slender a creature failed to get through and make its escape, but on closer examination I saw that its passage was blocked by the enormous distension of its stomach, which contained a fish measuring about 3 inches in depth ; if ever a snake could express disgust at an awkward situation resulting from its own greed, that snake certainly did. The same haul of the net brought up a young Sawfish, and the tremendous power exhibited by the thrashing blows of the saw against the sides of our canoe as the fish twitched its head from side to side in the convulsive movements of death was quite a revelation to me. What with an angry poisonous snake entangled in the net, and a lusty young Sawfish leaping about the floor of a crank canoe cumbered with fishing gear, we had quite a lively time of it until the fish received its quietus, and the snake found its last resting-place in a jar of spirit. The fish found in the snake's stomach was *Chorinemus toloo*, one of the Horse-Mackerel tribe : it is provided with a strong dorsal and two strong pectoral spines.

Dr. Annandale[1] records the occurrence of this Sea-Snake in great quantities in Patani Bay, Malay Peninsula, and states that they feed very largely on Siluroid fish and others provided with strong spines. As he took many specimens of the snakes with these spines protruding from their bodies, and as they did not seem

[1] *Fasciculi Malayenses, Zoology*, Pt. I. (1903), p. 167.

to be inconvenienced in the slightest degree thereby, he believes that the fish-spines are eliminated from the body of the snakes by passing simply through the wall of the alimentary canal and through the body-wall to the exterior. It is difficult to see how the spines of such a fish as *Chorinemus toloo* could pass out of the snake's body in any other way. The same naturalist confirms an observation that I have made more than once, that Sea-Snakes, when irritated, do not hiss but utter a low gurgling noise.

It is of interest to find that in each of the three sections of *Colubridæ* there is one sub-family of aquatic snakes. In the section *Aglypha* we have the *Acrochordinæ*, powerful crushing snakes, living in the sea near the shore and in rivers; in the section *Opisthoglypha* we have the *Homolopsinæ*, some species of which are commonly found in mud on the banks of rivers, others in the rivers themselves, others on the sea-shore; and in the section *Proteroglypha*, the *Hydrophiinæ*, which in their structure are far better adapted to an essentially marine life than either of the other two sub-families.

This short and incomplete review of the snakes of Sarawak may conclude with some remarks on their coloration and its significance. We have seen that certain poisonous snakes, the Vipers, as well as certain non-poisonous snakes, are coloured in harmony with their surroundings. This resemblance of animals to inanimate surroundings is a very common phenomenon in Nature, and in the case of plant-eating defenceless creatures has a protective purpose and is termed "protective resemblance." In the case of snakes, animals which prey on other animals, this resemblance plays a double role, for it enables the snakes to escape not only the observation of their enemies, but also the observation of the creatures that form their prey, and has been termed "aggressive resemblance." We have also seen that other poisonous snakes are conspicuously marked with alternate bands of colour (*Hydrophiinæ*, the Banded Krait), or are brilliantly coloured (*Doliophis*, Red-Headed Krait), or display characteristic warning signals when annoyed (Cobra, Hamadryad). It is another common phenomenon in the animal world that creatures protected by poisonous, or nauseous, properties advertise these qualities by bright and conspicuous colouring or by warning signals. It may be asked why such deadly snakes as the Rattle-Snake and the Cobra should trouble to advertise their dangerous character, the one by springing its rattle, the other by expanding its conspicuous hood; they are, it is argued, sufficiently armed against all possible enemies by their poison, and therefore they need neither fear nor warn their enemies. But snakes, both harmless and deadly, have numberless enemies. Captain Wall has compiled a long list of them, drawn from records in scientific literature, varying from man to ants. An Elephant, a Deer, or Buffalo plunging through the jungle might tread on a Cobra and crush its life out had the snake no means of advertising its presence in a conspicuous manner; the Cobra in its dying convulsions might inject a deadly dose of poison into the animal that had trodden on it, but how would the cobra be benefited by that dying effort? The whole conception of a poisonous snake as a ferocious animal that stealthily pounces on and kills every creature that disturbs it, wittingly or unwittingly, is quite erroneous; the belief that the Hamadryad will chase a man, if he disturbs it, is a pure myth. All who have observed these deadly snakes in their natural conditions agree unanimously in stating that the Cobra and Hamadryad are only anxious to get away from those who disturb them, and they have no desire to waste their precious supply of poison on an animal too large for them to devour subsequently. Professor Minchin when in India came suddenly on a Cobra in the road ; the Cobra reared up and displayed its hood in the best approved manner, but while Professor Minchin was watching it he perceived that the tail of the Cobra was moving about the surface of the ground, and eventually slipped into a large fissure for which the snake had evidently been feeling, and, in less time than it takes to write it, the Cobra had slid down into the fissure and was gone. The late Colonel Bingham encountered in a Burmese jungle a pair of large Hamadryads, male and female ; he was cornered between them, for one was on his right, the other on his left ; but they made no attempt to attack him, and when they realized that he had no intention of attacking them, they lowered their erected crests and silently glided away. Many other observations of a similar nature could be quoted, but these suffice to show that we can safely regard a poisonous snake as a somewhat timid creature, admirably equipped with a complicated poison mechanism for the capture and destruction of its prey, but resorting to the use of this for purposes of defence only in the last extremity, though advertising the possession of it by signals which to the knowing eye read as plåinly as the printed words *Nemo me impune lacessit.*

The question of mimicry amongst animals is one that will be discussed at greater length in a later

chapter. Here let it suffice to state that, when an
animal which is not protected by some special means
of defence imitates the colours and form of some
other species that is so protected, the imitating species
is termed a mimic, and the assumption is that the
mimic thereby acquires a certain amount of immunity
from attack, since its enemies are deceived by the
resemblance to an animal which experience has taught
them to avoid. The best examples of mimicry amongst
snakes are furnished by some harmless South American
species which imitate very closely in their colouring
certain poisonous species ; but instances are not lacking
amongst Oriental snakes. The' Indian Viper *Echis cari-
nata* is apparently mimicked by one of the Opistho-
glyphous *Colubridæ*—*Dipsadomorphus trigonatus*,[1] though
it is possible that a large part of the resemblance is
due to the fact that both species are coloured in
harmony with the desert surroundings in which they
occur. A better example of true mimicry is furnished
by *Chersydrus granulatus*, one of the *Acrochordinæ*, an
aquatic sub-family belonging, as already pointed out,
to the harmless section of the *Colubridæ*; this species
in its young stages is conspicuously banded with
black and white, and is remarkably like several of the
poisonous Sea-Snakes proper (*Hydrophiinæ*). They are

[1] *Dipsadomorphus dendrophilus* seems to be a close mimic of
Bungarus fasciatus. Both snakes have exactly the same colouring,
black with yellow bands, and live coiled up on branches of trees
in the mangrove swamps or over rivers. At a little distance it is
impossible to distinguish them apart. *Bungarus fasciatus* is a very
vicious poisonous snake. *Dipsadomorphus* when caught has a
habit of ejecting from the anus a large quantity of very foul-
smelling brown liquid by way of a defence (*Journ. Roy. As. Soc.
S. Br.*, No. 32 (1899), p. 199).—H. N. R.

found in the same situation as the Sea-Snakes, and are
of approximately the same size. The adult, which is
more capable of taking care of itself and a good deal
larger than an average Sea-Snake, is frequently found
at some distance from the sea, and is not conspicuously
banded. A young specimen of this species was caught
in a cast-net at the mouth of the Sarawak River, and
when it was brought to me I was so convinced that I
had to deal with one of the poisonous *Hydrophiinæ*, that
I exercised the utmost caution in transferring it from
the net to a jar of spirit, and only discovered that my
caution was unnecessary when I attempted some days
later to identify the species. The habit of the Cobra
and Hamadryad of rearing up the head and expanding
the hood is simulated by more than one species of
non-poisonous snakes. Mr. H. N. Ridley records [1] of
Macropisthodon rhodomelas that when irritated " it
sits up after the manner of a cobra, and seems to
flatten out its neck as if it was trying to imitate that
species, while from the bluish patch on its neck are
exuded some drops of a white viscid liquid represent-
ing the well-known cobra marks. I noticed that my
dog, seizing this snake in its mouth to worry it, presently foamed at the mouth, as if he had been licking
a toad, and soon dropped the snake." The *Macropisthodon* is not coloured at all like a Cobra, being
terra-cotta with a black **V** on its neck and a black line
down the back, but the dilatation of the neck and the
rearing-up of the anterior part of the body are certainly
Cobra-like habits. Just as in the Cobra, this attitude
is a warning signal advertising the poisonous bite, so
in the *Macropisthodon* the same attitude advertises the

[1] *Journ. Roy. As. Soc. S. Br.*, No. 32 (1899), p. 108.

nauseous excretion of the skin-glands at the back of
the neck, and may have been evolved independently
of mimicry altogether. *Zaocys carinatus* is in colouring
very like a Cobra, but I am not aware if it imitates its
attitude. Its near ally *Zamenis mucosus* is said by
Captain S. S. Flower[1] to rear up its head like the
Cobra and to dilate its neck ; this, however, is not
effected by lateral extension as in the Cobra, but by
the ventral shields, which are thrust out so far as to
become acutely keeled, the skin on the side of the
neck being widely stretched, and showing up the yellow
skin between the brown scales just as in the Cobra. The
resemblance between *Coluber radiatus* and the Cobra
has already been noted. The same authority states
that the similarity in colouring between the harmless
Lycodon subcinctus and the deadly *Bungarus candidus*
is very close, but it is to be noted also that though
the geographical ranges of these two species overlap
they do not coincide entirely, for the poisonous species
is unknown in Borneo, although the non-poisonous
one occurs there. Brilliant scarlet in combination
with other colours is, as we have seen, characteristic
of three of the Bornean poisonous snakes, and it has
often occurred to me that this scarlet colour when
appearing in other snakes may possibly be regarded
in these cases also either as warning colours advertising distasteful properties, or as mimetic of warning
colours. For instance, one of the harmless Colubrines
Calamaria leucogaster [*leucocephala ?*—C. H.] has a red tail
and belly : again in *Cylindrophis rufus* the red on the
tail is conspicuously displayed when the animal is in
a posture of defence, whilst its near relation *C. lineatus*

[1] *P.Z.S.*, 1899, pp. 666–7.

has, like the Red-Headed Krait, a scarlet head and
tail, though otherwise it is not at all like the poisonous
species. If these are examples of mimicry, the mimicry
is very far from being exact, and it may well be asked
how such imperfect resemblance can be of any value
to these defenceless snakes. It is perhaps a legitimate
answer that snake-enemies have, through the action of
natural selection, learnt instinctively to regard scarlet
as an advertisement of poisonous properties, just as it is
almost certain that animals and birds avoid poisonous
plants and fruits, not from experience of the ill-effects
of eating these, but from an instinct called into being
by selection. If a patch of scarlet colour inspires
dread or even only caution in a snake-destroying
animal, the display of this colour by a non-poisonous
snake will suffice to scare away a certain number of
its enemies. Theories of this nature, however, require
a large body of experimental evidence to support them
before they can meet with wide acceptance, and such
evidence is unfortunately entirely lacking in the instances just quoted.

Note, p. 92.—Malayan Cobra. The Ringhals, or Spugh-slang
("Spitting Snake"), *Sepedon hæmachætes*, of South Africa, has
the same habit. The discharged saliva is very acrid and a
powerful irritant. This snake is nearly related to the Cobra.—
H. B.
See *The Snakes of South Africa*, by F. W. Fitzsimons, F.Z.S.,
1912, pp. 183–91 ; pp. 488–9.—G. B. L.

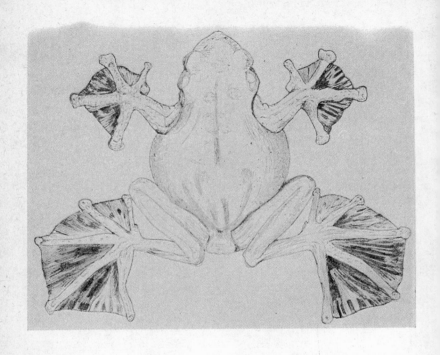

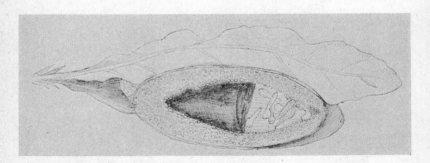

Above, the Bornean Flying Frog, *Rhacophorus nigropalmatus*. Below, the tadpoles of some tree-haunting frog which, like *Rhacophorus*, surrounds its eggs with a mass of froth enclosed between leaves. (From drawings found among the author's papers.) (See Note 9, p. 314.)

Plate XIII.

To face p. 105.

CHAPTER IV

CROCODILES, TURTLES, AND TORTOISES

OF all the reptiles of Borneo by far the most important, when it is considered in relation to man, is the Crocodile. I explained in a previous chapter that cases of snake-bite in Sarawak were extremely rare, but the Crocodile exacts a considerable annual toll from the native population. Some rivers are positively infested with these grisly creatures, and the Sarawak Government pays a reward of 36 cents (about 9d.) per foot for every one killed, and a couple of cents for every egg destroyed. At Kuching alone several hundreds of dollars are paid annually for Crocodile rewards.

The species which occurs in Malayan waters is *Crocodilus porosus*, and all who have observed it, whether in captivity or in a state of nature, are agreed that of all the Crocodile tribe it is the most savage member. Muggers, Alligators, Caimans are more or less amenable to kind treatment, and may even become comparatively tame, but the Malay Crocodile never.

I have seen a young one, scarcely 4 feet long, which had been brought to the Museum for me to inspect, when released from its bonds rush with open jaws at the natives who were standing by, so that it was a case of *sauve qui peut*. Even this youngster could deliver a blow with its tail which stung the legs like the lash of a heavy cart-whip.[1]

I once had a batch of eggs of this Crocodile brought to me, and on opening some of them they proved to contain nearly fully developed embryos. I was much amused to find that if the egg membranes were stripped from off these blind unborn babes and their muzzles gently tickled with a lead pencil, they instantly seized it between their jaws. Thus early does the ferocious instinct manifest itself in this cruel reptile. *C. porosus*, like all the members of the Crocodile tribe, is fond of sunning itself on river-banks with its jaws widely open —a habit, the object of which it is not easy to explain.[2] I am inclined to suppose that it is connected with the respiratory needs, for I have observed more than once that if a Crocodile has its jaws tightly lashed together, and is then exposed to the full blaze of a tropical sun, it will die in an amazingly short space of time—in fact, this was the usual way in which we killed the specimens that were brought to the Museum.

I once received from an officer in the Sarawak service a number of pebbles, which, together with some peculiar-looking objects, he had removed from the stomach of a large Crocodile killed in his district. The latter I could not at first identify, but at last came to the conclusion that they were the empty and de-flated eggshells of some species of Turtle (probably

[1] When the head is cut off the eyes continue to blink, and it will snap its jaws on a stick for some little time.—C. H.

[2] Natives say that sandpipers pick something off the teeth of the Crocodile.—C. H.

Trionyx subplanus), surely a very curious article of diet for a Crocodile. The presence of large water-worn pebbles in the stomach was of great interest, for the place where the reptile was killed was situated in the vast delta of the Rejang River—an area made up of nothing but swamps, where one might search for a year without finding a pebble. It is evident, then, that this Crocodile had travelled some hundreds of miles towards the head-waters of this, or some other river, in order to get the stones, and it is equally evident that the stones played some important part in its digestive economy. Doubtless these creatures swallow stones, as many birds do, for the purpose of triturating their food. The observation is of further interest because water-worn pebbles have been found in juxtaposition to the bones of Ichthyosauri, and it has been suggested that these were swallowed for the precise purpose mentioned above.

Large balls of hair about the size of a man's head are not unfrequently found in Crocodiles' stomachs. These are generally formed round some nucleus which appears to be of a concretionary nature, and are, of course, derived from the hair of the Crocodile's victims.[1]

The common Macaque, in spite of its wiliness, frequently falls a prey to the Crocodile. The monkey, as I have already stated, is fond of feeding on the crabs which abound in brackish waters: in the eagerness of his pursuit he draws too near to the huge reptile lying immobile on the mud and looking like some old log; nearer and nearer he draws, there is a sudden swish of the huge tail, and the monkey is

[1] In many cases the hair is found to be that of wild pigs and deer.—C. H.

knocked flying into the river, where his inferior powers of swimming avail not to save him from his foe.

It has been asserted by competent observers that the Crocodile, if it has seized a victim too bulky to be swallowed at once, thrusts its prey deep into the mud of the river bottom and leaves it there until putrefaction has reduced the corpse to such a state that it can be readily torn into pieces.

The eggs of *C. porosus* are long ovals measuring about $3\frac{1}{4}$ inches by $2\frac{1}{4}$ inches; the shell is pure white and of a texture like porcelain; the yolk has a peculiar rank odour, and is not fluid like the yolk of a bird's egg, but rather viscous, and granulated in appearance. Thirty to forty are laid by a single female in a depression which she makes in the mud, amongst the stems of the Nipa-palms, usually at some little distance from the river-bank. It seems that the mother may exercise a certain amount of supervision over her nest, as the following instance shows. My friend Mr. E. A. W. Cox, of the Sarawak service, when returning with some native followers and his dogs from a day's hunting in the swamp-land of the Baram River, came across a Crocodile's nest and proceeded incontinently to destroy all the eggs in it. The natives besought him to fly the spot at once, alleging that the mother was close at hand and would certainly come to wreak vengeance on the destroyers of her progeny. Mr. Cox determined to wait and see what would happen, and, sure enough, after some time a large female Crocodile made her appearance on the scene, and after a prolonged and exciting struggle succumbed to the spear-thrusts and sword-wounds delivered by the waiting hunters. The only other Crocodilian in Borneo is the Gavial [Garial], *Tomistoma schlegelii*. This has a long slender snout and is said to be harmless to man, feeding principally on fish. At one time it was regarded as peculiar to Borneo, but it has recently been discovered in the Malay Peninsula. In Borneo its distribution is very local—in fact, the only river in Sarawak where it can be said to occur in any abundance is the Sadong; only stray specimens have been taken elsewhere.

The Green Turtle, *Chelone mydas*, is very abundant in the seas round Borneo. At the close of the Northeast Monsoon the females lay their eggs in the sandy beaches of some coral islands that lie off the mouth of the Sarawak River. The round eggs are enclosed in a leathery shell, which can easily be torn open with the fingers. The yolk is stiff, pale yellow in colour, and not transparent. These eggs are considered a great delicacy, but the taste for them is certainly an acquired one. The egg-laying has been described as follows [1] :—

"The turtles on arrival extend round the shore and pair, during which process great fights take place among the males for the females. The latter ascend at night the small sand beaches, which occur at intervals along the coast, and dig deep holes in the sand, the fore-flippers being chiefly used for the task. . . . The number of eggs laid is about 200 : and the females are supposed to come up the beach twice in each season [with an interval of about a month—C. H.]. They always ascend with one flowing tide and go to sea again on the next ; consequently a night with the tide becoming high at sunset is the

[1] Fryer *Trans. Linn. Soc. London,* (2 *Ser.*) *Zool.,* XIV. (1910–12), p. 422.

most favourable [during the months of February, March, and April—C. H.]. The young turtles hatch in 40 days and go straight down the beach to the sea. The hatching of all the eggs in a nest takes place almost simultaneously, and the young turtles dig their way up out of the sand as fast as they can be counted and crawl down to the sea in a long procession. By what sense they find the right direction was not discovered; their eyes are not open but even if placed on a flat surface [or taken into the forest for a hundred yards or so] they know their way to the sea. The hatching of the whole nest only takes about 10 minutes and forms a remarkable and pretty sight."

In Sarawak the Green Turtle is rigorously preserved, the destruction of one entailing a heavy fine. Owing to the large number of eggs laid and the ready demand for them, the Turtle islands yield a considerable revenue, which by an agreement with the Sarawak Government, appertains to the principal Malay chiefs of the State in turn. At the commencement of the egg-laying season watchers are stationed on each of the islands whose duty it is to mark the places in the sand where the eggs are laid; these are dug up next morning and sent off by boat to Kuching. The fat of the Green Turtle, which figures so largely in civic banquets, is not appreciated by Oriental natives; indeed, the Turtle soup which is frequently served at the dinner-parties of Europeans in the Far East invariably comes out of a tin.[1]

The Hawksbill, or Tortoiseshell Turtle, *Chelone imbricata*, is far less abundant. According to Mr. Fryer (loc. cit.) it ascends the beach in the daytime to lay

[1] Not in Singapore where one gets fresh Turtle.—H. N. R.

its eggs [usually early morning before dawn—C. H.], which hatch out in sixty days, and the female is said to come at least twice, at an interval of from a fortnight to a month, to lay in the same place. Like the Green Turtle, the Hawksbill is a vegetarian, feeding on *Algæ*. The Malays are said to remove the tortoise-shell scales from this animal by laying it back downwards on an iron plate covered with sand, beneath which a fire is lit. Under the action of the excessive heat the scales peel off, and the wretched animal is returned to the sea again, Malays believing it can grow fresh scales to replace those that have been removed.

The Logger-Head Turtle, *Thalassochelys caretta*, is unknown in Sarawak waters, but was found in South Borneo by Dr. Bleeker.

Of Land and Fresh-water Tortoises there is a whole host in Sarawak, but I have little to say concerning them. The most interesting is perhaps the large Land Tortoise, *Testudo emys*. One of the commonest, *Geomyda spinosa*, is found amongst dead leaves, to which, the young ones especially, bear a cryptic resemblance. This concealment is due to the flattened form of the Tortoise and to the fact that the marginal scales of the carapace are produced and sharply pointed, looking like the tips of leaves. Another common species was the Box Tortoise, *Cyclemys amboinensis*. One of these was confined for several years in a shallow tub nearly full of water, just outside the taxidermy office in the Museum grounds. This animal presented an example of steady perseverance before which all those mentioned in the works of Samuel Smiles pale into insignificance. Nearly all day and every day, and so far as I know every night, that

Tortoise endeavoured to escape from its prison. Standing up on its hind-legs, it could bring the centre of its plastron against the edge of the tub, and by scrabbling violently with its front legs it would manage to hoist itself out of the water on to this edge, where for a few seconds of awful suspense it would balance itself, but invariably its centre of gravity was on the wrong side of the staves, and it would flop back into the water. To my certain knowledge this daily struggle went on for three years, until one day the tortoise managed somehow or other to shift its centre of gravity an inch or so further forwards, and it fell over the tub-side on to the ground. A Dayak attendant discovered the animal crawling away and was about to return it to its tub when I intervened and gave it the liberty it had earned so well.

Callagur picta is a large Water Tortoise. Young and half-grown individuals have the shell pale yellow striped with black, and the nose is brilliant scarlet. They are often found in mangrove swamps and are fond of resting on submerged snags with just the head exposed above the water. In this position the nose is a very conspicuous object, but it is difficult to see what purpose its brilliant coloration serves.[1]

Borlitia borneensis, of G. R. Gray, is another very large Water Tortoise which occurs not uncommonly in the lakes of the Batang Lupar district. For long it was represented in the British Museum by a solitary and very juvenile specimen, obtained by Dr. Bleeker

---

[1] This is really a River Tortoise which goes to the mouth of the river to lay its eggs, at which time the scarlet marking disappears altogether or is only very faint. It lays 15 to 20 long, oval-shaped eggs in February and again in March.—C. H.

at Sintang, Borneo, and the identity of the adult remained in great doubt. It was described in the *Sarawak Gazette* by my predecessor, Mr. E. Bartlett, as *Brookeia baileyi*, by Baur as *Adelochelys crassa*, and again by Mr. G. A. Boulenger as *Liemys inornata*. Finally, by the study of young specimens sent by me, and an adult by Dr. C. Hose, Mr. Boulenger was fortunately able to establish the identity of the small British Museum specimen with the adult, and Gray's specific name, *borneensis*, therefore stands. This Tortoise lays long, oval eggs with a shell of porcelain-like texture ; in fact, they are like little Crocodile eggs. It may be noted here that whilst the eggs of Turtles have leathery shells like those of Snakes, those of Tortoises have hard shells like Crocodile's eggs. Mud-Turtles of the genus *Trionyx*[1] were common enough in Sarawak, but I have nothing fresh to record about their habits. They are vicious creatures, capable of inflicting bad wounds with their powerful jaws.

[1] A figure of *Trionyx subplanus* is given by S. S. Flower in *P.Z.S.*, 1899, Pl. XXXVI, opposite p. 600. They live chiefly in holes along the banks of small rivers, and lay a small round egg with a hard shell. They kill waterfowl.—C. H.

CHAPTER V

COCKROACHES, MANTISES, AND STICK-INSECTS

THE insects forming the subject of this chapter constitute three families of the order *Orthoptera*: the other families of the order, including the Earwigs, Grasshoppers, Locusts, and Crickets, I will neglect for the present, since these are familiar insects to all who have paid any attention at all to natural history in England.

The common Cockroach[1] or "black beetle" is familiar to all of us, and too familiar to some, for in many houses it swarms in multitudes. It has a disgusting smell and a repulsive appearance; still it has been asserted that it is an enemy of those loathsome parasites the bed-bugs. Its scientific name is *Blatta orientalis*, and it has been known under that name to

[1] Americans have abbreviated this word as "roach," perhaps by a reversed analogy with "robin," "cockrobin." As "roach" is good Anglo-Saxon for a species of fish the use of the word for an insect is objectionable. "Cockroach" is derived from the Spanish "cucaracha," a word of obscure etymology but possibly derived from some South American Indian word signifying this insect. "Cuco" in Spanish means a sort of caterpillar or bug, and "cucaracha" is possibly connected with this: if so the elision of the first syllable of "cockroach," the syllable which originally gave the word its significance, is doubly objectionable.

naturalists since the days of Linnæus. Curiously enough it has not been met with in a truly wild state until quite recently; the first specimens that were found were caught in houses, and though it has always been assumed that it was imported into Europe from the East, I am not aware that it has ever been found in Asia except as an unwelcome guest in human habitations. The discovery[1] of specimens in the Crimean peninsula living under dead leaves, vegetable detritus and stones, in woods and copses far from any human habitation, is a fact of considerable interest, and it is perhaps permissible now to regard Southern Russia as the centre whence this ubiquitous insect has spread.

Cockroaches have a great *penchant* for human food and articles of human manufacture, and thus with the march of civilization some species have become disseminated throughout the world. *Periplaneta americana* is another of these cosmopolitan species; it is even more repulsive than its relative the "black beetle," for it is very much larger. It is common on board ships and is probably the species of which Captain John Smith, of Virginia fame, wrote in 1624— "a certaine India Bug, called by the Spaniards a Cacarootch, the which creeping into Chests they eat and defile with their ill-scented dung." *Periplaneta australasiæ* is yet another cosmopolitan cockroach and the specific names of these three forms, *orientalis*, *americana*, and *australasiæ*, indicate that the old naturalists regarded the East, America, and Australia as the three centres whence the species spread to Europe;

[1] *Ann. Mus. Zool. St. Petersburg*, XII. (1907), p. 401 [see Note 10, p. 314].

but, as we have already seen, *orientalis* may have originated in Europe, and it is certain that *australasiæ* is only a rare immigrant to Australia, and I believe that tropical Africa or perhaps South-Eastern Asia was its original home.

In Sarawak *P. australasiæ* was a serious Museum pest, for it devoured labels, the covers of books and anything with starchy or sugary constituents. Consequently I used to regard with a benevolent eye the presence in the Museum of a certain small Hymenopterous insect, *Evania*; this little creature has an absurd triangular and flattened abdomen suspended from a slender waist, and it deposits its eggs in the horny egg-case of Cockroaches. These egg-cases, or oothecæ, have been compared in appearance to Gladstone bags : the comparison is not very apt, but it serves to illustrate the fact that they are hollow, and made up of two halves which, when the contained young are ready to emerge, open along the top of the case. By means of her cleaver-like abdomen the *Evania* is able to prise open the egg-case of the cockroach at the line of closure, and then, thrusting in her ovipositor, she deposits her eggs or an egg on the eggs of the Cockroach, which are later devoured by the larvæ of the *Evania*.

The egg-case of the Cockroach is formed inside the body of the mother, and when ready and full of eggs it is in many species partially extruded and carried about for several days until a safe hiding-place is found for it. Thus the little cosmopolitan species *Phyllodromia germanica* forms a long flat leathery case, which is carried about extruding from the apex of the abdomen till just a few hours before the contained eggs hatch out. Other species form a horny egg-case which, however, is always retained within the brood-pouch of the mother and the young are born alive. In yet other viviparous species no egg-case is formed at all, but the eggs, enclosed in a thin transparent membrane, develop within a large brood-pouch.

Viviparous Cockroaches are by no means uncommon ; in fact, I am inclined to believe that almost half of the known species bring forth their young alive. The eggs and embryos of the viviparous species are of course protected from the attacks of the *Evania*, but on the other hand the death of a pregnant mother results in the death of all her offspring, and, since Cockroaches have many enemies, we cannot be certain whether the viviparous habit or the ootheca-forming habit is the more efficient in securing the safety of the developing young. All the species belonging to the sub-family *Epilamprinæ* are viviparous, and in Sarawak I once captured a female of a species belonging to this sub-family, *Pseudophoraspis nebulosa*, with the under-side of her body covered with newly hatched young ones clinging to it. I have no doubt that the young were born alive and then swarmed on to their mother. Their appearance was different from hers, for they were clothed with fine hairs on the margins of their bodies, and the thoracic shields were pitted or punctate. A Ceylon species of Epilamprine, *Phlebonotus pallens*, has been found with the young running about on the upper side of the abdomen of the mother and covered over by the tegmina, or wing-covers. In this species the wings of the female sex are much reduced in size, so that the insect cannot fly. Nevertheless the wing-covers are large and arched, and as beneath them the upper side of the abdomen is depressed with the sides raised up, a sort of box or chamber is formed inside which the newly born young can be carried about very comfortably. The maternal instinct is met with so seldom in the insect world, outside the great Hymenopterous order, that it is quite pleasant to be able to record new examples of it.

It must not be supposed that all Cockroaches are as repulsive in appearance as those mentioned at the beginning of this chapter. The great majority of species are found, not in houses, but in forest and jungle; some forms burrow in decaying wood or in the ground, others are found in flower-heads, others skulk under stones or dead leaves; others, wonderfully mottled and streaked, are found on the trunks of trees, and harmonize admirably with their background. A few species are gorgeously coloured, and some so closely resemble ladybirds and plant-feeding beetles, not only in their colour and markings, but also in their shapes, as to deceive all but an expert entomologist.

On Mt. Matang, in Sarawak, I discovered some immature Cockroaches lurking beneath the vegetable debris that bestrewed the banks of a stream trickling down the hillside. When disturbed these Cockroaches took to the water and swam and dived with ease. I was so interested in what appeared to be an unknown habit in this family of Orthoptera that I kept some specimens under observation in a glass tank for some weeks. I observed that my captives were unable to endure total immersion for any length of time; if they were confined in a corked tube quite full of water they were drowned in a few minutes after some violent struggles. This is quite in accordance with some experiments carried out by Professor Plateau, of Ghent, on aquatic and terrestrial insects ; the Belgian savant found that terrestrial insects can sustain total immersion for prolonged periods—22¼ hours to 97½ hours ; they may present all the appearance of death, but they soon recover when removed from the water. Aquatic insects, such as Water-Beetles and Water-Boatmen, on the other hand, when placed in water and denied all access to air, struggle violently and soon drown, for when removed from the water they do not recover.

It was concluded from the above-described observations that aquatic insects by their violent struggles rapidly exhaust all the air contained in the tracheæ, or breathing-tubes, ramifying throughout their bodies, and, being unable to renew the supply, they become asphyxiated ; whereas terrestrial insects do not struggle so violently when immersed in water, and consequently do not use up their supply of air at once. From such experiments and observations as I have made, I do not believe that this explains the whole secret of the endurance shown in water by terrestrial insects. In the first place a typically terrestrial insect, such as the common Cockroach of Borneo, *Periplaneta australasiæ*, when immersed in water will struggle quite as violently as the aquatic species, and yet will endure total immersion for some hours before finally succumbing. If a *Periplaneta* be thrown into a basin of water it flounders about on the surface, and all its efforts will not suffice to take it under the surface ; even when the wings and wing-covers, which conceivably might help to buoy it up, are removed, the creature is still helpless on the surface. The reason of its inability to sink is found in the simple fact that it is lighter than the water. A full-sized *Periplaneta* will weigh more than a small Water-Cockroach, yet the latter can swim in mid-water or even remain quietly at the bottom. If the bodies of these two insects, so similar in structure yet so unlike in their habits, be cut open, a striking difference in the appearance of their tracheæ is seen. The terrestrial Cockroach has these breathing-tubes thread-like, silvery, and dilated to their utmost extent with air; but in the aquatic form they are strap-like, not silvery in appearance, and with only an air-bubble here and there to expand them. If any terrestrial insect be examined it will be seen that its tracheæ are like those of *Periplaneta*, and it seems probable that these organs function very largely as storehouses of air, respiration is slower than in aquatic forms, and the tracheæ are always distended with air so that the insect is rendered buoyant, and can accomplish with ease movements of running or flying, but on account of their buoyancy they are helpless in water.[1] With the Water-Cockroach and many other aquatic insects the case is very different; it is essential that they should be able to swim and dive with ease, and this can only be attained if the insects lose their buoyancy; hence the tracheæ must be empty, or nearly so, but as it is necessary that the tissues of the body be constantly aerated, air must be

---

[1] Insects with strongly developed chitinous exoskeletons are, of course, relatively very heavy, and when thrown into water sink like stones; but it is astonishing to find how many massively built insects are very buoyant when tested by immersion in water.

quickly taken in and quickly expired, none being stored up or allowed to accumulate. As a natural result, when insects so constructed are deprived of their normal supply of air they are soon asphyxiated.

Such a purely aquatic insect as the little Water-Boatman, *Notonecta glauca*, common in English ponds and streams, has limbs well adapted for swimming ; it carries a supply of air about with it under the wing-covers, and is in consequence very buoyant, so much so that it is only by powerful strokes of the oar-like hind-legs that it can force itself below the surface of the water, and directly it stops swimming it comes bobbing up to the top like a cork. But even these insects die very soon if their air-supply is cut off, so it is evident that they do not carry a great quantity of air inside their tracheæ. The limbs of the Water-Cockroach are not specially adapted for swimming, but since the tracheæ are always deflated, and since it carries about no adventitious supply of air, it is not at all buoyant, but can swim easily in mid-water, and can lie at the bottom of a pool without clinging to some sodden leaf or stone as a Water-Beetle, such as *Dytiscus*, is forced to do. As a matter of fact the Water-Cockroach spends very little of its life entirely submerged ; it rests amongst decaying vegetation at the side of a pool or stream, with the greater part of its body under water, but always with the tip of the abdomen projecting above the surface. If closely watched, it will be seen that the abdomen gently moves up and down with a regular action, and that there appear at the submerged thoracic spiracles at regular intervals bubbles of air, which grow in size and then break away to give place to fresh bubbles,

This, indeed, is the way in which the creature breathes ; air is taken in at the abdominal spiracles, and, passing through the tracheæ, emerges at the thoracic spiracles, the exchange of air being as rapid as in warm-blooded vertebrates.

The structure of the thoracic spiracles of the Water-Cockroach, of which there are two pairs, is different from that of the abdominal, of which there are eight. The former are slits opening between a pair of thick, lip-like valves that shut and open by means of muscles attached to them. If a living Cockroach be held in the fingers and the thoracic spiracles be examined with a lens, it will be seen that the lips open and close with rhythmic regularity. The abdominal spiracles, on the other hand, are circular or oval openings, which remain open permanently, but they have an internal valvular arrangement which cuts off communication with the tracheæ with which each is connected. The spiracles of the terminal pair in the Water-Cockroach are situated each at the base of a short tube projecting from the last segment but one, and it is these which are thrust above the surface of the water, and through which the animal draws in its air-supply.

In order to make sure that it was the terminal abdominal spiracles which were inspiratory—and inspiratory only—in function, and the thoracic spiracles expiratory only in function, I submitted some Cockroaches to experiment. They were pinioned back downwards by cotton threads to strips of cork, placed in glass tubes containing water, some being placed with the attached Cockroach upside down, others with the Cockroach right side up. In the former the surface-level of the water was regulated so as to reach just to the middle of the abdomen, and consequently these specimens had the thoracic spiracles submerged, but the terminal abdominal spiracles exposed; the others had the whole abdomen covered with water, but the thoracic spiracles exposed. It was most instructive to observe that the latter series all died in eight to twelve hours, whilst the reversed specimens were quite lively and well after twenty-four hours, in spite of their constrained position. In the reversed specimens the respiratory movements went on quite regularly, the abdomen rhythmically moving up and down, and air-bubbles issuing at intervals from the thoracic spiracles; but in the other series of specimens the respiratory movements of the abdomen soon ceased.

The experiments showed .very clearly, first that normally the Water-Cockroaches inspire air by the terminal abdominal spiracles and expire it from the the thoracic spiracles; secondly, that a certain amount of air can be taken in by the thoracic spiracles so that pinioned specimens with these orifices exposed to air live much longer than specimens whose air-supply is entirely cut off.

I hoped that similar experiments with terrestrial insects would produce similar results, but I was doomed to disappointment. When Stick-Insects of the genus *Lonchodes*, terrestrial Cockroaches, e.g. *Panesthia javanica* and *Periplaneta australasiæ*, and large Passalid Beetles were experimented with, there was no uniformity in the results obtained. Sometimes the specimens with the abdomen exposed would die before those with the abdomen submerged, and examples of the same species would behave in quite different ways. All the insects struggled violently at first, and air issued rapidly from all the spiracles, both abdominal and thoracic, but later they appeared to become comatose and respiration seemed to come to a standstill, even though the insects were not dead.

Dr. N. Annandale[1] was the first to discover Water-Cockroaches, finding them in the Malay Peninsula, the wingless females resting en floating logs, whence they dived into water when disturbed. The winged males were seen to rise from the surface of the water but never to enter it. Since then Dr. Annandale has captured in Lower Burma a winged male which he found swimming on the surface of a pool, and the wingless females and immature males have also been found at Chota Nagpur, whilst another species has been taken in Japan. All the species belong to one sub-family, the *Epilamprinæ*, and most of them to the genus *Rhicnoda*.

Truly aquatic Orthoptera are distinctly rare, but a good many will jump into water when hard-pressed.[2] Once when collecting insects by the margin of a stream at the foot of Mt. Santubong, Sarawak, I saw a tiny Grasshopper of the sub-family *Tetriginæ* leap from a rock on which it was resting right into the water and with a few vigorous kicks of its powerful hind-legs it soon reached the bottom of the stream where it clung to a stone. I dislodged it and frustrated its valiant struggles to reach a *pied-à-terre*, whereupon, owing to its invincible buoyancy, it came bobbing up to the surface like a cork. An Australian species of this sub-family

---

[1] *Entomologist's Record*, XII. (1900), p. 75.

[2] Dr. Annandale in a letter pointed out this to me as a very usual occurrence amongst small Indian Orthoptera, and I have observed it frequently in Borneo.

has been found resting on the stems of water-plants,
6 or 7 inches below the surface of the water, and
when disturbed they dived to the bottom. Mr.
Froggatt states [1] that a little black Cricket (*Nemobius*)
in Australia when disturbed often jumps into water
and swims along the surface, and I have seen larval
Tryxaline Grasshoppers do the same in Borneo.

None of the above-mentioned insects are specially
modified for an aquatic life, though perhaps we may look
on the Australian Tetrigine as being on the high road
to becoming a truly aquatic insect.   There are, however, one or two Orthoptera that are endowed with
structures fitting them for life in or on water. Such
are the little *Tetriginæ* belonging to the genus *Scelimena*
found in India, Ceylon, and the Malayan region.
Dr. G. B. Longstaff caught some specimens of *Scelimena
logani* in a rapidly running river at Dambulla in
Ceylon,[2] and has kindly supplied me with the following
note : " Most of the specimens were seen on the rocks
or sand quite close to the water. When at rest they
were very cryptic, closely resembling the rock. They
were easily frightened, when they would fly 2 or 3
yards and settle again. Several were seen in the water,
under the surface, swimming by a succession of short
jerks, apparently propelling themselves by the hind-
legs." On examining the hind-legs of this species it
is seen that the end of the shin, or tibia, of the hind-
leg and the first joint of the next segment of the leg,
the tarsus, are furnished with membranous expansions,
thus converting the hind-leg into a very efficient swim-

[1] *Australian Insects*, Sydney, 1907, p. 48.
[2] *Butterfly-hunting in Many Lands*, London, 1912, Pl. IV.,
fig. 11. See also the figure of a swimming leg on p. 375.

ming-organ. Moreover, the oar-blade is curved in such a way as to increase its efficiency. Other species with the hind-legs similarly modified are found in Borneo and Java. It is most interesting, though perhaps not unexpected, to find in a group of Grass-hoppers, many members of· which are fond of damp situations by the margins of ponds and streams, and many of which take to water when scared, that in one genus the obvious advantages of increased swim-ming powers has been secured by the simple modifica-tion of pre-existing structures.

[The author had added the following note on the Paraguayan Grasshopper *Cœlopterna acuminata*, one of the *Œdopodinæ*. This insect "lives upon aquatic plants and often must swim, hence the peculiar de-velopment of hind tibiæ and their spurs."[1]]

In Viti, one of the Fiji Islands, a Cricket, *Hydro-pedeticus vitiensis*, has been found in great numbers dancing about on the surface of a swift stream. It has also been observed to jump from the water to a height of 6 inches. In this insect also it is the hind-legs which are specially adapted for the mode of life; they are very long, and from each side of the tibiæ at their ends project some slender spines fringed with delicate hairs. This Cricket is very small, being only 11 millimeters in length, and is so light that when it gives a vigorous push with its hind-legs the surface-film of the water is not broken owing to the resistance offered by the fringed spines of the legs, and con-sequently the insect is enabled to leap forwards or upwards from the surface of the stream; it is, in fact,

[1] Lawrence Bruner, "List of Paraguayan Locusts," *Proc. U.S. National Mus.*, XXX. (1906), p. 637.

like a man shod with snow-shoes running along on the surface of the snow.

One other aquatic Orthopteron may be mentioned, the Brazilian Stick-Insect, *Prisopus flabelliformis*. This curious-looking creature hides under stones in mountain-streams.[1] The under-side of the body is hollowed out and is fringed with long hairs. It has been supposed that the air is expelled from this hollowed-out portion of the body, and a vacuum being formed the pressure of the water keeps the insect closely applied to the stone on which it is resting. I think it is far more likely that a store of air is held in the hollow beneath the body, and that the insect is enabled to cling to the stone by means of the sucker-like pads known as pulvilli that are found on the tarsal joints, otherwise it is difficult to see how the insects can breathe.

Very closely related to the Cockroaches are the Praying Mantises, quaint hobgoblins of insects of which only a few species occur in Europe, though they are abundant enough in the tropics. I kept many specimens in captivity during my time in Sarawak, and found that they made interesting pets. They were fed on a diet of insects which is their natural food, and some individuals would become comparatively tame, that is to say they could be held in the hand and

[1] These "aquatic habits," described by Murray, have been shown by C. J. Gahan to be a delusion. A closely allied species, *P. fisheri*, exhibited by him at the Ent. Soc., London, December 6, 1911 (*Proc. Ent. Soc.*, 1911, p. lxxxiii), possessed the same adaptive features as *P. flabelliformis*, and yet it had been taken on a tree or a sapling. Furthermore, Gahan showed that these features are such as to promote concealment on lichen-covered bark.—E. B. P.

would take food that was offered to them without making violent efforts to escape.

In a state of nature *Mantidæ* do not obtain their prey by hawking it on the wing as Dragon-Flies do, and since, with an exception to be noted later, their method of progression by walking is slow and uncertain, they cannot run down their victims. They lie in wait for their prey, and as a result of this habit, all or nearly all *Mantidæ* in a state of repose very closely resemble their inanimate surroundings; some are coloured green to match the green of the leaves amongst which they hide, others are mottled in shades of brown to resemble dead leaves and bark; some South African and South American species look like sticks or wisps of vegetable fibre, and these resemblances culminate in the remarkable forms which look like flowers.

It is very interesting to watch a captive Mantis, such as one of the common green species of the genus *Hierodula*, attack a large Butterfly that is introduced into its cage. The movements of the Butterfly are closely followed, the Mantis turning its head from side to side [1] in a watchful manner. When the Butterfly comes within striking distance the Mantis raises the forepart of its body, or prothorax, the raptorial front legs are drawn up close against its sides and slightly rotated outwards so that their inner surfaces, of a clear yellow, are displayed; meanwhile the abdomen is strongly dilated so as to show the contrasting black of the intersegmental membranes. Then a sudden snatch is made and the Butterfly is in the grip of the destroyer. The Mantis nearly always commences operations by biting

[1] I know of no other insect which moves its head in this remarkable manner.—G. B. L.

through the costal nervures of the fore-wings, but if the position in which the Butterfly is held is not favourable for this method of attack, the Mantis bites into the chest of its prey so as to sever the wing muscles. A large Butterfly when first seized will dash its attacker with great violence against the sides of the cage in its mad struggles for freedom, but I have never yet seen a Mantis relax its hold, and by its tactics of severing either the main ribs or else the muscles of the wings it soon reduces its prey to impotence.

Mantidæ are very cleanly insects, and if during the struggles of their prey they become plentifully dusted with scales and hairs, their first action after a meal is to rid their head and legs of these clogging atoms; the strong spines that arm the raptorial pair of legs are picked over by the mandibles; the antennæ, too, are combed clean by the same organs; the middle pair of legs are hooked up to the mouth by the raptorial claws and held in position there whilst the pads of the tarsi are licked clean, and finally the front claws are rubbed over the eyes and top of the head, very much in the way that the common house-fly cleans its head and eyes. A number of genera of *Mantidæ* have a special structure situated on the front femora adapted for cleaning the head and eyes : a little brush of fine hairs occurring in a well-defined patch, which is developed even in the newly hatched young.

Most of the *Mantidæ* that are coloured and shaped so as to harmonize with their surroundings are very brightly coloured on parts of their body or limbs that are not exposed to view when the insects are in a state of repose. For instance, a species that looks, when still, very like a dead leaf, *Deroplatys desiccata,* has the inner side of the fore-femora bright red-brown, blotched with black and pearly white in a small oval patch on the front border; the under-side of the prothorax is also red-brown, and the under-sides of the wing-covers are blotched with madder and white. In another dead-leaf-like species, *Deroplatys shelfordi*, the inside of the fore-coxæ are red in the basal part, pale bluish in the apical part, and the fore-femora are heavily blotched with black in the middle; the under sides of the elytra are bluish grey with four large fuscous patches, while the wings are coal-black streaked with innumerable pinkish lines except along the front border, where the colour is uniform yellow. When these insects are irritated, or when they are excited by the approach of their prey, these brightly coloured parts are exhibited to their best advantage. *D. desiccata* then assumes the attitude described in the case of *Hierodula*: the front part of the body is raised, and the raptorial claws are drawn up against the sides of the prothorax and their inner sides turned to face the aggressor; *D. shelfordi* not only rears up but also stretches out the raptorial claws at right angles to the body and at the same time raises the wing-covers and spreads out the wings like a fan; if seen with the light behind it the dark patches on the under-sides of the wing-covers are seen through their semi-transparent texture.

A still more remarkable appearance is presented by *Hestiasula sarawaca*. This little Mantis, when at rest, is cryptically coloured in shades of brown and grey; its fore-femora are produced into large, flat expansions which make them almost like circular discs, and when the Mantis is at rest they are held close together in front of the body and the insect looks like a piece of wood or excrescence of bark. But when excited a wonderful transformation takes place; the prothorax is raised and the fore-legs are stretched out widely on either side, the wing-covers, wings, and abdomen are raised, the antennæ are agitated so rapidly that only an indistinct blur is seen in their place, the fore-tibiæ snap down on their femora with clockwork regularity and a continuous rustling sound is kept up by the spread wings; in addition to all this, the insect sways from side to side: now it is bolt upright, then right over on one side, and then with a swing over on to the other side. The exposed parts are very conspicuously coloured, the under-side of the prothorax is coal-black, the under-sides of the front coxæ are deep crimson, the femora bright yellow with a black sickle-like mark on the posterior border and two black spots on the anterior border, the wings are black streaked with hair lines of chrome-yellow.

How can we account for these brilliant colours and extraordinary attitudes? I believe that they come into the category of warning colours. *Mantidæ* have many enemies against which their well-armed raptorial claws can be of little protection, and so, like many other insects, they defend themselves by the unexpected display of brightly coloured parts. Explain it how we may, it is nevertheless a fact that a sudden alteration in an animal's apearance is very disconcerting and startling even to a human being. I do not think that I have ever been more thoroughly startled than once, when having gently touched a large white caterpillar of the family *Lymantriidæ*, the creature suddenly displayed in the middle of its body a coal-black patch which stood out in startling contrast against the chalk-white of the

rest of the surface. So too the flickering red filaments
that many *Papilio* caterpillars suddenly shoot out from
just behind the head when touched, are distinctly
disconcerting. A Mantis which at rest appears like a
dead leaf or knot of bark, when displaying its bright
colours and assuming extraordinary attitudes is without
doubt to some creatures a very alarming object. An
African species, *Pseudocreobotra wahlbergi*, has eye-like
markings on the wing-covers, or tegmina, and Mr. G. A. K.
Marshall thinks that these are of a terrifying character ;
of this species he writes : [1] " When the insect is irritated
the wings are raised over its back in such a manner
that the tegmina stand side by side, and the markings
on them then present a very striking resemblance to the
great yellow eyes of a bird of prey, or some feline
animal, which might well deter an insectivorous enemy.
It is noticeable that the insect is always careful to
keep the wings directed towards the point of attack,
and this is often done without altering the position of
the body."

The species of the Malayan genus *Creobotra* also
have eye-like marks on the wing-covers, but I have
never seen any of them alive, so cannot say if they
behave in the same way as the African species ; still,
I have little doubt that they will be shown to do so.
A great many, though not all, of the species that
" display " when irritated, also display when they
perceive their prey approaching, and it may be asked
why the same warning colours should be exhibited
when the insect fears attack and when it is expectant
of an immediate meal. It seems probable that any
excitement may provide the stimulus—pleasure at the

[1] *Trans. Ent. Soc.*, 1902, p. 399.

prospect of food as well as fear of attack—and it is significant that the same appears to be the case with poisonous serpents. The Cobra spreads its hood to warn off attack, and behaves in exactly the same way if a rabbit is introduced into its cage, but both with snakes and *Mantidæ* the primary meaning of the display is warning. On the part of the *Mantidæ* it is a case of "bluff," for these insects have no poison to inject into their foes, as wasps and bees have, nor is there any reason at 'all to suppose that they are unpalatable as so many insects undoubtedly are ; but such examples of "bluff" are common enough amongst insects, as any one who will read Professor Poulton's delightful work, *The Colours of Animals*, can find out for himself, and they need not cause us any surprise.

It is possible to trace fairly completely the evolution of these "displays" from their early beginnings to the wonderful exhibition given by an African flower-mimicking species *Idolum diabolicum*. A green *Hierodula*, at the approach of prey or when irritated, will, as already stated, raise the prothorax and draw up the fore-legs against its sides, displaying to view the ochre-yellow of the coxæ and femora. I do not regard this in the nature of a warning attitude at all. It is usual in green insects that parts not exposed to view when the insects are at rest are coloured less deeply than the exposed parts, and the attitude of the *Hierodula* just described is assumed because it is the most favourable one for making a sudden rapid snatch at its prey, but here is the germ on which natural selection has worked. In *Deroplatys desiccata* the same attitude is assumed at times of excitement, but here the inner side of the front femora is con-

spicuously marked, and its sudden display is perhaps
disconcerting to enemies ; but the heavy blotches on
the wing-covers are not displayed nor are the wings
opened. *Deroplatys shelfordi* extends widely the front
legs, and also elevates the wing-covers and wings, so
that their startling colours are shown to best advantage,
and the insect appears twice its normal size. The
same thing, though accentuated by remarkable movements and still brighter colours, is shown by *Hestiasula
sarawaca.*

A further advance is made by an Indian Mantis,
Gongylus gongylodes, the habits of which have been
described in great detail by Captain C. E. Williams.[1]
In this species the prothorax is a narrow elongate
stalk with a diamond-shaped expansion towards its
front extremity ; this expansion on the under side is
brilliant azure in colour, the margins tinted with purple
and in the centre a coal-black spot. When the Mantis
is at rest waiting for its prey it hangs back downwards
with the under side of the thorax directed upwards,
the prothorax then appears like a flower at the end
of a long stalk ; the upper side is coloured green or
brown, and the legs have leaf-like expansions upon
them, so that when the insect is viewed in this aspect
it is protectively coloured and shaped. Captain Williams
states that the green Tree Lizard, *Calotes,* is a formidable
enemy of this Mantis, but it is evident that the leaf-
like disguise of the insect must protect it to a certain
extent from foes approaching it from below, as it
rests on twigs back downwards waiting for its own
prey. The same authority states that many Butterflies,
both Skippers and large Papilios, are captured by this

[1] *Trans. Ent. Soc.,* 1904, pp. 125–37.

Mantis, and there seems every reason to suppose that they are sufficiently deluded by the floral simulation of their enemy to approach within striking distance. When the Mantis is irritated the "raptorial limbs, which are usually held folded together in front of the prothoracic disc, are now widely separated until they lie in the plane of the disc, the inner aspect of the coxæ being directed forwards; the femora and tibia remain folded upon them as before. It is now seen that the internal aspect of the coxæ is coloured a brilliant purple, dotted over with circular white or pale blue spots, and the femora have a warm red-brown coloration on this aspect" [p. 128]. This attitude is the same as that adopted by *Hierodula* when ready to seize prey, but in addition the abdomen is greatly distended, and in immature examples is curled up; the intersegmental membranes at the base of the abdomen are bright purple in colour, whilst on those at the hind part of the abdomen are black eye-spots. In this attitude the insect presents a terrifying appearance, which, in Captain Williams's opinion, would deter even a large Lizard from seizing it. This species is of great interest, as showing an intermediate stage between such a form as *Hestiasula* and that which will be next considered. It displays its warning signals when irritated by exposing to view the inner sides of the front legs which normally are concealed, but the under side of the prothorax, which in *Hestiasula* is part and parcel of the whole scheme of warning coloration in that insect's display, is in *Gongylus* wonderfully coloured to resemble a flower, and is displayed all the time that the insect is at rest and waiting for its prey. This is an instance of alteration of habit and colouring to meet the ever-present pressure threatening to crush organisms out of existence.

The culminating point in floral simulation by *Mantidæ* is reached in *Idolum diabolicum* from East Africa.[1] In this species, which is protectively coloured on the upper-side, the prothorax is enormously expanded into a plate-like disc, and the front pair of coxæ are also flattened and dilated ; the prothorax on the underside is white with a greenish band along its hindborder, the coxæ are purple throughout the greater part of their length, but pinkish-white at the apex. The creature rests like *Gongylus* back downwards on shrubs, waiting for its prey, but unlike *Gongylus* the raptorial legs are kept widely stretched out.   It catches its prey not by snatching at it, as other *Mantidæ* do, but by snapping the tibiæ down on the femora. The prothorax and front legs on their under surfaces present the appearance of some remarkable exotic blossom, and it is so attractive to flower-haunting insects that they hover over the Mantis or actually settle on it.   Here there is no trace of warning coloration ; all the parts which in other species are coloured with the object of scaring enemies are so coloured as to resemble the petals of a flower, and, so far as is known, the insect does not adopt any threatening attitude when irritated.   We may, perhaps, safely assume that while its floral simulation attracts its prey, the same adaptation as well as to its protective colouring on the upper surface enables it to elude the observation of its enemies. *Idolum* is, moreover, a large, robust insect, with very heavily armed raptorial

[1] Sharp, *Proc. Cambridge Phil. Soc.*, X. (1898–1900), pp. 175–80, Pl. II.

limbs, and it might be an awkward customer for any insect-eating bird or lizard to tackle.

Hymenopus bicornis, another floral simulator, is not uncommon in Sarawak and the Malay Peninsula. Newly hatched specimens are bright red with black spots, and present a close resemblance to the similarly coloured young of a very common and unpalatable plant-bug, *Eulyes amœna,*[1] and it is probable that this mimicry is of considerable advantage to the young Mantis. After the next moult *Hymenopus* becomes, and to the end of its life remains, flower-like. It is in the larval stages pink as a rule, but has, I believe, considerable power of adapting itself to its colour surroundings ; for I found a young larva on a jasmine-like plant that had yellow flowers with crimson stamens, and the Mantid larva was yellow with crimson lines on the abdomen and coxæ. I do not believe, however, that it can alter its colour to any extent without undergoing a change of skin.   Dr. N. Annandale has made some most interesting observations on this species, which he observed in the Malay Peninsula, and the following is an abridged account.[2] The general colour of the nymph is pink, and there is a bar of green across the base of the prothorax ; the dorsal surface of the abdomen is pink with some slender stripes of yellow-brown, and some darker transverse bars near the base.   As the nymph when at rest carries its abdomen curved over its back the dorsal surface is invisible, but the pink under surface exposed to view.   At the tip of the abdo-

---

[1] This interesting mimetic resemblance of the young *Hymenopus* was described and figured by Mr. Shelford (*P.Z.S.,* 1902, II., pp. 231, 232, Pl. XIX, figs. 16–19).—E. B. P.

[2] *P.Z.S.,* 1900, pp. 839–48.

men is a conspicuous dark patch. The limbs have
petaloid expansions pink in colour, with, on one edge,
a "slightly livid, bruise-like mark, such as one sees on
flowers that have been battered by tropical rain." Dr.
Annandale further remarks that the "whole surface of
the trunk and that of the flattened expansions of the
femur of the posterior limbs had that semi-opalescent,
semi-crystalline appearance that is caused in flower-
petals by a purely structural arrangement of liquid
globules or of empty cells." The specimen referred to
was found on *Melastoma polyanthum*, and was first
discovered resting on some of the pink flowers, which
it matched so closely that its presence was only detected
when it moved. It cannot be said that this Mantis
imitates with accuracy a flower or part of a flower of
the *Melastoma*, but, owing to the close mimicry in colour
and texture this is not of first-rate importance. The
green bar at the base of the prothorax divides the
insect into two, and as the Mantis is much larger than
a *Melastoma* flower, the protective value of this green
bar is obvious, for it gives the effect of two smaller
flower-like structures. When the Mantis was placed
near a branch of the *Melastoma* it was seen that it
selected as a resting-place a twig bearing flowers, after
trying others that bore only leaves or unripe buds.
When the Mantis was at rest, several small flies that
haunt the *Melastoma* settled on it, and at a short distance the black spot at the apex of the abdomen
appeared very like one of these small flies. The Mantis
was indifferent to these little flies, but seized and
devoured a large fly that settled quite close to it.
When the Mantis left its resting-place and walked
about, the abdomen was straightened out, and then the

insect presented a resemblance to a fallen orchid, the
lines on the dorsal surface of the abdomen looking
"like the 'honey-guides' of many orchids. The darker
transverse bars seen in the shadow cast by the head
and thorax gave an idea of hollowness, such as might
be expected round the nectaries ; while the abdomen
itself resembled the labellum, and the limbs the other
petals of the orchid." Before the Mantis left the in-
florescence on which it was resting, the abdomen, which,
as stated, is carried curled up, was seen to droop slowly,
until gradually it came to lie in the same line as the
thorax, and then the insect made a sudden leap to the
ground. It is suggested that this gradual drooping of
the abdomen, bringing into view the brown streaks and
bars of the dorsal surface, may represent the fading of
a petal of the *Melastoma* flower, for the fading of flowers
in the tropics is a rapid process. The observations of
Dr. Annandale show that every detail in the scheme
of coloration of this species—the texture, the structure,
the habits—assist in adding to the sum-total of the
floral simulation ; the black spot on the apex of the
abdomen, and the green bar on the prothorax, which
render the insect conspicuous when seen in unnatural
surroundings, are deeply significant when it is seen in
the surroundings which the insect is careful to select
—the pink *Melastoma* flowers. The adult Mantis is
cream coloured with a brownish suffusion at the base of
the wing-covers, and is then far less like a flower than
in its younger and more helpless stages ; but even then
it is sufficiently flower-like to gain protection and
delude its prey when in its natural haunts. Neither the
nymphs nor the adults adopt any sort of warning attitude when irritated, nor do they extend the fore-limbs

to resemble petals, as does *Idolum diabolicum*. Natural selection has gone, if not a step further, at least along a different line, and has produced an insect that from every aspect and in every detail is so flower-like that warning attitudes and protective colouring of one surface in contradistinction to an alluring colour of another are lost in the effort to attain perfection along other lines.

Some *Mantidæ* supplement their warning displays by making a hissing or rustling sound, and many of those that show no brilliantly coloured parts of the body or its appendages produce the same sound. The late Professor Wood-Mason[1] was the first to draw attention to this stridulating habit in the *Mantidæ*, and other observers, among whom I may include myself, have confirmed his observations. The sound is produced by the friction of the fore-edges of the two wing-covers against the legs or abdomen. According to Captain Williams,[2] when *Gongylus gongylodes* assumes a threatening posture the wing-covers are slightly raised and spread outwards and downwards, so that their fore-edges come into contact with the thighs of the hind pair of legs; the insect then sways from side to side, thus causing the edges of the wing-covers to scrape against the thighs. On examining these edges it is seen that they are serrated. Wood-Mason supposed that the sound was produced by the wing-covers scraping against the abdomen, but it is difficult to see how its soft and rounded sides could act as a scraper on the rasp of the wing-covers. He figures the edge of the wing-cover in

[1] *Trans. Ent. Soc.*, 1878, pp. 263–7.
[2] *Ibid.*, 1904, p. 129. See also p. 128 for an account of further details in the intimidating attitude.—E. B. P.

Hierodula gastrica, showing the dentate edge with a small seta springing from the side of each tooth.

Stridulation, though almost the rule rather than the exception among the saltatorial Orthoptera, is certainly exceptional amongst the non-saltatorial families. Most of the *Mantidæ* cannot produce a hissing noise, but only a rustling noise, which, since it is caused merely by the sudden opening and closing of the fan-like wings, does not come under the head of stridulation at all. Two African Cockroaches belonging to the genus *Nauphœta* possess the power of stridulating when alarmed or irritated, and in the case of one of them the noise made is a loud chirp, which can be heard to a distance of several yards.[1] It is produced by rubbing the edge of the wing-cover at the shoulder against the under-side of the prothoracic shield. The edge of the wing-cover is armed with rows of minute asperities, 400 to the millimetre, specialized develop-ments of the polygonal fields into which the chitin of the wing-covers is split up, showing that it was developed from cells. The under side of the pronotum at the edge against which the wing-cover file is brought to bear is transversely ridged. Since this apparatus is possessed by both sexes, it is probable that the stridulation is a warning signal, as it is in the *Mantidæ*, and not a love song, as in the saltatorial Orthoptera. Stridulation in the *Phasmidæ* will be discussed when we come to treat of that family.

I mentioned above that nearly all the *Mantidæ* had a very uncertain gait when walking, and that con-sequently they could not run down their prey. The

---

[1] Vosseler, *Deutsch. Ent. Zeitschr.*, 1907, p. 527.

members of the genus *Metallyticus*,[1] however, are an exception. These are brilliant metallic green, with red reflections, or bluish-black insects inhabiting the Malayan islands and peninsula; they are flattened like cockroaches, and with their long legs they scurry along on the floor of the jungle or over the bark of trees at a great pace; the young, which are chequered with white or orange on the back, I have taken in decaying wood. These Mantids prey almost entirely on Cockroaches, and they pursue their victims with great vigour, as I was amused to witness when I placed Cockroaches in a cage in which was confined a specimen of *M. semiæneus*. This creature was quite indifferent to the Butterflies put in its cage, and I was puzzled how to feed it until it occurred to me that the lack of protective coloration and the swiftness of the insect might be associated with active predatory habits. A diet of Cockroaches was much appreciated by my captive, and the pace at which a despairing Cockroach and its relentless enemy careered all over the cage had to be seen to be believed.

As is well known, the *Mantidæ* form rather elaborate egg-cases, which they attach to blades of grass or stems of plants. In the sub-family *Mantinæ* these egg-cases, which are somewhat pear-shaped, look something like small sponges of dense and springy texture. If one of these cases be cut open it is seen that there is an inner mass of eggs surrounded by a thick outer covering of the spongy material. The central cavity containing the eggs is divided by numerous membranous partitions into a series of flattened chambers, each

[1] *Metallyticus*, Westw. (= *Metalleutica*, Burm.) in Kirby's *Synonymic Catalogue of Orthoptera*, I. (1904), p. 208.—E. B. P.

containing twenty or more eggs ; these chambers along the front of the egg-case are quite close to the exterior, and the young larvæ, when ready to emerge, have only to force their way through the opposed walls of the membranous partitions to gain the outside world. The spongy outer covering is fabricated by the mother, and serves as a protection against the attacks of ants and other enemies of that sort. I once found resting on the egg-case of a Mantis a species of Braconid, a Hymenopterous parasite with a very long ovipositor, and it is possible that this insect was meditating an attack on the eggs of the Mantis. Its ovipositor was certainly strong enough to penetrate the outer spongy coat of the egg-case and long enough to reach the egg-mass inside. But my approach scared the creature away, and I successfully reared a numerous progeny of Mantids from that egg-case.

The newly hatched larvæ swarm out of their egg-case in scores all at the same time, and look rather like long-legged ants, and if not supplied with suitable food in the form of mosquitoes or other minute flies, they will commence to devour each other. Brongniart, who has studied the emergence of the larvæ of some Algerian *Mantidæ*, states that the newly hatched young do not leave the egg-case at once, but for several days remain hanging from it by means of two slender filaments emerging from a pair of jointed appendages, the cerci, at the end of the body. Then the larvæ cast their skins, which are still left hanging to the egg-case, and drop to the ground. I have observed the emergence of the young of many species, but have never seen this appearance ; the young have always walked straight out of the egg-case and wandered about in search of food at once.

In other sub-families of *Mantidæ* the egg-case is very different in appearance from that just described. *Hestiasula sarawaca* lays a long double row of eggs on a branch, and then covers them with an irregular shaped mass of spongy texture, sea-green in colour. A very interesting egg-case in the Hope Collection at Oxford is spherical and green in colour, resembling some unripe berry : this is the outer cover ; in the centre is the smaller egg-mass, fastened by strands to the outer cover and surrounded by an air-space ; unfortunately, I am entirely unable to determine the species to which it belongs. Again, *Hymenopus bicornis* deposits her eggs on a branch in a long double row, but then covers them with a sort of hard enamel. Another species, *Theopropus elegans*, makes a similar egg-case and spends a good deal of her time seated astride it—another case of maternal instinct in the Orthoptera.

Captain Williams [1] has been fortunate enough to witness the making of an egg-case by the Indian species *Gongylus gongylodes*, and his account is so interesting that I transcribe it here : "The insect, having taken up her position, proceeds to pour out secretions from the accessory genital glands, with which she builds up the ootheca. These secretions appear to be of two kinds ; the one is a thick viscid semi-transparent fluid which very rapidly hardens to the consistency of horn ; the framework and nearly the whole bulk of the structure is formed of this material, and the eggs are extruded and placed

[1] *Trans. Ent. Soc.*, 1904, pp. 130–32.

in rows, with their long axis vertical to the branch on which the ootheca is built. The second secretion is thinner in consistency, and as it pours out is beaten up into a white foam or lather-like mass, by the very rapid rotation of two small spatulate organs which are protruded at the sides of the genital orifice. This lather-like substance envelops the egg at the moment of extrusion, so that the manner in which it is placed in a position at right angles to that it occupies during its exit from the oviduct cannot be made out. As the eggs are placed in position the lather is constantly being swept aside by the end of the abdomen until it occupies a position on the outside of the ootheca, which it entirely clothes throughout to a depth of $\frac{1}{8}$ of an inch. Its function appears to be, in the first place, to protect the egg from parasitic insects until it is firmly placed in its matrix, and secondly, as an outer covering to the ootheca, to shield its contents from the direct rays of the sun and from the desiccating effects of the hot air. The lather is full of air-bubbles, and at first is sticky, adhering to the fingers like bird-lime, gradually changing to a firm spongy consistency. It is quite tasteless and free from odour. . . . The ootheca is roughly square in section. The eggs are arranged in a single layer, four abreast, and are usually about forty in number. The viscid secretion which forms the matrix of the case hardens with remarkable rapidity, so that even a few seconds after the egg is laid it is not possible to dislodge it with the point of a knife. It may be that the lather-like secretion has the function of protecting this fluid from the hardening effects of the atmosphere while the egg is being placed in position.

11

" It may further be noticed that the female uses her cerci which are attached to the last ventral segment, in the manner of a pair of callipers to shape her egg-case and to arrange the lather-like substance in regular parallel rows along its exterior, corresponding in position to some degree, with the rows of eggs within.

"The ootheca is finished off at either end with a sort of rostrum formed by a vertical plane of matrix substance projecting in the middle line of the structure. That formed at the commencement of the construction is short and rounded, while that formed at the end of the process is drawn out into a sharp point, as the insect moves away. These rostra are covered with the lather, in the same way as the rest of the ootheca. Each female makes about five of these egg-cases during four or five weeks ; a single union with the male appears to suffice for the fertilization of the whole series of eggs laid in the season. . . . In some way the embryo softens the end of the cell in which it lies, and this falls outwards as a small disc hanging by a silken thread, and setting the nymph free. At the moment of hatching the nymphs come pouring out of their cells, and hang each by a silken thread suspended in the air ; this silken thread is not attached to the cerci, which have not, I think, the function of spinnerets as figured for another species by Brongniart. The thread appears to be a single one of twisted strands, and to be attached at one end to the silk lining of the egg-case, and at the other to a very delicate silk membrane which enfolds the body of the nymph. The nymphs, clad in this membrane, have a distinctly maggot-like appearance. They soon free themselves from this covering, which remains hanging from the ootheca, and enter upon an independent existence within a quarter of an hour of hatching."

Stick-Insects, or *Phasmidæ*, occur in astounding numbers in Borneo. Most of the species, as their name implies, resemble sticks and twigs very closely, and one, *Cuniculina nematodes*, is of such extreme tenuity that one is led to wonder where room can be found for the internal organs within so slender and yet so lengthy a body. A great many forms are winged, and though in a state of repose they appear indistinguishable from the leaves or bark on which they rest, many become highly conspicuous when they fly, as their wings are then seen to be very brightly coloured ; *Marmessoidea quadriguttata*, for instance, is green, but the part of the wings unfolded during flight is bright rosy-pink, and the insects form beautiful objects as they take short and slow flights from one shrub to another when disturbed. All the species are vegetable-feeders and most of them feed on leaves, but I have found one burrowing in rotten wood.

A South American sub-family, the *Anisomorphinæ*, have very distasteful properties, exuding when irritated a whitish fluid from the bases of the legs. They are mostly wingless and, far from being stick-like, are very conspicuous, being either brightly coloured or of a shining black. So far as is known, all the other sub-families are palatable to birds and other insect enemies, so that the presence of gaudy colours on the parts of the wings exposed during flight is a fact the reason of which is difficult to explain. In spite of their marvellous resemblance to vegetable structures, these insects are preyed on extensively by Trogons, a family of birds that affects a diet of Orthoptera in preference to one of other insects. An enthusiastic anti-Darwinian to whom I related this fact rejoiced at having found an argument to combat the belief that the imitation of sticks and leaves was of protective value to the insects, but inasmuch as every believer in natural selection supposes that these resemblances have been evolved through the elimination of insufficiently perfect and of unfit individuals by their enemies, and supposes further that evolution is progressing to-day with unabated vigour, the joy of the unbeliever appears misplaced.

A good many of the *Phasmidæ* are nocturnal feeders, and I have noticed a peculiar habit in some that I have kept in captivity : during the daytime the insects were quiescent, resting for hours together with their long fore-legs stretched out in front of them and their other legs sticking out at various angles to the body, but at night they were somewhat more active, moving about over their food-plant and munching the leaves greedily. That the presence of light had practically no effect on these two modes of living was shown by the fact that the insects were quite as active after dusk had fallen whether the room in which they were placed was brilliantly illuminated or not, and conversely, some specimens kept in a bathroom that was only imperfectly illuminated by a grating in one wall were as quiescent in the middle of the day as specimens exposed to bright sunlight. The same fact has been observed of plants that at night adopt a sleeping attitude, the leaves being turned at a different angle from that which they adopt in the daytime ; if such a plant be placed in a dark room and examined suddenly by day it will be found that the leaves are in the waking

attitude, i.e. turned so as to catch the full strength of
sun-rays, which for it are practically non-existent,
while at night the plant adopts the sleeping attitude
even if the room be brightly lit. In fact, all attempts
to turn the plant's and the Stick-Insect's nights into
days, and days into nights, are a failure. The inherited rhythm of action is much stronger than the
suddenly reversed stimuli of light and dusk ; the Stick-
Insect will rest and the plant will wake in the day in
spite of artificial darkness, and conversely at night in
spite of brilliant illumination.[1]

Most of the winged species of *Phasmidæ*, especially
some with brightly coloured wings, are diurnal feeders,
or at any rate feed as readily during the day when
in captivity as during the night. Dr. Annandale has
stated that during the great heat of the day in Malayan
jungles, when insectivorous birds are not actively hunting their prey and when all nature seems to be at
rest, gasping in the heat, Stick-Insects are apparently
more abundant because they are more on the move
than early in the morning or towards the close of
day. I do not know if Dr. Annandale is referring only
to winged species : for my own part I have always
found the most stick-like apterous forms very difficult
to find at any time of the day [Note 11, p. 315].

[1] The results described are probably due to the persistence
of an individual rhythm already set up, and not to an inherited
specific rhythm. In order to prove the existence of the latter
it would be necessary to begin the experiment very early in life,
before any individual rhythm can have been set up. A note at
the end of this chapter shows that the author had intended to
refer to Sir Francis Darwin's Presidential Address to the British
Association (*Report*, 1908, p. 3), where the inheritance of acquired
characters is supported on similar grounds.—E. B. P.

Certain species of Phasmids are bulky creatures, and are protected by an elaborate armature of stout and sharp spines which renders them very unpleasant to handle, especially as they struggle valiantly when captured, scraping their spiny legs against the hands and fingers of the ardent entomologist. The male of one of the spiniest species, *Heteropteryx grayi* [Note 12, p. 315], has the power of stridulating quite loudly when irritated, by scraping the wings against the under-side of the wing-covers. The wing-covers and wings are reduced rudimentary organs in the male sex of this genus, and are quite useless for purposes of flight ; their function of producing a hissing sound is a secondary modification. The veins on both wings and wing-covers are very strongly developed and stand up as ridges ; the wing-covers are incapable of independent movement and lie as mere flaps over the short wings ; but these latter organs can be moved, and when the insect is irritated they are quickly raised up and down, lifting up the passive wing-covers and scraping against their under-surface with each movement. A good many *Phasmidæ* with larger wings, though scarcely large enough to serve usefully in flight, make a rustling sound by repeatedly opening and closing the wings, and this they do when irritated. A Brazilian species, *Pterinoxylus difformipes*, has in the female a stridulating apparatus something like that of the male *Heteropteryx*. The fore margin of the rudimentary wings is finely shagreened, and when the wing is raised this margin scrapes against the edge of the wing-covers. There is a large clear patch on the disc of the wings like a speculum, and it has been suggested that this is thrown into vibrations by the scraping of the wings against the wing-covers, thus increasing the sound, which is still further augmented by the dome-shaped wing-covers acting as resonators. Dr. L. Péringuey [1] states that the female of *Palophus haworthi*, a South African Phasmid, when irritated suddenly opens with a loud tearing sound the fan-like wings, which are too short to support the body in flight, and at the same time jerks the abdomen into the air. In one case the noise and attitude were sufficiently alarming to put to flight a cat that was cautiously investigating the Stick-Insect. Stridulation amongst these defenceless insects is even more of a " bluff " than in the case of the *Mantidæ* ; but if the bluff succeeds once in a thousand times its value to the species might be incalculable.

One and only one sub-family of the *Phasmidæ*, the *Ascepasminæ*, has the claws of the feet toothed like a comb, and it is difficult to know what advantages these Phasmids have over the vast majority of other species. Though I have kept some of them in captivity, I have failed to detect any particular use to which the pectinate claws were applied. The claws of insects differ in structure very considerably and pectinate claws are found in many orders, but they occur in a sporadic manner, some genera in the same family possessing them whilst allied genera have the ordinary simple type of claw. So far as we know the structure of the claws bears very little if any relation to the habits and modes of life of the insects, for species with very similar habits have different kinds of claws, and species with most dissimilar habits often have claws of the same type. The fact of the matter is that minute details of structures, which are

[1] *Proc. S. African Phil. Soc.,* XIV. (1903-4), p. vii.

of the greatest importance to the entomologist in enabling him to classify his collections, can generally be of no importance to the insects themselves in their struggle for life. What is termed a natural system of classification, that is, a system displaying the relationship of one form to another, cannot be arrived at if the classifier confines his attention to characters that must be of enormous biological importance to the animals themselves, such as the presence or absence of wings, the shape and colour of the body and its appendages. It seems to me that the claws of insects come into the category of structures whose form is indifferent to the species but of great use to the systematist. Perhaps we may learn some day the reasons for the persistence of such structures of taxonomic importance, even when they are of no value to the creatures possessing them, but at present we are standing on an isolated rock of knowledge, gazing down into the vast abyss of the unknown.

The eggs of *Phasmidæ* are extremely like seeds, and on this account have for long attracted the notice of naturalists. It is really one of the marvels of nature that insects, resembling plant structures so closely, should have the resemblance extended even to the eggs which they deposit, and it has even been stated that the microscopic structure of the egg-shells is identical with that of seed-coats. Many species lay large numbers of eggs, and they are dropped on the ground in the most casual manner possible while the females are feeding. The eggs, owing to their hard shells, are well protected from the attacks of ants and parasitic Hymenoptera, the foes that are most likely to destroy them. As a

further protection they are closed at the top by a
tightly fitting lid—the operculum, on which is generally
situated a little knob known as the capitulum. It is
probable that this knob is itself nothing more than
an imperfectly developed egg, formed beside and subsequently attached to the true egg in the ovarian tube
of the mother. There is, indeed, some evidence to
show that at one period of development the operculum,
too, is an imperfectly developed egg, so that the egg
as laid may be really a compound structure consisting of one perfectly developed and two imperfectly
developed eggs, the latter being modified to form a
capitulum and an operculum.[1]

Not the least interesting feature of Phasmid eggs is
a peculiar sculpturing on the egg-shell, the hilar area
and hilar scar, resembling very closely similar structures on some seeds ; in such eggs as I have investi-
gated the embryo lies with the head just under the
operculum and the ventral surface under the hilar
area.   The form of the egg varies greatly, and it is
possible to discriminate between closely allied species
by the well-marked differences that the eggs present.
Eurycnema herculanea, a large species that I kept in
captivity for some time, has a large smooth oval egg,
greyish in colour, with a spherical yellow capitulum.
Lonchodes uniformis lays a small dark-brown egg with
an orange capitulum shaped like the tuft on a gooseberry.   *Sipyloidea* sp. has a long pointed egg with
sculptured and rugose surface, and the capitulum is
long and pointed.   The eggs of the *Ascepasminæ* are
very peculiar, for they are exactly like the seeds of a

[1] Sharp, " Account of the Phasmidæ," etc., in Willey's *Zoological
Results*, etc., Cambr , 1902, p. 75.

small vetch—lenticular objects, dark brown in colour with a paler spot situated on one side, and they have no capitulum. The species of the genus *Marmessoidea* do not drop their eggs casually, but attach them in rows to leaves, and only a few, in comparison with the scores of other species, are laid. They are creamy white, but the upper side is covered with a black network, and the hilar area is marked by a denser pigment. In shape they are a long oval, and at one end on the upper side is the operculum, dotted with pigment except for a clear white crescent; there is no capitulum.

Some species of *Phasmidæ* have the power of parthenogenetic reproduction for several generations. In Sarawak I kept *Eurycnema herculanea* in captivity for eight generations. Although no males ever appeared the females laid eggs which in course of time hatched out, and the larvæ grew to maturity and in turn laid eggs also. I noticed that the later generations laid a larger proportion of eggs that never hatched out, and also a larger proportion of dwarfed infertile eggs. How long the race would have taken to become extinct in the natural course of events I cannot say, for a captive monkey broke loose one day in my absence and extinguished the whole brood by the process of eating them one and all; the specimens were all in the larval stage, and as I had no more eggs my observations came to an abrupt conclusion. The male of *Eurycnema herculanea* has, so far as I know, never been discovered, though the female is common enough in collections. Here in England I have still a small colony of an Indian Stick-Insect that has bred parthenogenetically for several generations; its

ultimate fate I hope to be able to witness uninter-
ruptedly.[1]

[1] Mr. Shelford exhibited, in 1908, a specimen of this stock bred by
Mr. H. Main (*Proc. Ent. Soc.*, 1908, p. lxxvi). Mr. Shelford's breeding
experiment is still (1916) being continued in Oxford by Mr. J. B.
Baker, M.A. The insects thrive upon privet. As yet no male
has been observed in Oxford, but a single one was bred by Mr.
K. G. Blair in London from the same stock (*Proc. Ent. Soc.*, 1911,
p. lxi). The parent is believed to have come originally from India,
but the species has not been made out with certainty. The insects are generally referred to the Indian species *Dixippus* or *Carau-
sius morosus*, although others have considered that they are an
undescribed species of *Menexenus*, or of *Lonchodes*. Mr. H. Ling
Roth has in recent years reared to maturity about 1,200 individuals
in four generations, at Halifax, Yorkshire. Among these one single
male appeared in the third generation. Mr. Ling Roth has made
careful measurements of the size of various parts, the length of
stages, etc., proving that variation is strongly marked in these
parthenogenetically bred individuals—a conclusion of great importance in relation to Weismann's well-known theory of the rôle
of sexual reproduction in causing variation.—E. B. P.

CHAPTER VI

BEETLES

ONE of the common beetles of Sarawak is a little blue Tiger-Beetle with red legs, *Collyris marginata*; it may be seen flying about in the sun and settling frequently on the leaves of trees and shrubs. It is, like the other members of the genus, more of an arboreal than a terrestrial insect, and so differs from the great majority of Tiger-Beetles, or *Cicindelidæ*, which are ground-beetles, running about on paths and open spaces, and depositing their eggs in the ground. Here the eggs hatch out, and the larvæ form burrows in which they lie in wait for their prey. The life-history of *Collyris emarginata* is rather different, for the eggs are laid in twigs of shrubs or trees, and in these the larva forms its burrow.

Dr. J. C. Koningsberger, of Buitenzorg, Java, was the first to call attention to this interesting habit,[1] and when I was at Buitenzorg in 1905 I saw in the museum there a preparation illustrating the life-history of the beetle, which at one time was rather a serious pest to the planters of Java on account of the injury done by the larvæ to the young coffee-shoots. At the

[1] *Mededeelingen uit's lands Plantentuin* (1901), XLIV. [See Note 13, p. 315].

time of my visit to Java Dr. Koningsberger was on leave in Europe, and I was unable then to get any further information about the beetle, but later on he was kind enough to supply me with several specimens of the larvæ in their burrows, and I was able to make an examination of their external anatomy.[1]

The burrow occupied by a *Collyris* larva is situated in the pith of very small twigs. It is generally half as long again as the larva, so that there is room for to-and-fro movements by the occupant. Just at the front end of the burrow is a small circular orifice passing through the woody tissue of the twig and placing the burrow in communication with the outer world. On examining a larva, it can be seen that it possesses no organs adapted for boring through the resistant woody tissue of the twig, and it is obvious that the egg must be placed in the soft pith by the mother beetle. An adult female of *Collyris emarginata* is provided with a complex armature of strong chitin, concealed within the terminal visible segments of the abdomen. The armature is really made up of three abdominal segments and their appendages, retracted within the abdomen, and highly modified for oviposition. The actual oviposition of this species has never been witnessed, but a glance at the chitinous armature of the female is enough to show that it is well suited for penetrating the relatively hard wood of the coffee-twigs, so that the egg can be placed safely inside the pith. All the *Cicindelidæ*, so far as is known, deposit their eggs *in* substances and not *on* substances, and the females invariably have some sort of boring apparatus concealed within the abdomen.

[1] *Trans. Ent. Soc.*, 1907, pp. 83–90, Pl. III.

The last ventral plate of the abdomen of *Collyris emar-ginata* has on its free terminal margin a pair of little decurved spines, and I believe that the function of these is to guide the egg safely through the hole bored in the wood on to the central cylinder of pith. Without these guides the beetle would be very liable to make a bad shot at the hole which she had bored, and lay the egg on the outside of the twig, where it would be exposed to all sorts of dangers, or it might fall to the ground. It is interesting to observe that these spines occur in other *Cicindelidæ* which are known to be arboreal. They are well developed in *Therates labiata* from Amboina, which Wallace states to be arboreal; very minute and perhaps functionless in some Bornean species of *Therates* which are more terrestrial than arboreal in their habits, and they are present in the arboreal Australian genus *Distypsidera*.

When the larva of *Collyris emarginata* hatches out it must proceed to form its burrow by digging out the soft pith of the twig, and we find that the front legs are well adapted for this purpose. In the larvæ of other *Cicindelidæ*, which live in burrows in the soil, the legs are long and slender, and act as stays to prop the larvæ up at the top of its lair; but in *Collyris* larvæ the fore-legs are flattened and shortened to form efficient digging instruments. The thigh or femur is not much longer than the plate-like first joint of the leg, the coxa: it is broadest at the distal end, and is produced at one point into a strong, flat-tened tooth, bearing in its turn smaller teeth. The next two joints, the shank or tibia and the tarsus, are extremely short, and have little teeth on the outer aspect. By means of oar-like movements of these strong spades the larva can soon dig out the soft pith, which is expelled from the opening made by the mother.

In all Cicindelid larvæ there occurs on the back of the seventh segment of the body a hump or process armed with two or more long spines. When resting at the top of their burrows the larvæ are bent into an S-shaped curve, and the spines, together with the legs, serve to prop them up and keep them steady when they are struggling with some large and strong victim that has fallen into their clutches. In *Collyris* larvæ the hump is small and beset with six little spines, which all point forward. In the specimens I examined there was no very pronounced S-shaped curve of the body, and it did not appear to me that the spines would be of very great service in holding the larvæ in their places when struggling with powerful prey. The *Cicindela* larva rests at the top of its burrow, closing the mouth of it with its large head and the first segment of the body. When any small insect running on the ground passes over this living trap-door it is seized in a pair of powerful jaws, and the larva drops like a bullet to the bottom of its burrow, there to devour its prey at its ease.

The action of *Collyris* is a little different, and has been observed by two entomologists, Mr. F. Muir and Mr. J. C. Kershaw, who studied the larva of a species of the genus at Hong-Kong. This species, like the Javan and Bornean *C. emarginatus*, lived in the stems of a shrub, and fed on ants and aphides which it seized by darting out of its burrow, and then retiring to shelter again. It is obvious with this different mode of seizing prey that the powerful dorsal spines

that are so useful to the *Cicindela* larvæ as props, and
possibly as climbing-irons, would hamper the *Collyris*
larva, and so, in accordance with the rule that structures are adapted to requirements, we find these hooks,
though more numerous, much reduced in size.

One interesting feature was seen in the piece of
stem bored by this Hong-Kong larva—the part of the
stem occupied by the larva was swollen, an evident
pathological result of the injury inflicted by the larva ;
I have seen similar swellings on plant stems tunnelled
by ants, and it is not unlikely that the huge bulbous
swellings on the roots of those remarkable plants
Myrmecodia and *Hydnophytum*, which afford perma-
nent shelters to colonies of ants, took their origin in
the first place from pathological swellings induced by
insects boring in normal tissues.[1]

Another very common Tiger-Beetle found, mostly in
old jungle, running about amongst the decaying vegetation, is *Tricondyla gibba*. Nothing unfortunately is
known of its life-history, which may be expected to
be different from that of *Collyris* and *Cicindela*. I am
inclined to suppose that the larva will eventually be
found burrowing in decaying wood ; but I must confess that I have no facts to back my belief.

A digression may now be made to consider very
briefly the adaptation of the fore-legs of many insects
for digging. These adaptations are strikingly apparent
when the fore-legs of certain burrowing insects are
compared with those of their non-burrowing allies.

The fore-leg of the Mole-Cricket *Gryllotalpa* is familiar to all entomologists, and it has been often figured

[1] There is no doubt that the swellings referred to *precede* the
insect attacks.—H. N. R.

in books on the natural history of insects. Less
familiar is *Panesthia javanica*, a Cockroach that swarms
in multitudes in decaying wood, and has fore-tibiæ that
are considerably shortened and strongly spined, but not
otherwise highly modified. The fore-limb in Passalid
beetles is only moderately adapted for digging, but the
Copridæ, which are ground-burrowers (although I have
also taken a species in decaying wood), have lost the
tarsus of the fore-limb, and the tibia is considerably
expanded. The fore-limb of the larva of *Collyris
emarginatus* has been already described (p. 158). A
very remarkable bug of the family *Lygæidæ*, found in
rotten wood, has a fore-limb approaching that of the
Mole-Cricket. With all these we may compare the
corresponding leg of the Sand-Wasp or Fossor *Bembex*,
which does not burrow in decaying wood, but digs
holes in sand for her young.

It may be pointed out that insects play a large part
in the production of the rich and fertile soil that
covers the floor of the jungle. The soil for the depth
of a foot or two is made up of vegetable detritus,
the deciduous leaves of trees contributing to it largely.
But occasionally storms sweep through the jungle and
bring down some of the older or weaker trees, especially those which have been attacked by the interlacing parasites of the *Ficus* order. The trees in their fall
involve others in their ruin, and great clear spaces, with
fallen trees cumbering the ground, may occasionally be
met with in any tract of jungle. An examination of
these trees shows that they are in all stages of decay,
from comparatively sound timber to little more than
mere cylinders of vegetable humus.

A newly fallen tree attracts for miles around all

those beetles whose larvæ bore into more or less sound wood—Longicorns, Weevils, *Scolytidæ*, and others. The tree-trunk, being now riddled in all directions by the tunnels of the borers, is exposed to the penetration of the ever-present moisture of a country with an average annual rainfall of over 130 inches, and the attacks of parasitic fungi follow. If the wood be of sufficient softness white ants make terrific inroads into it, and ordinary ants also colonize it ; but if the wood be of a nature not agreeable to the white ants it more slowly rots away, and in course of time becomes of so soft and friable a texture that it provides a home for scores of different insects, that live partly on the rotten wood and partly on the smaller organisms, such as *Scolopendrella*, *Thysanura*, and others, which swarm throughout the mass. Passalid beetles and their larvæ, Cockroaches of the genus *Panesthia*, a peculiar Lygæid bug, a Phasmid, and Heteromerous beetles are a few examples of the insects that I have taken in quantities from a decayed trunk. Ere very long the log, traversed in all directions by these borers, becomes converted into a cylinder of humus peopled by Mole-Crickets, Earthworms, the larvæ of many Diptera, and other soft-bodied grubs.

One of the most wonderful beetles known to science is *Mormolyce phyllodes*, a member of the great family *Carabidæ*. This insect, which is of considerable size, is very flattened in shape, the elytra have large semi-circular expansions, the prothorax is elongated and flattened ; the head has a long neck, and the antennæ are almost as long as the body. More than one species of this remarkable genus have been discovered, but they appear to be confined to the Malay Peninsula and the Great Sunda Islands, Borneo, Java, and Sumatra. The first specimens that reached Europe excited the wonder of all entomologists, and gave rise to many discussions on the true affinities of the species. In the middle of the last century the Paris Museum actually paid 1,000 francs for a single specimen of *Mormolyce phyllodes*, a disbursement which subsequently they must have regretted, for the beetle is by no means uncommon, and recently has been taken by the hundred.

The adults are generally found resting on the huge *Polyporus* fungi, which project from the trunks of decaying trees. The larvæ are found inside lenticular chambers, which have been excavated within the woody tissue of the fungus. These chambers communicate with the outside world by a small orifice situated on the under side of the fungus. There may be more than one chamber in a fungus, but I have never found more than one larva in a chamber. The larva, as it grows, continues to increase the size of the chamber, and when two chambers are placed close together it sometimes happens that the dividing wall is broken down by one of the larvæ, and then it appears as if two larvæ lived together in a single cell. The grubs feed on such insects as enter by the hole leading into their chamber, but occasionally on each other. Oviposition has never been observed, but it is probable that the female beetle bores a hole in the fungus and deposits her egg therein, otherwise the egg would fall to the ground; for in every fungus that I have examined the one and only entrance to the larval chamber is on the under surface of the fungus.

According to Heer Overdijk,[1] who was the first to discover the life-history of this curious beetle, the larval stage lasts for eight to nine months, during which five moults take place, and the pupal stage lasts eight to ten weeks. The larvæ are not very remarkable in appearance, closely resembling other Carabid grubs, but the pupa is sufficiently like the adult to present a very extraordinary appearance. I do not know how the imago manages to effect its escape from its prison. I once caught a newly emerged beetle, with the integument still soft and pale in colour, resting on a *Polyporus* fungus, but though the cell in the fungus was empty it was almost incredible that so large a creature could have escaped through the small hole leading to the cavity, even allowing for the softness of its tissues, which would, of course, be capable of a certain amount of compression. It is a curious fact that one or more adults are always found in close proximity to a fungus with larval chambers, and I have sometimes wondered if they assisted the newly hatched beetles to emerge by gnawing at the entrance to the larval chamber and increasing its size, but I have never found a fungus showing traces of such action, and so do not consider it probable. Overdijk states that the adults when handled caused such a burning and itching sensation that his fingers were disabled for a whole day. I have handled several living specimens myself, and cannot state that I have ever experienced any ill-effects whatever, nor have I ever heard complaints from my Dayak collectors, who had a still wider experience of living specimens.

[1] *Tijdschrift voor Entomologie (Nederland. Ent. Ver.)*, vol. I. (1857), pp. 41-3.

Every one who has collected insects in the tropics is thoroughly familiar with certain beetles, usually coloured red, or red and black, which on account of their soft leathery wing-covers bear a family resemblance to the "Soldiers and Sailors" so abundant in England. These beetles belong to the *Lycidæ*, one of the families of the group Malacodermata, to which the "Soldiers and Sailors" also belong. The *Lycidæ* are not only abundant, but expose themselves very freely on flower-heads, tree-trunks, etc. From observations and experiments made by Mr. G. A. K. Marshall in South Africa, and by myself in Borneo, there is every reason to suppose that the *Lycidæ*, owing to their nauseous properties, are very distasteful to insect enemies; but to this subject I shall return later. The larvæ are also very conspicuous creatures that may be found in some numbers crawling about on the trunks of trees or on the floor of the jungle.

I was successful in breeding the imagines from two kinds of Lycid larvæ, *Lycostomus gestroi* and *Calochromus dispar*. The first of these is in shape and certain details of anatomy not unlike the common Glow-Worm, which is the larva-like female of another member of the Malacodermata, *Lampyris noctiluca*. But in colouring the *Lycostomus* larva is very different, for it is black on the upper surface with a marginal series of orange spots, while beneath it is white with black spots. The larvæ, like the adults, are very distasteful, and their colouring is, no doubt, yet another example of warning coloration. The head, as in so many Malacoderm larvæ, is very small, and can be withdrawn inside the first thoracic segment; the antennæ are also retractile, and are little club-shaped structures of only two joints ; a well-defined crescentic area of the cuticle at the tip of the second joint is very thin, and as the body of the antenna is occupied by many nerve-fibres and large ganglia, these organs must be very sensitive. The larvæ crawl about with a looping movement something like Geometer caterpillars, and they constantly apply the tips of their minute antennæ to the surface on which they crawl. As their only visual organs are a pair of small ocelli, so simple in structure that it is impossible to imagine them capable of more than appreciating the difference between light and darkness, the antennæ are undoubtedly the most important sense organs that the creatures possess.

The larvæ feed either on Mollusca or else on such small soft-bodied creatures as *Scolopendrella*, *Thysanura*, and perhaps Dipterous larvæ, it is not certain which, for I was never able to find out exactly what they ate, though I was successful in rearing them when kept in decaying wood.[1] It is certain that the larvæ do feed on animal matter, for their mouth-organs are constructed on the same plan as those of the Glow-Worm, which, as is well known, devours snails. A more or less detailed account of the mouth-parts in *Lycostomus* larvæ will illustrate how admirably these organs are adapted for sucking the juices of the creatures on which they prey.

The mandibles are fine sickle-like blades, each enclosed in a delicate sheath, and perforated through-out their length by a delicate canal into which open

[1] Dr. D. Sharp, F.R.S., who has bred the English Lycid, *Eros aurora*, from the larva, tells me that he has never really discovered what the larva feeds upon.

the salivary ducts; the mandibular sheaths are open at the back and at their ends, allowing the tips of the mandibles to project freely. A portion of the next pair of mouth-organs, the maxillæ, known as the lacinia, is deeply grooved along its inner face, and into this groove the mandible of the same side accurately fits; the lacinia is of somewhat spongy texture. The way in which these organs are used must be somewhat after this fashion.

The sickle-like mandibles are plunged into the body of the prey, and as they are forced into the tissues they spring partly out of their sheaths, which remain outside the wound as do also the bluntly pointed spongy laciniæ of the maxillæ. A secretion from the salivary glands is forced through the mandibular canal into the wound, which serves to make the fluids of the animal's body more liquid, exactly as the Mosquito, preparatory to sucking blood, injects a salivary secretion, which is not only poisonous, causing an abominable irritation round the puncture, but also may contain the micro-organisms which are directly the cause of malarial fever. Outside the wound caused by the *Lycostomus* larva, the mandible is enclosed in a tube made of two half-tubes—the mandibular sheath open at the back and the lacinia grooved down the front; up this closed channel the juices, rendered more fluid by the salivary secretion, can be drawn into the mouth of the larva. It can be clearly seen from the structure of its mouth-parts that the larva is a suctorial insect, and does not bite or munch its prey.

After eight to ten weeks the larvæ pupate. Immediately before pupation they swell up and become very sluggish. The pupæ are white and the outer edges of the first two thoracic segments, and the "shoulders" of the future wing-covers, are beset with little spinous processes ; two such processes are also situated at the posterior angles of each abdominal segment, and the apex of the abdomen itself is furnished with a pair of slender processes, each terminating in a grapnel-like head. This complicated armature serves a particular purpose, that of securing over the back of the pupa the dorsal part of the last larval skin. When the final moult takes place the pupa is attached by its ventral surface to some tree-trunk. The ventral part of the last larval skin is lost, but the dorsal part is fixed over the back of the pupa, for the terminal grapnels and the tiny spines hold it quite securely fore and aft. Without a close examination it is not possible to distinguish a pupa from a larva owing to this overlying blanket of larval skin. The object of the retention of the larval skin is not far to seek. A pupa is a helpless object unable to escape or resist its enemies; the nauseous properties of the adult larval *Lycostomus*, which are their protection against foes and are well advertised by bright colours, are undoubtedly present in the pupa, but not coupled with a conspicuous advertisement. There is no doubt that nature could evolve a pupa with a conspicuous warning colouring, but she has other methods of arriving at the same result and here we have an example. The pupa, by retaining the last larval skin, borrows, so to speak, the warning advertisement of the larva, and thus acquires immunity from the attacks of enemies familiarized by experience with the larval colouring.

The larva of *Calochromus dispar* is very different in outward appearance from that of the *Lycostomus*. The

FIG. 3.   FIG. 2.

FIG. I.

H. Main, photo.

To face p. 163.

"Trilobite-Larva," upper side (Fig. 1) and under side (Fig. 2). An allied larva of different shape (Fig. 3). (From photographs of living examples brought, in 1912, from Sarawak to England, by J. C. Moulton. Reproduced by kind permission from Plate VII of *Proc. South London Ent. and Nat. Hist. Soc.*, 1912–13.)

Plate XIV.

back of the first thoracic segment is expanded into
a large shield, bright orange in colour; the last
segment of the body is also orange. The back of
the larva is black, and from the sides of the body
there project finger-like processes coloured black and
white, except those at the end of the body, which are
orange; the body terminates in a pair of antler-like
processes. The habits of this larva are like those of
Lycostomus, and in the same way the last larval skin
covers the pupa, and is held in position by very similar
devices.

Of very great interest are the large trilobite-like
larvæ, apparently of some unknown Malacoderm beetle.
Structurally they resemble the larvæ of *Lycidæ*, but
are very much larger not only than the Lycid larvæ
but than any adult Malacoderm beetle known to
science. Several species occur in Borneo, and one of
them is not at all uncommon; others are found in Java,
Sumatra, the Malay Peninsula, Burma, and Travancore.
The extraordinary fact about these larvæ is that no one
has ever succeeded in rearing them from the larval
stage to an adult, or even to a pupal stage, nor has
any one ever identified the species of beetle which
might be expected to be the adult stage. It is not
that the attempt to rear them has never been made,
for sundry entomologists, including myself, have kept
the creatures in captivity, have seen them moult and
increase in size, but have never witnessed the pupation
of a single specimen. Dr. Hanitsch obtained quantities
of another form on Mt. Kina Balu, in North Borneo,
his collectors bringing specimens to him literally in
handfuls until he stopped them from catching any
more; the larvæ were kept alive for some months in

Singapore, but eventually died. As in the case of the Lycid larvæ, it is not certain what these creatures feed on, but they seem to thrive if always kept moist and surrounded with plenty of rotten wood.

It may be observed that neither on Kina Balu nor in the neighbourhood of Kuching, where " Trilobite-Larvæ " also occur, does there exist, so far as is known, a Malacoderm beetle that could possibly be regarded as the adult of either of these larvæ, and this in spite of the fact that in the one place the larva is extraordinarily abundant and in the other common enough. I once put forward, in conversation with coleopterists, a suggestion that these larvæ underwent no metamorphosis at all, but that they merely grew in size, and when they attained full growth reproduced their kind, or in other words became adult without metamorphosis. The suggestion was scouted as too improbable to deserve discussion, but a consideration of the metamorphosis of some other Malacodermata, and an examination of the internal anatomy of the larva, convinces me that the suggestion may eventually be shown to be not very wide of the actual truth.

A very remarkable South American Malacoderm, *Phengodes hieronymi*,[1] is in the male sex completely winged, and quite a normal beetle, but the female is externally indistinguishable from the larva. Dr. Annandale is inclined to believe that the same is true of a common Fire-Fly, or Glow-Worm, of Calcutta, *Luciola vespertina*. These two beetles, *Phengodes* and *Luciola*, belong to two different families, and consequently there

[1] Mr. Gahan informs me that nearly all species of *Phengodes* have larva-like females and winged males. The species referred to in the text is figured in Sharp's *Insects*, Pt. II. (1899), p. 249.—E. B. P.

is nothing inherently impossible in the view that the same limited metamorphosis may occur in members of a third family; in fact, we may go further, and say that the female larvæ, and female adults of the Malayan Lycoid species, are in all probability indistinguishable in their external anatomy. But can it be possible for the male larva also to undergo no metamorphosis? I think it quite probable, for the following reason. In all winged insects the future wings and wing-covers of the adult are formed in the body of the larva; they are developed as thickenings and folds of that layer of the body-wall known as the hypodermis, and in this stage of development are known as imaginal rudiments. As the larva grows in size they grow too, and when the larva casts its last skin and becomes a pupa, the imaginal rudiments of the wings and wing-covers unfold and are visible as wing-pads. The legs, antennæ, eyes, and other adult organs are all developed from imaginal rudiments inside the body of the larva, so that we can truly say that a larva is not a distinct organism, which towards the end of its life suddenly changes into a pupa, the pupa eventually suddenly changing into an adult, but that a larva is a stage of gradual growth, containing within its body all the organs of the adult: it is merely an adult in embryo.

The adult female of the English Glow-Worm, *Lampyris noctiluca*, is larviform, that is, though in many respects different from the larva, yet it resembles it in the soft grub-like body and in the entire absence of wings and wing-covers. If we examine the larva of the female beetle we shall find that there are in it no imaginal rudiments of wings and wing-covers, but they are present in the larva of the male, because the male beetle has well-developed wings and wing-covers.

If, then, the adult male of the "Trilobite-Larva" is provided with wings and wing-covers, then its larva should possess imaginal rudiments, but a careful microscopic examination of male larvæ, ranging from a comparatively small size to nearly the largest, has failed to reveal the slightest trace of these organs. I can therefore declare with some degree of confidence that if an adult male of this larva be eventually found differing in its external anatomy from the larva, then it must be apterous. In spite of the abundance of these larvæ, in spite of the fact that they have been known to collectors for many years, a male of this description has never been found. I will venture to prophesy, moreover, that it never will be found, but that some day a "larva" with completely developed internal generative organs communicating with the exterior by ducts will be found, and such a "larva" will be to all intents and purposes an adult. If this is ever established we shall have a gradual transition from species exhibiting complete metamorphosis to species without any metamorphosis at all, as thus :—

Males and females undergoing complete metamorphosis

Lycidæ, etc.

Males and females undergoing complete metamorphosis, but female larviform ...   . *Lampyris noctiluca*.

Male undergoing complete metamorphosis, female not meta-morphosing, indistinguishable from larva ...   ... *Phengodes*.
? *Luciola vespertina*.

Male and female undergoing no metamorphosis, both indistinguishable from larvæ ...   . "Trilobite-Larvæ."

On Mt. Matang I found larvæ of a species of *Luciola* living in a trickling stream, or in the moss on its margins. They were phosphorescent, just like our English Glow-Worm, and like it also appeared to feed on snails. This may possibly be the same species as that found by Dr. Annandale in the Malay Peninsula [1] in a stagnant pool, which he observed to display their light only when the water was quite still and when they were resting on plants near the surface. When the water was disturbed the lights of the larvæ disappeared.

Dr. Annandale indulges in some philosophical speculations as to the display of phosphorescent lights by insects, and it is certainly difficult to explain the significance of the light in Lampyrid larvæ. The old explanation that the female *Lampyris* displays her light to attract the male fails to account for its display by the larvæ and by the males themselves. Dr. Annandale suggests that the light of the aquatic larvæ serves as a lure to attract surface or aerial prey, but I do not accept this explanation of its significance, as the larvæ probably prey on molluscs, for which they search.[2]

The same naturalist has discovered another aquatic Lampyrid larva in tanks at Calcutta,[3] among the roots of a floating water-plant, *Pistia stratiotes*. This is probably the larva of *Luciola vespertina*, a very

[1] *P.Z.S.*, 1900, p. 862.

[2] I should suggest that this light serves as a defence or warning. A small *Lampyris* flew into my verandah at Singapore and a young Gecko (*Hemidactylus*) advanced to attack it. Just as it was about to seize the *Lampyris* the latter flashed its light and the Gecko turned and fled [see Note 14, p. 315],—H. N. R.

[3] *Journ. and Proc. As. Soc. Bengal* (*N. Ser.*), II. (1907), p. 106.

common Fire-Fly in Calcutta. In nearly all Malacoderm larvæ there is at the termination of the body
on the under side a sucker, formed by and continuous
with the lining of the lowest portion of the intestinal
canal. In the terrestrial forms this sucker is used
when the animal crawls, being applied to the surface
over which it is moving and withdrawn when the
front part of the body is stretched out straight, to be
reapplied when the posterior end has been brought up
to the anterior, and so on.

Mr. E. J. Bles informs me that a Malacoderm larva
which he observed in Paraguay, before proceeding to feed
on a snail, smeared its head all over with its terminal
sucker, and it is possible that glands opening on the lips
of the sucker pour out a secretion, perhaps for the purpose of dissolving the snail's slime, which might hinder
the larva in its attack [Note 15, p. 315]. Dr. Annandale
finds in the Calcutta larva that the sucker is modified
into a star-shaped funnel which can be withdrawn into
the body or completely extruded ; the funnel is connected with a pair of large air-tubes which run along
the sides of the body and send out fine branches
amongst the internal organs. The under side of the
floating leaves of *Pistia stratiotes* holds films of air and
the funnel is thrust into these air-reservoirs, and thence
air is drawn into the respiratory system. We thus
see that a structure with only slight modifications can
serve as an organ of locomotion, an organ accessory
to feeding, and an organ of respiration.

Another common Calcutta Fire-Fly is *Luciola gorhami*,
which is winged in both sexes, but Dr. Annandale
believes that the female of *Luciola vespertina* is practically indistinguishable externally from the larva, for

specimens which, after having been kept and fed for some months in an aquarium, died and sank to the bottom, were, when dissected, found to be full of eggs. The final proof of the similarity between larvæ and female adults by breeding has yet to be established, but it may be noted that a winged female of *L. vespertina* similar to the winged female of *L. gorhami* is not known.

The *Cassididæ*, or Tortoise Beetles, are of considerable interest on account of their very remarkable larvæ. The adults are plant-feeders, and some of them are most gorgeously coloured, though the brilliant hues disappear in dried specimens. The two commonest species in Sarawak are *Prioptera octopunctata* and *Aspidomorpha miliaris*. The former is something like a Ladybird, convex in shape, orange or yellow in colour, with several black spots on the wing-covers and pronotum ; the latter, which is flattened, is also yellow and marked, but in a different manner, with black spots.

The larvæ of *Cassididæ* are also plant-feeders, various species of *Convolvulaceæ* being a very favourite food-plant of the family. Their bodies are covered by the old shed skins and excrementitious matter, which are attached to long, slender processes at the end of the body. These processes can be turned forwards so that the matter which they carry forms a sort of umbrella over the larva. Some larvæ also, when irritated, have the habit of flicking the processes with the attached matter at the enemy.

Dr. D. Sharp and Mr. F. Muir [1] have given [pp. 2–6] a detailed account of the egg-laying and larvæ of some

[1] *Trans. Ent. Soc.*, 1904, pp. 1–21, Pl. I–V.

African species, and as the egg-case and larva of *Aspidomorpha miliaris*, which I once found in some numbers at Malacca, are very like those of the African species, *A. puncticosta*, the *modus operandi* of the egg-laying females must be very similar. In some species of *Cassididæ* the eggs are deposited in an ootheca of variable structure, which very roughly resembles that of the *Mantidæ*. In the genus *Aspidomorpha* the egg-case, which is attached to a leaf or stalk of the food-plant, contains a number of cells, formed by opposed membranes, each containing an egg. The way in which the ootheca of the African species is formed is as follows : The beetle, having selected a suitable spot, plants her front feet firmly and does not move them throughout the operation ; the hind pair of legs are held up out of the way. "The abdomen is then extended and the oothecal plates extruded. Placing the tips of the plates against the surface of the leaf, she exudes a small quantity of colleterial fluid which adheres to the leaf. [This fluid is secreted by certain glands, accessory to reproduction, situated at the hind-end of the body.—R. S.] Then compressing the oothecal plates together and moving the abdomen upwards this fluid is drawn out between the plates as a thin membrane. Having attained the limit of the upward movement, the two oothecal plates are moved laterally upon one another, so that the membrane is cut off. It rapidly dries and becomes hard on exposure to the air, and is then tough and elastic. To form a second membrane she brings the tip of the abdomen again to the surface of the leaf, but a little on one side of the point of attachment of the first membrane, again exudes some colleterial fluid, and,

elevating the abdomen, another membrane is formed.
Having thus fastened a few membranes firmly to the
leaf, the beetle now begins to add the deposition of
eggs to the process. An egg after passing down the
oviduct becomes covered with colleterial fluid. This
egg is placed about the middle of the membrane
behind it (it is of course one previously deposited :
the formation of the ootheca proceeds from behind
forwards). The egg adhering in this position, the
abdomen is moved downwards (i.e. towards the leaf),
but when it has reached the limit of movement in
this direction it does not touch the leaf, but, moving
in a parallel direction with that of the preceding membrane, is turned upwards so that the membrane is
doubled, and the movement continuing upwards the
end of the membrane is left free at the top, when the
limit of upward movement is reached. . . . The egg
and membrane having been thus deposited, another
egg is placed by the side of the first (and of course
on the anterior face of the membrane), and the process
is repeated. The series of four rows of eggs is attained
by means of slight lateral movement of the abdomen.
. . . The membranes are soft and pliable when extruded from the oothecal cavity, and rapidly become
solid, and thus retain the form they are made to
assume during the construction. The cells are made
to a large extent by the eggs pushing apart the membranes in some places, and pushing them together in
others, but they are partly due to the shape of the
membranes, which are, each one, curvate, and moreover are doubled so that sometimes two concave
faces are brought together ; in other cases the outside
edge of a membrane projects somewhat, and thus

13

keeps the next membrane a little way off. These
various facts are seen by examining those cells, at the
two ends, that contain no eggs : at these places the
cellular structure still exists, though in more irregular
fashion than in the area of the egg-containing cells.
The outer row of cells on each side is quite different
in form and never contains any egg."

The value of these remarkable egg-cases appears to
be that the eggs are protected from drought and
from any sudden changes of temperature. Though the
egg-case just described is a very beautiful structure,
Mr. Muir and Dr. Sharp consider that no skill is shown
in its production—"The operation seems to be more
comparable with the action of a machine." The
insect cannot see what it is doing, since the egg-case
is constructed between the lower surface of the abdomen
and the leaf, and it is doubtful if the " brain " (or cerebral
ganglia) is concerned in the operation at all. The formation of a Mantis egg-case is similarly a purely mechanical action, for an Italian observer has noted that a partially
decapitated Mantis can still construct its egg-case.

I have frequently found the egg-cases of the common
Oriental species *Aspidomorpha miliaris* attached to the
under sides of leaves of species of *Ipomœa*, but I have never
witnessed their manufacture. There is little doubt that
the method is in all essentials the same as that employed
by the African species, for in structure and appearance
they are very similar. There are eight rows of cells, the
four central ones occupied by eggs, and on each side of
this core are two rows of empty cells, and at the hind-
end of the case are some rather loosely attached
membranes which are plainly the rudiments of cells.

The larvæ are whitish and black-spotted, and that

are gregarious, feeding and resting in serried masses on their food-plant. When a larva moults, the skin is not thrown right off the body, but remains attached behind, and that next moulted is attached to the previous one, and so on, till a full-grown larva is furnished with a long chain of old skins, borne erect on a process at the hind-end of the body. The larva also has the habit of fastening particles of excrement to the spines of the last moulted skin, but they are very loosely attached and soon fall off. It is a habit which, as we shall see, has descended from a far more elaborate one. When the larva is ready to turn into a pupa, it fastens itself to a leaf and then partially throws off the last larval skin —a part, however, still remaining attached to the pupa— while the chain of old skins is thrown off entirely. The pupæ are found in little groups and are conspicuous objects.

The female of *Prioptera octopunctata* does not form an egg-case, but deposits her eggs singly on the under sides of leaves. She first lays down a thin membrane, or layer of viscous secretion which hardens to a membrane, and on this is laid an egg, which is again covered with another membrane, the egg being thus enclosed in a flat semi-transparent case. But this is not all, for over this case is placed a sort of roof to which particles of excrement are attached ; this accomplished, at another point on the same leaf, or even on another leaf, the process is repeated again and again until all the eggs are laid.

The larva is a conspicuous white-spotted creature, and it has the habit of covering the spines at the end of its body with excrement, forming a solid shield with an irregular sort of fringe along the hind-border. The

larval skins, as they are moulted, become involved in
this mass, and are more or less completely hidden in it.
The excrement is laid on to the spines in a very peculiar
manner : the anus is evaginated for a considerable
distance and plasters the excrement smoothly over the
surface.   This shield is generally carried turned forwards
over the back, but the larva can flick it backwards and
forwards when irritated.   Just before pupation the larva
casts the excrementitious shield, and then fastens itself
securely to a leaf of its food-plant.   The pupa is a broad
and somewhat flattened object, with curious spinose hooks
projecting from the first, second, and third abdominal
segments.   Portions of the last larval moult are retained
at the end of the body, but otherwise the pupa is freely
exposed.   Another species, *Metriona trivittata*, forms an
egg-case described as follows by Mr. W. Schultze [1] :—

" It is laid on the upper or under side of the leaf and
always contains a single egg.   The egg itself is inclosed
within a very thin primary case and the latter is placed
under a remarkably perfect, roof-like cover fastened to
the leaf.   This cover is thin and has two nearly parallel,
longitudinal carinæ, which are somewhat excurved at one
end, but run together at the other end where they are
bent and erect.   The area between the carinæ has a
semicircular impression, but the area outside of this is
sloping. . . . Numerous regular, fine striæ are visible.
The egg of this species is always free from any excre-
mental covering.   The color of the egg-case is a very
pale green."

The young larva attaches particles of excrement to a
pair of long spines at the end of the body, forming a
sort of cross-bar between them, but subsequently it does

[1] *Philippine Journ. of Science*, (*Ser. A.*), III. (1908), p. 267.

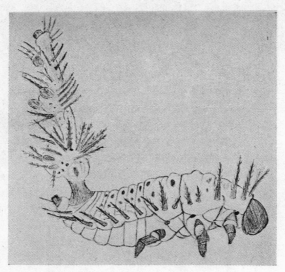

FIG. 1.

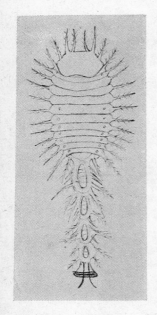

FIG. 2.

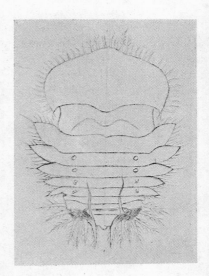

FIG. 3.

FIG. 1.—Larva of *Aspidomorpha miliaris*, with its chain of moults and attached excrement. FIG. 2.—Larva of *Metriona trivittata*, with its chain of moults and "cross-bar" of excrement on the earliest. FIG. 3.—The pupa of *Laccoptera* sp ?, retaining the shield of excrement and moults. (From the author's drawings, Figs. 1 and 2 after W. Schultze.)

Plate XV.

To face p. 181.

not add to this little mass. The moulted skins are not
entirely thrown off, but each one is added to the preceding until a long string is formed, just as in *Aspidomorpha
miliaris*, but at pupation the skins are not thrown off,
but still carried, turned over the back of the pupa.

Laccoptera sp. ? [Note 16, p. 315], makes egg-cases
rather like those of *Prioptera* 8-*punctata*, and, as in that
species and *Metriona trivittata*, there is only one egg in
each case.[1] The larva forms a solid shield of excrementitious matter, which is turned over the body and the cast
skins are worked into the mass. The pupa does not dis-
card this mass, as does *Prioptera* 8-*punctata*, but retains it
just as it was left by the larva.

Hence in these four genera we get the following
variation in habit :—

Aspidomorpha : Larva retains chain of moults with
particles of loosely attached excrement. Pupa does not
retain the chain of moults.

Metriona : Larva retains chain of moults with a
" cross-bar " of excrement on the last (viz. the earliest
moult). Pupa retains the chain of moults.

Prioptera : Larva forms a shield of excrement with
moults embedded in it. Pupa does not retain the shield.

Laccoptera sp. ? : Larva forms a shield of excrement as
in *Prioptera*. Pupa retains the shield.

It may now be asked what is the value to the species
of the peculiar habits of egg-laying and covering the
body with excrement. It has been suggested that the
formation of egg-cases protects the delicate eggs from
drying up and also from the attacks of parasitic enemies.
This may well be so, for the eggs are laid in exposed

---

[1] *Laccoptera chinensis* lays *more* than one egg in the case.
Kershaw and Muir, *Trans, Ent. Soc.*, 1907, p. 250.

situations unprotected by horny egg-shells. Without some form of protection they would be exposed to all sorts of dangers, hence that they should be enclosed in a special covering is only natural. That the protection is not absolute is certain, for Mr. Muir observed a small Hymenopterous parasite depositing her eggs in those of an individual *Aspidomorpha puncticosta* [*Trans. Ent. Soc.*, 1904, p. 18], as fast as they were being laid. But then we know that none of the multifarious protective devices of Nature are absolutely successful. If there were no destruction of individuals of any given species we should be overrun by countless hordes of them in a very short space of time.

The shields of excrementitious matter and chains of moulted skins play a double rôle. The larvæ and the newly formed pupæ have the habit of twitching or flicking up and down these appendages whenever irritated, and these movements might be quite sufficient to drive away any but the most persistent of parasitic enemies. But I think that they serve also to render the larvæ and pupæ conspicuous objects. The adult beetles are certainly very distasteful creatures. Most of them are abundant, they are gaudily coloured, and some species are mimicked by other insects. *Prioptera* 8-*punctata*, at any rate, exudes an acrid fluid when handled. These are characteristic features of nauseous species. I have not the slightest reason to doubt that the larvæ are equally distasteful, and the necessity for advertising their distastefulness is urgent. The larvæ of *Aspidomorpha miliaris* are conspicuous enough objects, being white, black-spotted creatures, and this conspicuousness is accentuated by their habit of bunching together when at rest, as well as when feeding. The pupæ, although they have discarded the chain of moults, are also conspicuous enough, because they, too, are found in little clumps. The great black shields of *Prioptera* and *Laccoptera* render their owners very plain to see on the leaves of their food-plant, and in addition *Prioptera* has the habit, both in the larval and pupal stages, of bunching together, and then the groups of larvæ look like masses of black fungoid growth. As is so often the case, a protective device can play many parts, and in *Prioptera* 8-*punctata* I believe that the shield serves to keep off parasites, perhaps defends the larva from too-scorching heat, renders the creature a conspicuous object, warning off prospective foes, and even protects it from other foes by its resemblance to a fungus.

The *Brenthidæ* are closely related to the true Weevils, or *Curculionidæ*, and occur in considerable numbers in the Oriental tropics. Very little is known about their habits or life-histories, but the majority of species in their larval stages bore in wood, and some adults live in wood all their lives. Some of these forms are very remarkably modified for boring habits, the body being grooved or compressed in places, allowing the limbs to fit closely against its sides and so not to break the perfectly cylindrical outline. Some of the species are much infested with mites, which cluster round the legs and on the long prothorax. I was much interested to find one day a species with a deep channel running along the greater length of the prothorax crammed with little mites. A good many species of *Brenthidæ* have shallow open grooves along the prothorax, but in this species the groove is deep, and, though wide, is almost completely roofed in, only a narrow slit putting it into communication with the exterior. This modification of structure for the accommodation of what appear to be mere parasites is very remarkable, but it is not without parallel in the insect kingdom.[1] Another case may be mentioned here. The *Anthribidæ*, like their allies the *Brenthidæ*, are also much infested with mites, and one species has a deep crescentic slit in the prothorax which is filled with the parasites.

[1] The following exceedingly interesting examples are described by Dr. R. C. L. Perkins in *The Entomologist's Monthly Magazine*, XXXV. (1899), pp. 37–9. The female bees of many species of the genus *Koptorthosoma* (*Xylocopinæ*) possess, in the basal abdominal segment, a special chamber which always contains, and sometimes is entirely filled by, *Acari* of large size. Somewhat similar accommodation for minute *Acari* is provided by a female wasp of the genus *Odynerus* from Arizona and Mexico.—E. B. P.

CHAPTER VII

ANTS AND PLANTS

WHEN the traveller first visits the tropics, the surprising number of ants in every conceivable situation is a feature which cannot fail to attract his attention. The sugar-bowl on his tea-table will soon be besieged by hordes of a tiny ant (*Monomorium pharaonis*), a cosmopolitan species. The long line of ants which he frequently sees crossing his dining-room floor can be traced to some fragment of food dropped at a previous meal. If a naturalist, should he carelessly leave on some table or shelf a specimen destined for the museum or collecting-box, in an hour or two he will see this specimen a revolting, seething mass of ants. When he takes his walks abroad, the same abundance of ant-life presents itself. There in the jungle he will see solitary individuals of a gigantic *Camponotus* hurrying along; or perhaps a long train of *Cremastogaster* with abdomen, shaped like the ace of spades, held aloft. If he brushes incautiously against some shrub growing in an open space, he may soon feel the vicious bite of the " Keringa " (*Œcophylla smaragdina*), which forms its nests by sewing living leaves together with the silk of its larvæ. Let him beware of that band of shining black ants crossing the path yonder, for that is *Sima*, one of the

Ponerine tribe, and it is of a ferocious nature with a cruel sting.

An immense deal of work relating to the habits of tropical ants has yet to be done. The tropics have still to hail their Huber, their Lubbock, and their Wheeler. A good deal of attention has, however, been directed to the very remarkable relations which exist between ants and the vegetable world. We find several very different plants exhibiting curious modifications of structure, such as huge bulbiform swellings galleried in all directions, tubular stems and roots, and curious appendages, which structures are constantly inhabited by ants. We will discuss some of these structures in the present chapter, and then ask ourselves, " Are they developed by the plants for the benefit of the ants, or have the ants taken advantage of the structures as asylums, although they were originally developed for quite a different purpose ? "

The table on p. 187 is a list of the Myrmecophilous plants which have been described from Borneo, but that it could be greatly extended is quite certain. On account of the great singularity of their structure, and of the great interest which attaches to the problem of the relations between the plant and the ant-guests, I will consider first the two Rubiaceous genera, *Myrmecodia* and *Hydnophytum*.

These two genera have long excited the interest of botanists and entomologists alike, for no plants exhibit more remarkable structures—to all appearance admirably and purposely adapted for the harbouring of ants. The genera have a wide distribution, ranging from Cochin China and the Malay Peninsula right down to New Guinea and the Solomon Islands, and away east

to the Fiji Islands. Such a wide distribution of plants
whose seeds are not adapted for transportation by
wind or ocean currents itself argues in favour of their
dispersal by birds; now we find that the seeds of these

Nat. Order.	Species of Plant.	Nature of Modification.
Euphorbiaceæ	*Macaranga caladifolia*, Becc.	Stems enlarged and hollow
Verbenaceæ	*Clerodendron fistulosum*, Becc.	
Palmæ	*Korthalsia horrida*, Becc. " *echinometra*, Becc. " *cheb*, Becc. " *scaphigera*, Mart. " *angustifolia*, Bl. *Calamus amplectens*, Becc.	Portion of leaves modified to form with stem ant-shelters
Rubiaceæ	*Myrmecodia tuberosa*, Jack *Hydnophytum coriaceum*, Becc. " *borneense*, Becc.	Galleried tubers
Nepenthaceæ	*Nepenthes bicalcarata*, Hook. fil.	Peduncle of pitcher hollowed
Melastomaceæ	*Pachycentria macrorhiza*, Becc. " *microstyla*, Becc.	Tuberous and galleried roots
Filices	*Polypodium (Lecanopteris) deparioides*, Bak. *Polypodium (Lecanopteris) carnosum*, Blume *Polypodium sinuosum*, Wall.	Rhizomes hollowed
	Polypodium quercifolium, L.	Sterile fronds as shelters
Asclepiadaceæ	*Dischidia rafflesiana*, Wall. " *shelfordi*, Pears.	Modified leaves as pitchers

Rubiaceæ are surrounded by a viscous pulp which is
attractive to fruit-eating birds such as pigeons, and,
even if the seeds are not actually swallowed, they
may by virtue of the viscous pulp adhere to the feet

or feathers of birds hunting in the vicinity of the plants for other food. The plants are all epiphytic, growing upon trees, but not as true parasites like mistletoe, which sends its rootlets into the bark of the tree on which it grows. The viscous seeds when dropped on the branch of a tree adhere to it and send out little rootlets and leaves. A full-grown specimen of *Myrmecodia tuberosa* has a large tuber measuring 30 centimetres in length by 20 in diameter; its surface is ridged, and on the ridges are sharp spines, homologous with the numerous rootlets whereby the plant is attached to the bough on which it lives. The tuber has the consistency of an apple, and it is tunnelled in every direction by an elaborate system of galleries tenanted by ants, either *Cremastogaster difformis* or *Iridomyrmex cordata*, var. *myrmecodiæ*. These galleries communicate with the exterior by means of numerous pores, the larger of which are situated at the base of the rootlets. The walls of the galleries are marked with pimples, which are not, as originally supposed, glands secreting a sweet fluid pleasant to ants, but lenticels or rudimentary breathing organs. The species of *Hydnophytum* have large spineless tubers, also galleried, and the leaves are much more fleshy than those of *Myrmecodia*. There are two views about these remarkable galleried tubers. Beccari holds that the galleries are the work of ants; that it is impossible for young plants to come to maturity without the intervention of ants; that their tunnelling causes the tuber to grow enormously, whilst its weight is not proportionally increased; and the galleries increase the absorbent surface. Treub, on the other hand, regards the ants as of quite secondary importance. He has seen the young plants develop,

and has noted that the first galleries, at any rate, are
produced by a mere breaking down of tissue without
the help of ants at all, whilst tubers transported from
the jungle to the botanical garden were often entirely
deserted by ants and yet flourished well, putting out
new leaves, producing flowers and seed. In opposition to Beccari, Treub considers that not only the
tubers, but the galleries in them, are part of the normal
development of the plant, the galleries serving for
aeration. The ants he regards as mere opportunists
who have taken advantage of the conveniently galleried
tubers to make their home there. The ingenuity of
Beccari's arguments is matched by the uncompromis-
ing clarity of Treub's observations and experiments.
When the seed of *Myrmecodia* germinates, the hypo-
cotylar axis, i.e. the part of the seedling underneath
the two first leaves or cotyledons, begins to swell and
continues to grow until a little tuber is formed, and
later, when the seedling has become a plantlet, a hole
appears leading from the exterior into the tuber, which
is now hollowed : this is the first gallery. If a cross-
section of a developing tuber be cut, it will be seen
that it is made up of large thin-walled cells, called parenchyma, and in the middle is a single vascular bundle.
Later on, other peripheral vascular bundles appear,
and then arises around the central bundle a ring of
different cells termed meristem—a ring within which
all the cells dry up and become flocculent, so that a
cavity, the first gallery, is formed. The meristem,
seen as a ring in cross-section, is really a cylinder of
cells, conical towards the tip of the little tuber, but
at its base abutting on the outer cork-layer, which
spontaneously breaks down, and so the first opening is

formed. The meristem has the power of producing
on its outer side new parenchyma cells, and it does
so with such vigour that the tuber quickly grows in
size, and new galleries are formed in it just as the
first gallery was formed; and this goes on until the
tuber becomes nothing more than a scaffolding of laminæ
separating galleries. When we examine the structure
of the swollen rhizomes of the ant-harbouring fern, *Polypodium carnosum* [Note, p. 205], we find that the galleries
therein are formed in very much the same way, and, moreover, their arrangement is symmetrical to correspond
with the symmetry of the fern, and quite unlike the
random burrowings of ants in a more or less homo-
geneous structure. There is nothing, therefore, very
startling in the view that the galleries of *Myrmecodia*
and *Hydnophytum* are spontaneously formed by the plants
in their normal development. But, at the same time,
the function of the galleries seems obscure. If the
tuber is a reservoir of moisture in time of drought,
the removal of a large portion of it by the galleries
must surely impair its efficiency. Why not an un-
galleried tuber? Treub regards the cavities as air-
shafts, and supposes that the fleshy tuber is aerated
by means of these moist chambers without undue loss
of water. But this mechanism for exchange of gases
is extraordinarily elaborate, its necessity is not proved,
and finally the tubers are not green, and therefore
cannot assimilate. Until we know more about the
physiology of these remarkable plants we must be content to theorize. Between the view of Beccari that
these plants cannot develop and cannot flourish without the intervention of ants, and the view of Treub
that ants are not in the least necessary for their de-

velopment or growth, it is perhaps possible to steer a middle course. If once we realize the ubiquity of ants in the tropics, and their marauding, plundering nature, we shall recognize that plants which have juicy, succulent, unprotected fruits, or large fleshy organs suitable for excavation—such as the tubers of *Myrmecodia*—offer to ants attractions which these insects will certainly not resist, and which may well prove destructive to the plants. The plants, in order to escape annihilation, must either develop other structures to protect them from ants or else must modify the attractive structures to accommodate the ants, whilst at the same time their original functions are preserved. It is, of course, well known that plants can develop certain structures in direct response to the stimuli of insect attacks : the oak-gall is merely one instance out of hundreds. Such structures are rightly regarded as pathological ; but it must be noted that, given the same plant and the same attacking insect, the structure is invariably the same. That is to say, the power of producing this structure is inherited. Now, it does not seem to me a very long step from this inherited power to produce a definite structure in response to a given stimulus, to a power to produce a definite structure *in anticipation* of a given stimulus. That an epiphytic plant furnished with a large fleshy tuber would have this tuber attacked and tunnelled by ants is almost certain in lands that swarm with ants, and that many of the plants so attacked would perish from this extensive destruction of their tissues is equally clear. The advantage of having an elaborate system of galleries all ready and prepared for the ants is obvious, and I see no reason why

natural selection should not have brought into existence this power to produce such structures. If the
presence of the ants is of advantage to the plants in
protecting them from other enemies, so much the
better, and perhaps in some myrmecophilous plants
the need for this protection has called into being
definite ant-harbouring devices. But this does not
seem to be so with *Myrmecodia* and *Hydnophytum*, for
not only has it yet to be shown that they need this
protection, but Treub's experiments show, on the con-
trary, that without the ants the plants flourish quite
well. It is a fact worthy of consideration that in
Borneo it is one species of ant which, to the almost
entire exclusion of other species, lives in nearly all the
myrmecophilous plants ; it is found in the species
of *Korthalsia,* in both genera of myrmecophilous
Rubiaceæ, in *Polypodium* spp., and in the species of
Dischidia. It may also be noted that the same ant is
frequently found in the hollowed-out branches and
twigs of shrubs not specially adapted for harbouring
ants, and we may believe that these tunnels are excavated by the ants themselves. It is thus evident that
Cremastogaster difformis is a species that habitually lives
in any convenient hollow or tunnel that it can find,
and, if it cannot find one ready, it will excavate one.
The very ubiquity of this ant tells against the view
that there is a real symbiosis of ant and plant. In
true cases of symbiosis one species of animal lives on
or in another species of animal or plant : we do not
find one species living on or in half a dozen or more
other species, and, failing to find a convenient companion, living an independent life. That ants can be and
are of immense service to some plants is certain. The

Chinese, the most expert of agriculturists, recognize this fact. In a Chinese orange-grove it is quite usual to see lengths of bamboo connecting some of the trees, and these are placed to serve as bridges to conduct ants from ant-infested trees to trees infested by destructive insect pests. If ants were as abundant in the orange-groves of Florida as they are in the tropics, we should perhaps hear less of the ravages of that very destructive pest, the Orange-Scale. Nevertheless, I believe that the benefits conferred on myrmecophilous plants have been greatly over-rated, and I regard some of the wonderful developments of plant structure as protective devices against the too pressing attention of ants, rather than as devices to attract ants. If one plant can inherit the power to produce a definite pathological structure, I do not see why another cannot inherit the power to produce a structure adapted to harbour with least damage to itself guests that certainly will not fail to make their appearance.

We may now pass to the consideration of the other plants of my list.

Macaranga caladifolia is a little shrubby plant about 3 feet high; the stem is hollow, slightly swollen, and here and there perforated by little holes. The leaves are peltate, with veins running out to the margin in a radiate manner, and those at the base of the leaf terminate on the margin each in a large glandule which secretes a sweet fluid. Ants are found in the hollow stems.[1]

[1] The story of the truly myrmecophilous species of *Macaranga* in the Malay Peninsula is described by H. N. Ridley in the *Annals of Botany*, XXIV. (1910), pp. 470-83. There are two series, in both of which the stem, at first solid, becomes hollow by dilatation

Clerodendron fistulosum is a shrubby herb about
5 feet high. It has a straight unbranched stem, woody
at the base, herbaceous at the summit. The lower
part of the stem is hollow. The internodes into
which the stem is divided are here short and rather
swollen. Exactly under the insertion of the leaves is
found a round hole, or two holes, with a prominent
thickened lip. As the leaves are opposite we should
expect to find two holes to each internode, one under
each leaf-insertion, but very often one of the holes is
absent, but is represented by a little circular patch of a
different texture and structure from the surrounding parts.
Occasionally there occurs an internode without any
holes at all. The cavity of one internode does not
communicate with the cavities of the internodes above
or below it, but every internode is separated from its
neighbours by a thick partition. An ant, *Colobopsis
clerodendroni,* has been found running in and out of
the holes. The singular fact about these holes is the
regularity of their position ; they occur under the leaf-
insertions always, whereas the holes in the stem of

and the disappearance of the pith. In one class, the bud-bracts,
which cover the bud, bear some curious bladder-glands. The
bracts eventually become recurved into a ring-like chamber round
the stem, which contains "food-bodies" developed from the
bladder-glands. They are small white balls used as food by the
ants, which live in the hollowed stem or branch. In the other
class the bracts do not bear bladder-glands or food-bodies, but these
are borne on the under side of the young leaf, which remains for
some time with its lobes deflexed. To this class belongs *Macaranga
caladifolia.* These modifications are not due to any action of
the ants, as they occur whether ants are present or not, but are
of no advantage to the plant unless ants are present. Observations showed that when ants were absent the plant suffered
severely from the attacks of caterpillars.—E. B. P.

Macaranga caladifolia are arranged in a quite haphazard way—in fact, they occur just wherever the ants desire to effect an entrance. Beccari found ten dead ants in an internode of a specimen of *Clerodendron fistulosum* which he had dried and pressed for his herbarium ; in this internode there was only one hole, and that was covered over by a leaf. Beccari asks why the imprisoned ants had not gnawed their way out, either through the leaf covering their solitary exit or through the wall of the internode at the point where the other hole ought to have been—a point marked by a circular patch of softer tissue. If we make the obvious answer that the ants did not bore their way out because they were not able to do so, we must then assume that ants do not make the holes which are found in the internodes, but that these as well as the cavities are part of the *normal* structure of the plant.[1] Then immediately arises the question—for what purpose are these holes and cavities formed ?

Many rattans of the genus *Korthalsia* have a special organ which seems to be adapted for harbouring ants. It is known as the ocrea, an appendage of a leaf-sheath which may be likened roughly to an upturned flat-bottomed boat. One species attracted Beccari's attention by a peculiar sibilant rustling, which was produced by the passing of ants over the ridged and dry ocrea, which acted like a sounding-board. The ocrea is very closely pressed to the stem of the rattan, and in order to get underneath it the ants have to bore holes through it. These holes may be

[1] The openings into the stems of *Macaranga* and *Clerodendron* are made by the ants themselves.—H. N. R.

either in the middle or near the margin, and their position is quite irregular.

Calamus amplectens is another rattan which harbours ants. The two lower segments of the leaves are folded back and embrace the stem in such a way that it is enclosed by them, very much as a stick held between hands clasped together.

Nepenthes bicalcarata is one of the most remarkable Pitcher-Plants in the world. It is found climbing up trees, and its stalk is often 20 feet long. The pitchers are of two shapes ; those which grow from the lower leaves are like bladders truncated at the mouth, and their transverse diameter is about equal to their length. The stem of the pitcher is straight, and the pitcher is joined on to it at right angles, its lower end is swollen, hollowed out and perforated. The pitchers springing from the upper leaves are smaller, infundibuliform, and rather constricted at the base. They are attached to the pitcher-stem in a curve, and the stem itself is always twisted into one curl of a spiral. This curl is swollen and hollow, and is perforated by a single hole. There is no direct evidence that these peculiar cavities are inhabited by ants, but their structure leads me to suppose that this is their purpose, and as glands are found in the tissue of the pitcher-stems, it is quite likely that these serve as nectaries for the ants.

The species of the genus *Pachycentria* are all epiphytic, or pseudo-parasitic, and some of them are provided with tuberous swellings on the roots, which are much frequented by ants. These tubers are filled with a spongy tissue, and it is probable that ants destroy this tissue and live inside the tubers.[1]

[1] *Pachycentria.* I have seen many of these, including the

In ferns there appear to be two devices for harbouring ants. In the tropics a great many ferns grow on trees, and their roots are more or less exposed to the air, and in order to prevent their drying up some of the sterile fronds are developed into roof-like shelters. In *Polypodium quercifolium* these sterile fronds are concave on their upper surface, like dried paper in consistency, and they are pressed closely to the trunk of the tree on which the fern grows; in the cavity so formed are found rootlets, and ants. Beccari asserts that in cultivated specimens these sterile fronds are not so papery nor so concave, and he thinks that these differences are due to the absence of ants. But the conditions of life under cultivation are so unlike natural conditions that these slight differences may well be attributed to other causes than absence or presence of ants. In *Polypodium carnosum* and *P. sinuosum* it is the rhizomes which afford shelters for ants, and Professor R. H. Yapp has made a very careful study of these two species.[1] Both have large fleshy rhizomes which are tunnelled by a system of galleries, and both are invariably inhabited by colonies of ants. The former species grows on the higher branches of trees in thick encrusting masses, often several feet in length, completely encircling the branches of its host. *P. sinuosum* grows nearer the ground on the trunk or lower branches of a tree, and its creeping rhizomes do not form such massive

species described by Beccari. The tubers are not hollowed out or inhabited by ants, but when they have become cracked or split, ants may at least temporarily make a nest there, as in *Ficus irregularis* (*Annals of Botany*, XXIV. (1910), p. 482).—H. N. R.

[1] *Annals of Botany*, XVI. (1902), p. 185.

growths as those of *P. carnosum*. In *P. carnosum* the branching of the rhizome is very extensive, and the branches arise very close together, so that the final result is a close tangled mass of interlacing branches, so tightly packed as to form practically one solid mass which embraces the branch of the tree on which it grows. From the upper surface of the rhizome spring the leaves or fronds, and the stems of these are articulated to the rhizome by means of conical projections or leaf-cushions, but it must be noted that a great many of these leaf-cushions do not bear any fronds at all. If a cross-section be taken through a rhizome a number of hollow spaces in the ground-tissue will be seen; these are the ant-galleries, and if they be traced up towards the apex of the rhizome, it will be seen that they are replaced in this the younger part of the rhizome by a fragile tissue made up of large, thin-walled cells which are filled with water. These cells disintegrate gradually as the rhizome grows forward, and the space formerly occupied by them becomes an ant-gallery. The system of galleries consists of a large central ventral gallery running right along the rhizome and giving off alternately on either side lateral galleries to the branches of the rhizome, and a dorsal series of chambers leading into the leaf-cushions. Now though these galleries originate from the breaking-down of thin, water-containing cells, which of course once occupied the spaces now given up to galleries, they are increased in size by the ants which inhabit them nibbling away at their walls; moreover, they communicate with the exterior air by means of holes gnawed by the ants, and generally opening on the lower surface of the rhizome. The actual function of these galleries is not quite clear, but their regularity and symmetry is in definite relation to the branches of the rhizome and to the arrangement of the leaf-cushions. The ant which Professor Yapp found inhabiting *Polypodium carnosum* growing on a mountain in Perak was a new species of *Cremastogaster*, which has been named after its discoverer. In Sarawak I have found the ubiquitous *C. difformis* in the galleries of this fern. Professor Yapp believes that the ants are of no service to the ferns, and their presence may be accounted for in the same way as in *Myrmecodia*. The galleries are possibly for the aeration of the rhizome. Professor Yapp points out that there are no stomata on the stem, and there are no intercellular spaces in the rhizome tissue. In the absence of these adaptations for gaseous exchange in tissue which is capable of assimilation, there must be a tendency to partial asphyxiation, which however is obviated by the galleries, which function as air-passages. It is also possible that when the hot sun shines on the exposed fern, water vapour condenses on the walls of the galleries and is re-absorbed when the temperature falls. Rain-water also may find its way into the galleries and be absorbed. For my own part I prefer to regard these galleries as produced for the same purpose as those which I have alleged for *Myrmecodia*.

Finally, we come to those very singular Asclepiads, the species of *Dischidia* with pitchers, several of which are found in Borneo, though only two appear to have been described. All are epiphytic plants with slender liana-like stems straggling over the branches and twigs of trees on which they grow. In the majority of species none of the leaves are abnormally developed, but are rather fleshy, kidney-shaped organs, concave on the under side, fitting very closely to the bark of the tree on which the plant grows, so that the little hollow spaces underneath them afford a shelter to the adventitious roots which spring from a point near the petiole, and push their way under the leaves. This adaptation is undoubtedly for the purpose of protecting the rootlets from excessive drought and heat, whilst the rootlets can absorb any moisture that transpires from the inner surface of the leaves when these are heated by the sun. Very often ants and other insects are found under the leaves, but they cannot be regarded as special ant-shelters. *Dischidia rafflesiana* has certain of the leaves, especially those growing on the older part of the plant, modified to form long urn-like pitchers with open mouths. The development of the pitcher has been followed out in detail, and it is now known that it is formed not by the growing together of the leaf-margins but by the bending of the apex of the leaf towards the base. This is really brought about by the arrest of the apical growth of the leaf; a rapid growth of the central portion of the leaf ensues, and so the apex is brought round towards the leaf-stock or petiole, and a pitcher is the result. The inner surface of this pitcher is the morphological under surface of the leaf, and the apex of the leaf is at a point in the margin of the pitcher exactly opposite the insertion of the petiole. These hollow pitchers are filled with adventitious rootlets, with fragments of soil and leaf-detritus, and are usually swarming with ants. As both outer and inner surfaces of the pitchers are coated with wax they are obviously not absorbent organs, but are adapted to the purpose of protecting the rootlets with which they are filled. No doubt the ants which colonize the pitchers bring in a certain amount of soil, dead insects, leaf particles, and so forth, and from these the rootlets can derive a little nourishment. After a heavy shower of rain the pitchers become more or less filled with water, and some have supposed that they are true insect-traps like the pitchers of *Nepenthes*; the insects which fall into the water in the pitchers, or the insects already in the pitchers when surprised by the rain-shower, being drowned, and the products of their decomposing bodies being absorbed by the rootlets. As a matter of fact there is practically no evidence for this point of view. Dr. Treub examined numbers of pitchers of *D. rafflesiana* growing in the Buitenzorg Botanic Gardens, and found that in the wet season most of the pitchers were more or less full of water, but only a very few contained one or two drowned insects. Beccari regards the pitchers as comparable to galls, and as produced by the action of ants, in fact he supposes that if it were not for the ants there would be no pitchers. That the pitchers can only develop after a stimulus applied to leaves by ants is certainly untrue, for the development of normal pitchers has taken place in specimens acclimatized at Kew, to which ants had no access. Treub roundly asserts that the ants, far from being of use to the plant, are positively harmful, for they nibble the rootlets inside the pitchers ; he regards the pitchers as part of the normal development of the plant and adapted purely and simply to the purpose of protecting the rootlets, and not at all as ant-shelters. It seems more likely that the associa-

tion of ants with these plants has played at least a
small part in the development of the pitchers, and
some observations of Mr. H. H. W. Pearson [1] on
Dischidia shelfordi deserve consideration. In this
species the pitchers are double, that is to say, a small
pitcher is found inside each large pitcher. The large
pitchers are kidney-shaped, and are borne on very
short petioles ; the entrance to them is a small round
orifice just under the petiolar attachment, and it lies
at the bottom of a funnel-shaped depression. If a
pitcher be cut open it will be seen that the interior is
filled with numbers of rootlets, which springing from
the petiole or stem grow through the orifice of the
pitcher. The inner pitcher is formed by the inflexed
margin of the outer pitcher, the infolding taking
place in the funnel-shaped depression opposite to the
insertion of the petiole, it is therefore of the nature of
a pouch or pocket, and its walls are thickly beset with
small glandular hairs. In the large outer pitchers, in
addition to the rootlets are found a certain amount of
earth and numbers of ants—*Cremastogaster difformis*.[2]
In the inner pitcher of a species from the Philippines,
Mr. Pearson found a number of small irregularly
shaped masses sweet to the taste, and he came to the
conclusion that they were decomposition products of
cells in the neck of the inner pitcher, brought about
by punctures of ants, and the growth of fungi from
these wounds. Moreover, microscopic examination of
the inner surface of the outer pitcher revealed the
presence of a " dense waft of superficial mycelium,"

---

[1] *Journ. Linn. Soc. Bot.*, XXXV. (1901–4), p. 375.

[2] In another undescribed Bornean *Dischidia* with double pitchers,
a species of *Dolichoderus* (probably *D. bituberculatus*) has been found.

which grew from definite centres or rosettes of an appearance vividly recalling structures found in the well-known fungus-gardens of the South American ants of the genus *Atta*. An examination of the extremely elaborate nature of these double pitchers, the presence of a sweet substance in the inner pitcher, and the peculiar fungoid growth on the inner wall of the outer pitcher, point strongly to the view that the pitchers are adapted for harbouring ants in addition to their original functions of sheltering the rootlets and storage of water. I say "original functions" because it is plain that these pitchers, like those of *D. rafflesiana*, are developed from the shell-like leaves of the pitcherless species of the genus, but their development has been carried even farther than that of the above-named species. It seems highly probable that in both species the plants benefit to a certain extent by their association with ants on account of the soil brought into the pitchers by these insects, for particles of soil are found adhering in a perfecily normal manner to the root-hairs. What is the function of the inner pitchers in *D. shelfordi* ? Mr. Pearson has put forward the ingenious suggestion that they serve as harbours of refuge when the outer pitchers become nearly filled with water after a shower of rain, the mouth of the inner pitcher being so arranged that water cannot enter into it until the outer pitcher is three-quarters full. This theory could easily be put to the test, and I did so by immersing a plant with several pitchers growing from its stem in a bowl of water. As I expected, the ants instantly came swarming out, and by reason of their natural buoyancy came floating to the surface of the water. The risk of ants drowning

in the water contained in the pitchers of *D. rafflesiana*
and *D. shelfordi*, is indeed infinitesimal. As pointed
out in a previous chapter, terrestrial insects take an
unconscionably long time about dying from drowning,
and, owing to the numerous rootlets in the pitchers,
they have an easy means of exit when their quarters
become flooded. I feel convinced that it will eventually be shown that the inner pitchers are designed
for the purpose of producing a food-substance attractive to ants ; the sweet decomposition products already
mentioned may be the pathological results of ant-
punctures, but they may also be normal katabolic
changes, whilst the presence of numerous gland-cells
in the inner pitcher walls points to the conclusion
that these too may secrete a substance palatable to
ants.

In conclusion, it is reasonable to regard the pitchers
of *D. shelfordi* as developed with a double purpose—
to store water and protect rootlets, and to attract and
shelter ants. They thus differ from such simple
structures as the hollow stem of *Macaranga caladifolia*, punctured casually by ants, and from all
accidental ant-shelters ; they differ, too, from the
remarkable tubes of *Myrmecodia* and the swollen
rhizomes of *Polypodium carnosum*, which are developed
to harbour ants at least inconvenience to the plants ;
and they differ, too, from those structures which are
developed purely for attraction of ants, as the thorns
on the Neotropical *Acacia cornigera*. In fact, they
take their place in a long series leading from simple
beginnings to complex endings. To assert, as some
have done, that all " myrmecophilous " plants derive
great benefit from their association with ants, and

that the most varied structures have been expressly
modified for the purpose of affording shelter to
beneficent guests, appears to me as wide of the truth
as to assert that the association of ants with all
"myrmecophilous" plants is purely accidental, sheer
opportunism on the part of the ants, and that none
of the elaborate structures of the plants are more than
part of their normal development. My study of
natural history, if it has taught me nothing else, has
taught me that biological phenomena will not fit into
Procrustean beds of theory, every case must be taken
on its merits, and when the honest student observes
that exceptions to a rule are more numerous than the
examples of the rule he need not be disconcerted, for
he will have learnt that Nature has endless ways of
adapting means to ends and of meeting every kind of
emergency.

Note, p. 190.—*Polypodium carnosum.* I have met with this fern
growing high up on the branches of very tall trees—tunnelled, but
without an ant visible.—C. H.

CHAPTER VIII

MIMICRY

THE subject of this chapter is a theme around which so much controversy has raged that echoes of the clash and clang of argument have penetrated beyond scientific circles. This being so, it is unnecessary for me to do more than give the briefest possible account of what mimicry amongst animals really means.

In 1866 H. W. Bates enunciated his celebrated theory. From a study of the butterflies of the Amazon Valley, he noticed that some comparatively rare species resembled in a very exact manner certain dominant conspicuous species belonging to families totally different from those to which the "imitating" species belonged; these resemblances could not be due to relationship: to what, then, were they due? Bates supposed that the conspicuous "imitated" species possessed nauseous properties which rendered them distasteful to birds and other enemies, and that the "imitating" species, by their deceptive resemblance to the nauseous species, escaped the attacks of enemies, although they might be themselves quite palatable. This was the theory in its original simplicity; elaborations were soon introduced. Fritz Müller, a German naturalist living in

Brazil, in 1870, drew attention to the fact that in a given area there was a sort of family resemblance between all the distasteful conspicuous butterflies, although they belonged to different genera and sub-families. The conspicuous colouring of these species, he said, was a warning signal to prospective enemies of their distasteful properties. Further, he said that if a certain arrangement of colours were common to a congeries of distasteful butterflies, it was obvious that all these species would share in a common advantage. It would be easier for the butterfly foes of a given area to associate nauseous properties with one or a few simple patterns than with scores of patterns. Professor Poulton has neatly expressed the difference between these two kinds of mimicry by likening the palatable mimic of Bates's theory to a fraudulent trader who imitates the advertisement of an honest trader, whilst the distasteful mimic of Müller's theory may be compared to an honest trader who enters into combination with other honest traders to exhibit an identical advertisement of the same class of goods. An assemblage of insects exhibiting a close similarity of colouring is now known as a Müllerian association, or better as a convergent group. Latter-day entomologists, more especially Professor E. B. Poulton and Dr. F. A. Dixey, have elaborated the mimetic theory so that its originators would perhaps not recognize it as the offspring of their brains. There is a danger of the theory becoming overweighted with hypothesis, and there is certainly a demand for further observation of facts by highly skilled and unprejudiced field-naturalists.

It is an unfortunate thing that the vast majority of collectors and field-naturalists are poor philosophers, whilst a great many philosophic zoologists are sorry failures when it comes to observing the living animal in its natural surroundings. The collector is far too prone to kill at sight every animal he captures; he is usually a bird of passage, and has not the time to devote to the patient and difficult observation of an animal's behaviour and habits of life; even if he does observe a few facts here and there, his observations are either too incomplete to be of much value, or he does not see their bearing on current theories, and therefore keeps them hidden from the light of day in his private journal.

Scores of collectors will tell you that they have never seen a bird eat a butterfly; but if you ask these men what insects they have seen eaten by birds, they are completely nonplussed, and are fain to confess that they have rarely, if ever, seen an insectivorous bird feed at all. As a matter of fact, Mr. G. A. K. Marshall—most philosophical and competent of field-naturalists—has collected from a variety of sources abundant evidence to show that all manner of birds do prey on butterflies. It is difficult to see how mimicry, amongst butterflies and moths at any rate, could have been brought about except through the agency of winged enemies: in other words, mimicry is brought about by natural selection, and the mimicry hypothesis may be regarded as a corollary of the Darwinian hypothesis; they must sink or swim together.

The objections to the mimetic theory, when analysed, are not very serious, and it is significant that no rival theory has yet proved capable of accounting satisfactorily for these remarkable resemblances that exist between animals widely separated in classificatory

schemes. There is the naturalist who acknowledges
the resemblances but makes no attempt to account
for them ; that type of naturalist is fortunately becoming
extinct. There is also the naturalist who can detect
flaws in the theory when it is applied to particular
cases a few of which we will examine later on : meanwhile we will only say that this sort of argument is
perfectly valid, only it must be remembered that when
a great majority of observed facts support a theory,
while a few do not, it is more reasonable to suppose
that the few are capable of another interpretation than
that they subvert the theory.

Thus it is no argument against mimicry that birds
have been seen to capture and devour distasteful
species of insects ; not only are some birds—e.g. the
cuckoos—catholic enough in their tastes to devour
every kind of insect, nauseous or otherwise, but
we may be certain that if young and inexperienced
birds and birds with strong palates or with very
hungry appetites did not from time to time devour
butterflies of all sorts, there would be no mimicry at
all : it is the severity of the struggle for existence which
has brought about the present state of mimetic perfection. Some suppose that mimetic resemblances are
due to parallelism in development induced by similarity of environment, but such an argument will not
bear examination ; far more often than not the two
creatures, model and mimic, differ widely in their life-
histories. For example, in Borneo and elsewhere certain Pierine butterflies are closely mimicked by moths
of the sub-family *Chalcosiinæ*, yet the caterpillars are
widely different and feed on different plants. Again,
there occurs in Borneo a wonderful locust which

15

mimics most closely a large Tiger-Beetle, *Tricondyla cyanea*, var. *wallacei*: the mimicry is so exact even in dead and dried specimens that the famous entomologist Professor J. O. Westwood found the first specimen of this Locustid in a collection of Tiger-Beetles, while the French entomologist Duponchel actually labelled another specimen with the name of *Tricondyla rufipes*. And yet what two insects could lead more different lives ? The beetle hatches out from the egg as a small grub, which probably lives in a hole in the ground ; when full growth is attained the grub becomes a pupa, and after a short resting stage emerges as the adult beetle. The locust, on the other hand, hatches from the egg to all intents and purposes a locust, recognizable as such ; it hops about actively in search of its food, and from time to time it casts its skin, each moult marking a distinct increase of size until finally the adult stage is reached. The young and half-grown locusts do not mimic the adult *Tricondyla*, they are too small to produce the effect of their model : it is impossible for them to mimic the early stages of the beetle, but the difficulty is obviated by their mimicry of smaller species of beetles, the very young locust resembling a small *Collyris* (*C. sarawakensis*), the half-grown locust a small species of *Tricondyla* (*T. gibba*). Now can anything more different than the life-histories of these two insects be imagined ? Yet how close is the mimicry. Evidently similarity of conditions has not produced the likeness ; and scores of other cases, though perhaps none quite so remarkable as this, could be quoted.

I have heard it stated by more than one field-naturalist who has collected insects in the tropics that a mimicking butterfly can be, after a short experience, readily distinguished even when on the wing from its model, and that therefore it is only reasonable to suppose that the butterfly's enemies can readily penetrate the thin disguise, and consequently are not deceived by the deceptive resemblance ; in other words, the resemblance, not being sufficiently perfect, is valueless to the insect.

An observation of my own may throw a little fresh light on this question. On Mt. Penrisen in Sarawak, two of the commonest butterflies were *Caduga larissa* and *Tirumala crowleyi*, species belonging to the sub-family *Danainæ*. These butterflies are black with streaks of green on both surfaces of all the wings. Like all the other members of the sub-family, these two species were conspicuous by their abundance and by their slow flaunting flight, and habit of settling in exposed situations, so that they were quite as conspicuous when at rest as when on the wing. The *Danainæ* are regarded as a sub-family of distasteful insects advertising their distasteful properties by the means noted above. Before very long I had secured enough specimens of both these two butterflies to satisfy me, and subsequently when out butterfly hunting I used to ignore them. One day I saw approaching me a butterfly which I took to be *Caduga larissa*, and it was not until the insect had passed me quite closely that I realized from its quicker flight and from a slightly different style of wing-marking that here was no Danaine, but a mimic—*Elymnias lais*. The critical moment, however, was past, and the butterfly was out of reach. I saw it settle in a little thicket of thorny rattan, and cautiously approached, but no sign of it could I see until a rash movement startled the butterfly, and it darted up from under my very nose and was in full flight again. *Elymnias lais* has the under side of the wing mottled with brown and white, and when the insect is at rest with the wings closed it is almost impossible to detect it among its inanimate surroundings. From that day forward I kept a keen look-out for *Elymnias lais,* and in course of time I did manage to secure a fair number of specimens, but more than once I was deceived as to the nature of the insect until it was so close to me that I had not time to get my net ready before it was gone ; in fact the critical moment of capture was not seized simply because I failed to recognize the deception quickly enough. Now I see no reason whatever to suppose that the faculties of a trained entomologist on the sharp look-out for a definite species of butterfly are less keen than those of a bird in search of a meal, the constituents of which may be scores of different species of Lepidoptera. Such a bird if it had learnt by repeated experiment that *Caduga larissa* was bad to eat, would ignore those butterflies when out hunting and, unless particularly sharp-set and keenly on the look-out, would be prone to ignore the mimic too, at any rate at first. But the escape of a few individuals suffices to preserve the race ; no one is so foolish as to suppose that all the individuals of a mimetic species escape destruction, for if this were so there would be no checks on their unbounded increase.

My observations on this butterfly lead to another consideration. Is it possible to tell a Batesian mimic from a Müllerian mimic ? One or two naturalists spend a good deal of time selecting from the cabinet specimens of butterflies which resemble each other more or less closely, and call the asssemblage "a Müllerian association." The process is analogous to that of matching colours in a Berlin-wool shop, and is perhaps less useful. Without direct knowledge of the living insects it must always be hazardous to assert dogmatically that this or that species is a Müllerian mimic. But it appears to me that a useful criterion is afforded by the colouring of the under side of the butterfly. For example, *Elymnias lais* has a double defence : when the upper wings are exposed to view, as in flight, the insect resembles a distasteful Danaine, when the insect is at rest the under surface only of the wings is seen, and it harmonizes perfectly with the inanimate surroundings. Now the safety of a distasteful butterfly lies in its bold advertisement of nauseous properties, whether the butterfly be at rest or in flight, and it is a significant fact that all those butterflies which have been proved by direct experiment to be nauseous to birds and reptiles are conspicuously coloured on *both* wing-surfaces, and freely expose themselves at all times ; such as, e.g., the *Heliconinæ* and *Ithomiinæ* of the New World, and the *Danainæ* and *Acræinæ* of the Old World. If we, for the sake of argument, assume that *Elymnias lais* is a distasteful Müllerian mimic, we may imagine that the following combination of circumstances would often occur ; a bird, searching for prey, would discover and seize some protectively coloured butterfly, and finding it good to eat would, on encountering an *Elymnias lais* at rest, naturally associate palatability with the under-side pattern of this species ; seizing it the bird would then discover that it had made a mistake, but by this time it would be too late, for the butterfly would be dead; in fact, it would forfeit its life for aping the wing-pattern of a palatable species, and its protectively coloured under-side would be simply a source of danger to it. Batesian mimicry is a far less efficient means of safety to a butterfly than distasteful properties associated, as they always are, with conspicuous colouring and such toughness of integuments that they withstand all but the most determined onslaughts. Batesian mimics are comparatively rare and isolated species, whereas distasteful species are extraordinarily abundant not only in species but in individuals.

By those who hold that a cryptic under side is no criterion of palatable properties it will be urged that *Elymnias lais* has two kinds of defence—its distasteful properties causing it to be a Müllerian mimic, and its cryptic under-surface colouring. But it must be remembered that distasteful properties are no protection at all unless sufficiently advertised. Careful observation of the living insects is worth any amount of arm-chair theorizing, however ingenious, and those who are thoroughly familiar with the habits of such groups of nauseous butterflies as the *Danainæ* and *Acræinæ* sometimes find it a little difficult to accept the views of men who perhaps have never seen a tropical butterfly alive.

Feeding experiments with captive mammals, birds, reptiles, and amphibians have only a limited value. In many cases the captive is either sulky from recent capture and will refuse to eat, or is so bored with a long captivity and monotonous diet that it will devour anything offered to it. I have seen captive Macaques, fed for months on bananas and rice, devour with the utmost gusto Danaine butterflies, Lycid beetles, and even Pentatomid bugs endowed with a most nauseating odour. Are we to conclude from this that none of these insects are unpalatable in a general sense? I prefer to believe that the facts prove very little, except that Macaques have strong stomachs and poor palates. I am equally disinclined to attach a very great deal of importance to the fact that a Japanese Salamander has manifested signs of disgust when fed with caterpillars of the European Gooseberry Moth, *Abraxas grossulariata*. The foes with which these caterpillars have to contend certainly do not include the Japanese Salamander. We have really no grounds for saying that because the Salamander finds the caterpillars unpalatable, therefore they are nauseous to European lizards and amphibians. This is as indefensible as Professor Plateau's view, that because he himself found *Abraxas grossulariata* larvæ quite pleasant to the taste, therefore all animals must enjoy them. When, however, a large number of experiments show that these particular larvæ are distasteful to a great many animals—birds, beasts, and reptiles—then certainly we have grounds for supposing that the larva is not good to eat. If the animals experimented on can reasonably be regarded as *natural* enemies of the larvæ the value of the experiments is accentuated. I have already drawn attention to the fact that Trogons feed very largely on *Phasmidæ*, and apparently exclusively on Orthoptera, and there is good reason to suppose that the diet of most animals is more or less restricted. Consequently to offer as food to animals insects which never form any part of their diet cannot lead to very definite conclusions,

This seems to be the proper place in which to describe an experiment which I conducted with a large spider, *Nephila maculata*, because I am conceited enough to believe that this experiment did yield information of importance, since it was carried out as nearly as possible under perfectly natural conditions. On Mt. Matang, one July morning in 1902, as I was setting forth for a little insect-hunting walk, I almost blundered into a large outspread web of *Nephila maculata*, with the huge body of the maker hanging in the centre waiting for prey. I just avoided wreaking a catastrophic disaster on the elegant structure, and, as I recoiled, a little Dammar Bee, *Melipona apicalis*, flew into the web. The behaviour of the spider was interesting to watch. She[1] rushed towards the bee, cut with her falces all the strands in which it was entangled, retaining hold, however, of one strand at the end of one hind-leg. The bee thus hung suspended. The spider then violently agitated its hind-leg, until it succeeded in jerking the bee some distance away from the web. The bee spent a little time in cleaning itself, then spread its wings and flew away. This incident suggested to me that I might introduce different insects into the spider's web and observe the results. My first experiment was with a second specimen of *Melipona apicalis*, which the spider treated as it had treated the first. Then I introduced *Melipona lacteifasciata*, a fulvous species with white wing-tips ; this the spider seized in her jaws, but after mouthing it a little dropped it, and it fell to the ground, so this bee, too, was evidently not to the

[1] The male of this species is a minute creature not one-tenth the size of the female,

spider's liking. *Melipona apicalis* is a black insect with
white wing-tips, and it is not only common but there
are one or two other species of the same genus coloured
exactly like it. These black and white Meliponas are
mimicked very closely by many other insects, e.g. by
two Braconids, by a Chalcid—*Megalocolus notator*, by
two Diptera—*Toxophora* sp. and *Holocephala* sp., by a
Longicorn beetle—*Epania singaporensis*, by a Plume-
Moth, by a Reduviid bug, by a Capsid bug, and a
Homopterous bug. *Trigona lacteifasciata* is not so
common, and I have only found two mimics of it, a
Capsid bug and a fly. It was interesting, then, to see
that the spider instantly recognized the distasteful nature
of the common, widely mimicked species, but had to
seize the rarer species in its mouth before deciding
that it was bad to eat. The Trigonas are stingless,
but they swarm round the head of any one disturbing
their nests, and bite with great vigour; they have,
moreover, a rather disagreeable odour. To return to
our experiments. A Muscid fly flew into the web of
its own accord, and was instantly captured and its
juices sucked. A small brown plant-bug, *Riptortus* sp.
(Fam. *Coreidæ*), which I put into the web, was also
eaten. The little black and yellow Reduviid, *Cosmo-
lestes picticeps*, a very conspicuous and abundant species,
was at once treated like *Trigona apicalis*. The similarly
coloured but much larger species, *Velinus nigrigenu*,
was approached with great caution by the spider. She
just touched the bug with her palpi, and then started
away, probably nervous of the powerful rostrum of
this species; the strands in which the insect was
entangled were cut at a greater distance from it than
usual, so that a large hole was left in the web after

it had been thrown out. Both of these bugs were quite unhurt by their temporary captivity, and made off after freeing themselves from some of the glutinous silk of the web. The next insect tried was a Phytophagous beetle, *Antipha* sp.; this was seized at once but not devoured, merely mouthed and palpated, and the spider finally decided to keep the insect for future investigation, and thereupon proceeded to envelop it in a wrapping of silk until it formed an amorphous bundle, which was suspended from the centre of the web by a single strand. The method by which the beetle was enveloped was curious : it was held by the front pair of legs of the spider, and turned round and round by the help of the mouth-parts, whilst the hind pair of legs were applied alternately to the spinnerets, and led away each time a single strand, which was wrapped round the revolving insect. The action was very rapid, and the spider looked like some machine for winding thread round a spool, the thread being pulled in alternate strands from the spinnerets. The butterfly *Terias hecabe* was at once eaten, and so was *Ypthima pandocus*, but a very conspicuous and common day-flying moth of the genus *Deilemera* (*Hypsidæ*) was instantly thrown out of the web without a moment's hesitation. This is interesting, because *Deilemera* is the only genus of Lepidoptera which *Mantidæ* consistently refuse. It is curious that no mimics of the genus are known. Another *Terias hecabe* and *Ypthima pandocus* were thrown into the web simultaneously, and both were pounced on ; they struggled violently, and so were both enveloped in a silken shroud, which—hanging by a single strand from a posterior tarsus of the spider— was then hoisted up to the centre of the web, and made fast alongside the other bundle. The spider towing her bundle behind her was a comical sight. At this point I left off to make a midday meal, intending to resume operations later on, but a heavy thunderstorm almost entirely destroyed the web, and I was compelled to leave Matang early next morning. All the insects introduced into the web were captured in its immediate vicinity, and it may reasonably be supposed that any of them might have flown into the web of their own accord. From the experiments one gathers that *Nephila maculata* not only has very pronounced likes and dislikes, but also possesses great powers of discriminating between insects without employing her organs of taste. Anything more prompt than her rejection of the yellow and black bugs could not be imagined, and it was a striking demonstration of the efficiency of warning coloration which may be commended to the notice of scoffers.

With such enthusiasm do recent supporters of the mimetic theory pursue their studies that they are prone to regard every butterfly as protected either by (1) nauseous properties duly advertised, (2) mimetic features (Müllerian or Batesian), or (3) cryptic colouring, these latter being considered palatable. They seem inclined to maintain that if a butterfly is not cryptically coloured then it is either a mimic or a warningly coloured nauseous species. And yet there are many facts which do not accord with this Procrustean method. One of the commonest butterflies in Sarawak was the little obscurely coloured *Ypthima pandocus*; on mountains it is more or less displaced by the equally abundant *Y. fasciata*. According to current theories of mimicry these two species are protected

by their obscure cryptic coloration, but cryptic colouring is of no protective value if the insects possessing
it do not hide themselves as much as possible in
suitable situations; and this is exactly what the two
species of *Ypthima* do not do. They expose themselves freely, fluttering with weak and uncertain flight
close to the ground, settling only for a few moments,
and then not in particularly obscure spots. We cannot suppose that these butterflies are distasteful, for they
exhibit none of the characteristics of known distasteful
forms. Many more instances could be brought forward,
e.g. *Melanitis ismene, Precis iphita, P. atlites,* are all
cryptically coloured species, and yet expose themselves quite freely, and are excessively abundant. In
my opinion these species are abundant by virtue of
great fecundity, enabling them to maintain their
numbers in the face of a heavy destruction. This
is a mere suggestion, for in truth we are profoundly
ignorant of the reasons whereby one species may be
abundant and another, perhaps closely allied, extremely
rare. That the balance of forces regulating the abundance or rarity of any species is liable to be upset at
any time is shown by the overwhelming numbers in
which a species may appear from time to time.

One such instance came very forcibly under my
notice. One day at 2 p.m. [the date is not recorded]
there suddenly appeared at Kuching an enormous
swarm of the Nymphaline butterfly *Cirrochroa bajadeta* ?
For the space of fifteen minutes there poured over the
entire town countless numbers of the butterflies. All
were travelling in an east to west direction, and they
flew at a good pace. I am anxious not to exaggerate,
so will not say, like the Irishman, that the butterflies

were "fairly jostling" each other; but the air seemed
to be full of them as far as the eye could see, and
by standing on an open lawn I was able with one
sweep of a net to catch half a dozen. I can never
hope to see such a remarkable sight again. Identi-
cally the same phenomenon occurred at Sadong, a
place thirty to forty miles north-east of Kuching, and
I am sure that the swarm was continuous over this
great tract of country, and probably beyond it. A
friend residing on Mt. Matang, seven miles due west
of Kuching, reported that the butterflies arrived there
at about 4 p.m. Next day, at the same hour, the phenomenon was repeated, though on a much smaller
scale [Note 17, p. 316]. It is exceedingly difficult to
account for the sudden appearance of these vast
hordes. *Cirrochroa bajadeta* is normally a fairly abundant species, though not extremely common, and I could
gather no evidence whatsoever that the species preparatory to the great flight had been more abundant
than usual. We can only suppose that most, if not all,
the factors which normally held in check the increase
of the species had been at some time temporarily suspended, and we can realize faintly what would happen
if there were no such thing as a struggle for life. Even
granting this, it is difficult to account for the synchronous appearance of these hordes, whilst the object
of their migratory flight is equally buried in obscurity.
But it is evident that a vast multiplication of numbers
must affect the future history of a species very considerably, and a species once rare in a given locality
may, by the accession of large numbers, become quite
common, at any rate for a period of time.

Just as it is absurd to suppose that all obscurely

coloured butterflies are preserved by cryptic habits, so is it absurd to suppose that all brightly coloured butterflies are protected by nauseous properties. They can be equally well protected by habits of wariness, rapid dodging flight, and great fertility. The *Pierinæ* are for the most part very conspicuous butterflies, but there are no grounds for supposing that any but a few genera are distasteful; in fact, Mr. Marshall has shown that few sub-families are more preyed on by birds. White or yellow with black tips to the wings is the common type of colouring in this sub-family, and to allege—as has been alleged—that certain species so coloured mimic other similarly coloured species of the same sub-family, is about as sensible as to allege that every blue Lycænid is a mimic of or a model to every other blue Lycænid; in fact, if we will only recognize that the mimetic theory is not capable of universal application, if we will regard warning, cryptic, and mimetic colouring as only three factors amongst many others which help to ensure safety to insects, we shall gain a saner view of insect life, and perhaps thereby pacify our opponents.

I do not see why such scorn should be heaped on cases of imperfect or incipient mimicry. Apart from the fact that when we place side by side in an insect cabinet a mimic and its model, we submit the mimic to a test far more severe than any to which it is called upon to undergo in the field, we must remember that natural selection is operating to-day as in the past, and surely it is reasonable to suppose that if in the past this force has produced well-nigh perfect mimics out of imperfect, then it can do so now. Moreover, it may be argued that many an imperfect

mimic has found protection by other means than
mimicry; it has as it were discarded mimicry in
favour of greater fertility, rapid flight, or even distinct
nauseous properties of its own; its mimicry has become arrested, the stern necessity for it no longer
existing. If the mimetic resemblance be harmless to
the species it will not be eliminated, and the species
may actually develop warning signals of its own.
Such an example seems to be afforded by the Chal-
cosiid moth, *Pompelon subcyanea*. This distasteful
moth mimics the male of the Euplœine *Trepsichrois
mulciber*, a black butterfly with a most brilliant metallic
blue sheen on the fore-wings, but the mimicry is very
imperfect because the moth is so much smaller than
the butterfly and has a different flight, so that no one
could mistake the two. The tip of the moth's
abdomen is bright scarlet, and this is a very conspicuous feature. Now it seems to me that this scarlet
tip is of value to the moth as a signal of still more
distasteful properties than the butterfly possesses; the
moth, not content with advertising its unpalatability by
resembling an unpalatable butterfly, accentuates the
fact by developing an additional warning signal. This
is an extreme example, but the same reasoning applied
to other cases may explain much of the difficulty
which some find in regarding mimicry as efficient
when not quite perfect. That there is much which
cannot be explained by a facile application of the
theories of protective, warning, and mimetic colour and
form is very certain. Two instances may be noted
here. *Nezara viridula* is a little green Pentatomid
bug endowed with a positively nauseous odour; it is
cryptically coloured, for green in Nature is a cryptic

colour; it is excessively abundant, and has a wide distribution. It has the habit of flying into lighted houses at night, and when it enters in numbers the nuisance is considerable. I have seen a dinner-party in confusion and the guests driven from the table by an irruption of this noisome pest. Yet the bug does not advertise its nauseous properties—surely a very singular fact. Again, most of the Coreid bugs are cryptically coloured, and many of the species have flattened leaf-like expansions on legs and thorax, characters which we are accustomed to associate with palatability and strictly cryptic habits. Yet these bugs also have an extremely nauseating odour, and one asks again why do they not advertise this? The odour is often so strong that one can detect the presence of the bug before it is actually seen. Other *Coreidæ* are equally nauseous, and advertise themselves by bright colours, e.g. *Serinetha abdominalis*, which is vermilion, with the membranous parts of the elytra, the legs, and antennæ black; it is furthermore mimicked in the closest way by a moth, *Phauda limbata*, so that in a state of repose it requires a sharp eye to say which is which. Why then should some *Coreidæ* be so conspicuous, others so inconspicuous, when all seem to be equally nauseous? These are puzzling questions, which in the absence of experimental evidence I am not prepared to solve. It may be that the unpalatability is relative; in fact, the cryptic species may actually be palatable to some animals, although to our nostrils all stink equally vilely.

If the opponents of the mimetic theory regard natural selection as quite inefficient to produce the undoubted resemblances that do exist between insects of diverse orders, the mimetists retaliate by regarding every resemblance as a mimetic one. The generalized resemblance between one species of black and white or yellow Pierine and another is solemnly quoted as an instance of mimicry. But a vast number of *Pierinæ* are white or yellow with black tips or black borders to the fore-wings; such a type of colouring is almost as important a characteristic of the sub-family as (e.g.) the structure of the fore-legs or the method of pupation, and to assume that mimicry is the cause of the resemblance is unreasonable. We know that the *Pierinæ* of some islands in the Malay Archipelago are characterized by a certain amount of melanism, the wings being very heavily bordered with black; we know too that numbers of Celebes butterflies have the fore-wings long, narrow, and pointed, and we attribute these characters to similar environmental conditions acting in a similar manner on butterfly protoplasm. Natural selection will not affect the characters if they are harmless, while if they are correlated with characters of immense importance to the species in the struggle for life, natural selection may be said to have produced them. Whole-hearted supporters of natural selection regard variation as indefinite and infinite, and only controlled by natural selection; but I am heretic enough to believe that variation is defined and limited and controlled only partially by natural selection. I regard the lines along which variation in any organism can proceed as limited in number; to use a metaphor, I look on variation as an engine which can proceed only along certain rails; there may be numbers of such rails going in different directions, but the engine cannot get off the rails. I

16

first inclined to this idea after a study and arrangement of the large collection of *Phasmidæ*, or Stick-Insects, in the Oxford University Museum. In South America is found a sub-family of winged Phasmids known as the *Phasminæ*, and in Eastern Asia and the Malay Archipelago occurs the sub-family of winged species, the *Necrosciinæ*. The two sub-families are widely separated geographically and genetically, yet there exist numbers of species of *Phasminæ* which resemble most closely in colouring and form other species belonging to the *Necrosciinæ*. It is obvious that these resemblances are neither due to mimicry nor to genetic relationship, and they would be explained by nine out of ten entomologists as examples of convergent development. But to confess that certain species of a family exhibit convergence is merely to state in other words that their evolution has proceeded along very similar lines. . It is exceedingly common among the winged *Phasmidæ* for the insect when at rest to appear to be entirely green, and only in flight to reveal the greater part of the hind-wings as pink, the green colour being confined to a narrow strip along the front. This arrangement of colours crops up again and again in different genera belonging to quite different sub-families, living in different parts of the world. I regard this character as an expression of one of the lines of variation along which the *Phasmidæ* have moved; we cannot suppose that any other combination of colours, say yellow and blue, would have brought down destruction, would have been harmful to the species, and yet it is green and pink, not yellow and blue, which form the common widely distributed combination of colours; and in my opinion it is so because there is something inherent in Phasmid protoplasm which has caused variation to proceed along the green and pink "rails," and prevents it from going along blue and yellow "rails." So too with the black and white or yellow *Pierinæ*—that type of coloration is inherent in Pierine protoplasm.

A student of mimicry cannot fail to be struck with the fact that mimetic resemblances are due to a simulation of the model's characters and not to a direct imitation of them. A fly mimicking a wasp does not develop a second pair of wings to imitate the wasp's wings, but the wings of the fly may be so formed and so veined or grooved that they appear like the four wings of the wasp. Let us note one or two more instances of this from Borneo. A beetle of the distasteful family *Endomychidæ* and belonging to the genus *Spathomeles* has a strong stout spine on each wing-case, and this character of spiny wing-cases or elytra is common to all the *Amphisterni*. This particular *Spathomeles* is closely mimicked by a Longicorn beetle *Zelota spathomelina* ; the mimic is coloured like its model, and from each elytron springs what appears to be a spine, but on close examination is seen to be nothing but a finely pointed tuft of hairs. In other words, the spine of the model is simulated by the hair-tuft of the mimic. If natural selection is all-powerful, if it can guide variations into any and every direction, why has it not called into being a spine on the elytron of the Longicorn ? Spinosity of the elytra is unknown amongst Longicorns, pubescence is common, and natural selection must use the material to hand and make the best of that. To take another instance : there occur in Borneo numbers of parasitic Hymenoptera of the family *Braconidæ*. Some of these, mostly of the genus *Myosoma*, are black with reddish head and thorax, and they are mimicked by Longicorns of the genus *Oberea*. The *Braconidæ* fly about very freely, they are wasp-waisted like so many Hymenoptera, and when they settle on a leaf they have the habit of walking about waving the antennæ up and down in a very characteristic manner; the black wings are folded down over the back so that seen from above the wasp-waist is not visible. Now three species of *Oberea* resemble the Braconids in a very remarkable way; the colouring is the same, and a wasp-waisted effect is produced by a patch of silvery white pubescence on each side of the first and second abdominal segments; the part of the body covered with this pubescence tends to disappear from sight altogether, and the beetle looks as if the rest of the abdomen was slung on to the thorax by a mere pedicel as is really the case in the *Braconidæ*. It may be added that all the Obereas are active fliers, all have the habit of agitating the antennæ when walking about, and some of the species are so slender, and have the wing-cases so narrowed, that they look even more like Hymenoptera than the species with false wasp-waists.

This kind of colouring whereby certain parts of the body, or even the whole body, may be made to disappear from sight is very common in the animal kingdom, but it actually occurs that an organ can be so constructed that part of it is practically invisible even when exposed. The little Longicorns of the genus *Xyaste* mimic beetles of the family *Lycidæ*; now the *Lycidæ* have short thick, flattened antennæ, but the

Longicorns of the sub-family to which *Xyaste* belongs
have the antennæ long and slender. The effect of a
short flattened antenna is produced in a very interesting way : the first few basal joints are clothed
thickly with long black hairs closely set together,
whilst all the rest of the antenna is drawn out into a
fine slender thread which is hardly visible ; in fact at
a short distance it is quite invisible, and the antennæ
appear to be exactly like those of the model.

Examples of caterpillars resembling snakes have
been described more than once, but most of these
have resembled some weird monster rather than any
given species of snake. But in Sarawak I met with a
caterpillar which really did deceive me for the
moment : it is the caterpillar of a Hawk-Moth, *Chœro-
campa mydon*; the greater part of the body was hidden
behind a *Caladium* leaf on which the caterpillar was
feeding. The general colour was dark olive-brown,
becoming paler anteriorly ; at the junction of the third
and fourth segments on each side was an ocellus very
nearly the exact size of the eye of such a snake as
Dendrophis pictus ; the lower border of this ocellus was
margined with bright gold (the colour of the iris in
many snakes), giving an upward glance to the " eye."
The black of the ocellus was so intense and glossy
that an idea of depth was given, and it was difficult
to believe that one was not looking through a real
cornea into a real pupil. Running through the ocellus
on each side was a broad black stripe, just as in
D. pictus, while a wrinkled fold on each side of the
lower half of segments 2–4 gave an admirable impression of the division between the upper and lower
jaws of a snake. Not the least remarkable of these

simulatory devices was the flatness of the area bounded by the two "eye-stripes" on the dorsal surface of segments 3, 4. This area, together with segments 1, 2 was pink, reticulated with fine brown lines, giving an impression of the scutes on a snake's head; these were particularly well marked on the 1st and 2nd segments, looking extremely like the division between the internasal and prefrontal shields. When the larva was moving about with the anterior segments well expanded, the snake-like appearance was not so marked, but directly it was touched the anterior segments of the body were drawn together and turned towards the aggressor, and then the resemblance was striking.

Another remarkable mimetic caterpillar is a little reddish-brown larva of a Noctuid moth which Mr. H. N. Ridley found at Singapore on leaves much frequented by the savage Keringa Ant, *Œcophylla smaragdina*. Subsequently I was fortunate enough to see one of these caterpillars alive. Nearly all the segments of the body are furnished with fragile tentacle-like processes. The anal prolegs are large, and can be completely divaricated; just above each is a prominent black spot. When the larva is irritated, the posterior part of the body is immediately reared up, the anal prolegs are thrown widely apart, and the more posterior tentacles are violently agitated. When the larva is seen end-on it looks very like an ant, the anal legs mimicking the open jaws of the ant, the eye-spots like ant's eyes, the tentacles like the legs, while the antennæ are represented by the last pair of tentacles which are elbowed like these organs in an ant. It is very difficult to convey by a description, or

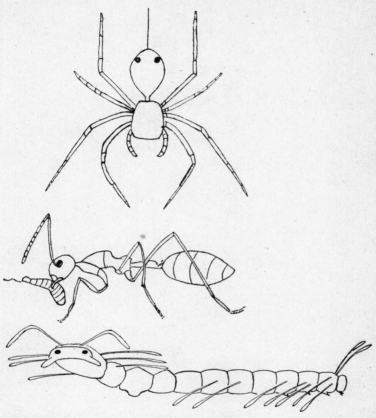

Spider, *Amyciæa lineatipes*; Keringa Ant, *Œcophylla smaragdina*; and Caterpillar. The posterior ends of spider and caterpillar bear eye-like sp ts,
and superficially resemble the head of the ant. The likeness is strengthened
by the movements of the insects, which live near the ant. The latter is
shown using one of its larvæ as a kind of sewing-machine to spin together
the leaves of its nest. (From the author's drawings of the mimics, probably from Singapore, of the ant, after Dr. D. Sharp, *Insects* Pt. II., 1899,
p. 147.)

Plate XVI.

To face p. 230.

even by a drawing, the very startling resemblance of this caterpillar to an ant, yet the resemblance will not really bear a close examination, for the caterpillar is much longer than the ant, and moreover the anterior part of the body plays no part in the likeness. It is more of the nature of an impressionist sketch, and like many impressionist sketches is startling in its likeness to the model, though not bearing close scrutiny. A little spider, *Amyciæa lineatipes*[1] also mimics the Keringa Ant: the body-form and colour correspond pretty closely, but curiously enough the head part of the ant is mimicked by the abdomen of the spider, which near its apex bears two black spots like the eyes of the ant. The spider preys on the ant, and I have taken one with an ant in its jaws. I do not, however, regard this as a case of aggressive mimicry; it is more likely that the spider escapes the attacks of its enemies by resembling the ants, and has acquired the habit of preying on them by always living in association with them.

Lepidoptera have always been studied so much more closely than any other order of insects, and they exhibit so very plainly the phenomena of mimicry on their large and brightly coloured wings,

[1] This spider always lives in the ant's nest or very close to it. It makes no web, but spins a little silk on the leaf on which it rests. As its abdomen with the last pair of legs resembles the head of the Keringa it moves in a backward manner, practically running tail first. When it seizes an ant it lowers itself from a leaf by a thread to devour it, practically out of sight and certainly out of the reach of the others. Living with the ants it is practically defended from all enemies, for no enemy would plunge into a Keringa's nest after it. I found the only way of detecting it among the ants was to present my finger; the ants would rush to attack it, the spider retreated.— H. N. R.

that more has been written about mimicry among
these attractive insects than among other orders. And
yet I feel sure that a close study of any other group
will convince the observer that mimicry is very wide-
spread throughout the insect class, and is everywhere
of as great interest as in Lepidoptera. Mimicry
amongst Oriental butterflies has indeed become almost
a hackneyed subject, and I will therefore leave them
alone. I will here give a short sketch of mimicry in
one class of beetles, the Longicorns, which I studied
closely whilst in Borneo.

The mimetic Longicorns of Borneo may be divided
into three groups : (i) those that mimic Hymenoptera ; (ii) those that mimic other beetles ; (iii) those
that mimic other and presumably distasteful species
of Longicorns. It may be mentioned here that the
Longicornia are divided into three families, the
Lamiidæ, the *Cerambycidæ*, and the *Prionidæ* ; the
latter contains no mimetic species in Borneo, and so
for our purpose may be ignored ; the other two
families are divided into several sub-families, most of
which include mimetic species.

In the first group we find many of the *Phytæciinæ*
a sub-family of *Lamiidæ*. These include the Obereas,
to which attention has already been drawn, and two
allied genera, all of which mimic *Braconidæ*. One
member of the huge genus *Glenea* resembles a little
blue sawfly. Turning to the *Cerambycidæ* we find in
the sub-family *Callichrominæ* three large species of
Nothopeus mimicking the formidable Fossorial Wasps of
the genera *Salius* and *Mygnimia*. The latter is known
to provision its nests with the huge poisonous
Tarantula Spiders, which it seeks out in their lairs,

paralysing them with its powerful sting, so it is
obvious that few, if any, insect enemies would care to
tackle an insect of such powers. The Longicorn
mimics of these Fossors have the elytra considerably
reduced, so that the large wings are easily seen even
when the beetles are not flying; in their rather
buzzing and noisy flight, and habit of curving the
abdomen down when seized, they copy the wasps
very closely, and I have seen my Dayak collectors
take the greatest precautions when transferring one of
these species of *Nothopeus* from the net to the killing-
bottle ; nothing that I could say would persuade them
that the beetles did not sting.[1] In the *Necydalinæ*
are three species mimicking Hymenoptera, viz. *Psebena
brevipennis*, resembling a Braconid of the genus
Myosoma, *Epania singaporensis*, which as already
noticed resembles a Dammar Bee ; and *E. sarawakensis*,
which is like an ant. Ants are also mimicked by two
tiny species of the sub-family *Tillomorphinæ*.

We now come to those Longicorns which mimic
other families of beetles. A very large number of
beetles which spend much of their life on the trunks
of trees are mottled in shades of grey and brown, so
that they harmonize closely with their background :
such are many of the *Anthribidæ* and *Curculionidæ*,
and a great number of Longicorns are similarly
coloured. Though it cannot be said that the Longicorns are exactly like the other beetles, they resemble
each other simply because all are coloured to look
like lichen-covered bark. This is not true mimicry,
but is known as syncryptic colouring.

[1] Dr. Longstaff records a similar experience with a Longicorn
beetle near Sydney, N.S.W., *Butterfly-hunting*, p. 485, Pl. VI. figs. 8, 9.

Other Bornean Longicorns mimic allies of the weevils—the *Brenthidæ*, curious long-snouted, slender beetles, generally cryptically coloured. Here again the mimicry is brought about by simulation, not by imitation. The Longicorns have the greater part of the antennæ clothed thickly with dense-set hairs, and they are carried closely apposed and sticking straight out in front of the head, the terminal joints diverging. They thus offer a sufficiently close resemblance to the rostrum of the *Brenthidæ* to be very deceiving. Such an example is quite enough to confute the argument that mimetic resemblances are due to similarity of conditions. Why should similar conditions produce a rostrum in one beetle and furry antennæ simulating a rostrum in another? One other fact may be noted : some of the *Brenthidæ*, which belong to the genus *Diurus*, are streaked or speckled with pale ochreous, and if one of them be carefully examined with a lens it will be seen that the pale colour is due to little ochreous scales, rather like miniature cartridge wads, set in deep punctures which are seriately arranged. The mimicking Longicorns, *Ægoprepis insignis* and *Ectatosia morei*, are also speckled with pale ochreous, but in these beetles the speckling is produced by small tufts of recumbent hairs on the elytra and thorax. So is illustrated once again the fact that a similar appearance may be produced by quite different means.

Six Longicorns belonging to three sub-families of the *Lamiidæ*, viz. *Mesosinæ*, *Hippopsinæ*, and *Agniinæ*, mimic the *Brenthidæ*. Two of these, *Alibora* sp., and *Elelea concinna*, mimic respectively *Baryrrhynchus dehiscens* and *Arrhenodes* sp., which are rich chestnut Brenthids with

yellow streaks. When Dr. Wallace was collecting in
Borneo in 1854–6 he noted the resemblance between
Elelea concinna and a Brenthid, and remarked of the
mimic that it carried its antennæ "straight and close
together, appearing like a *Brenthus*" [Note 18, p. 316].
When the insects are pinned out in the cabinet it is a
little difficult to convince sceptics of the close resemblance
between these mimics and models, for the antennæ of
the Longicorns in drying assume slightly unnatural
positions, so it is comforting to have one's observations on the living insects confirmed by so acute a
naturalist as Dr. A. R. Wallace.

Another of the Mesosines, *Zelota spathomelina*, has
already been noted as an Endomychid mimic. The
very aberrant *Trachystola granulata*, of the sub-family
Dorcadioninæ, is a good mimic of the powerful and
rather repulsive-looking black weevil, *Sipalus granulatus*. A very similar instance of mimicry has been
recorded from South Africa by my friend Mr. Guy
Marshall, but I confess that I am rather at a loss to
explain why the weevil should be mimicked by the
Longicorn ; the great hardness of the chitinous skeleton
may be the explanation, and certainly the weevil looks
to the human eye a highly indigestible morsel. Many
species of the large Lamiid sub-families *Saperdinæ* and
Astatheinæ resemble most closely Phytophagous beetles
of the family *Galerucidæ*. These latter are all brilliantly or conspicuously coloured, are excessively
abundant in species as well as in individuals, and
there is some evidence to show that they are unpalatable insects. It is not unlikely that their mimics
are also unpalatable and that the mimicry is Müllerian
rather than Batesian, but more information is required

before we can dogmatize. I confess to eating, in a moment of scientific enthusiasm, a few *Astatheinæ*, and I found that they had an acid taste reminding me forcibly of unripe gooseberries; but this experiment does not help us forward very much. I was most interested in comparing collections of Galerucids and Longicorns of the two sub-families noted above; if I picked out at random a Galerucid of striking coloration I could almost invariably match it with a similarly coloured Longicorn. How striking these colour-patterns may be is shown by the following little table, and it must be noted that both Galerucids and Longicorns exhibited these colours :—

1. Bright blue with white antennæ.
2. Yellow with blue band across basal half of elytra.
3. Dark shining blue, with apical half of elytra yellow or red.
4. Elytra dark shining blue, head and prothorax yellow or red.
5. Fulvous yellow or brown.

The parallelism may extend to quite minor details; e.g. the Galerucids *Antipha nigra* and *A. abdominalis* are coloured according to type 3, but the former has the abdomen beneath black, the latter yellow. Exactly the same difference distinguishes the two mimics *Astathes posticalis* and *A. flaviventris*.

One of the Saperdinids, *Entelopes glauca*, is red with black spots, and so looks like a common black-spotted Ladybird. Attention has already been drawn to the species of *Xyaste* which mimic *Lycidæ*. In the sub-family *Phytæciinæ* we find a little chalky-white beetle

banded with shining blue, *Daphisia pulchella*, which
bears a close resemblance to two species of *Callimerus*
belonging to the family of beetles known as *Cleridæ*.
This example is of interest because the *Cleridæ* themselves are essentially a mimetic family ; some of them,
for instance, mimic *Mutillidæ*, little Hymenoptera the
females of which are wingless ; others resemble *Coccinellidæ*, others *Lycidæ*. It has been suggested that
these mimetic *Cleridæ* are protected insects, and therefore that their mimicry is Müllerian rather than
Batesian.   It is often assumed that if one or two
members of a family or sub-family are distasteful therefore all are distasteful ; in fact, palatability or the reverse are regarded as deep-seated characteristics of the
group. I see no reason to believe that this is true in
every case ; it is no doubt true that amongst butterflies all Danaines, all the Ithomiines, all Acræines are
unpalatable, but I would hesitate to apply the same
canon to the *Cleridæ*.   Many Clerids are cryptically
coloured, and therefore presumably non-protected
species ; but though the species of *Callimerus*
mimicked by *Daphisia* are probably nauseous, I see
no reason to assume that the mimetic species of the
family are nauseous too ; they may well be palatable
Batesian mimics.   Turning now to the *Cerambycidæ*,
we find mimetic species amongst four sub-families,
Ephies dilaticornis (*Lepturinæ*), four species of *Erythrus*
and a *Pyrestes* (*Pyrestinæ*) mimic *Lycidæ*, while a
species of *Erythrus* mimics a green and red " soldier "
beetle. The Lycid mimics were found in great abundance on Mt. Matang, and though they are coloured
with the red-and-black livery of the *Lycidæ*, they
present quite a distinctive appearance of their own,

and I feel almost convinced that they belong to that great congeries of heterogeneous species which have nothing in common save their unpalatability and their Lycoid colouring. I will return to this later. *Collyrodes lacordairei* and *Sclethrus amœnus* of the sub-families *Sestyrinœ* and *Clytinœ* respectively mimic Tiger-Beetles.

We now come to our last section, the Longicorns mimicking other Longicorns. Just as amongst butterflies so amongst this group of beetles do we find that certain genera are protected and serve as models to many other genera. Amongst Longicorns the protected families are two only, both of the *Cerambycidœ*, viz. the *Callichrominœ* and the *Clytinœ*. The species of the former which serve as models all belong to one genus, *Chloridolum*; they are all bright metallic green beetles, occurring in great abundance on felled timber; they emit a strong, but to human nostrils by no means an unpleasant, odour proceeding from glands in the thorax, which open to the exterior by two pores. As the table on page 246 shows, they are mimicked by members of two Lamiid sub-families, the *Saperdinœ* and *Phytœciinœ*, and of three Cerambycid sub-families, the *Œmiinœ*, *Disteniinœ*, and *Lepturinœ*. The *Clytinœ* include the British *Clytus arietis*, a species which, as is well known, is marked like a wasp and when seized behaves as if it were about to sting. We cannot say for certain if this is a case of Müllerian or Batesian mimicry, but I am almost certain that the Oriental *Clytinœ* are for the most part protected. *Chlorophorus* (*Clytanthus*) *annularis*, a yellow beetle banded with black, swarmed in countless numbers on Mt. Penrisen, while round Kuching some species of

Demonax, grey, black-banded beetles, were amongst the commonest of all Longicorns. Their abundance, combined with the fact that they are widely mimicked, forces us to the conclusion that these two genera, at any rate, are protected, but we shall not be able to state with certainty whether all the genera of the sub-family are protected until we have larger collections to study and more observations on record. These protected *Clytinæ* exhibit three types of coloration : (1) yellow with black bands or stripes ; (2) grey with black bands ; (3) as (2), but with red thorax. The *Clytinæ* of type (1) are mimicked by a Lamiine, *Cylindrepomus comis*, by a Phytæciine, *Daphisia* sp., and by a Lepturine, *Leptura* sp. A species of *Leptura* also mimics a *Demonax* coloured according to type (3). All the other mimics, including six species belonging to four sub-families, resemble species of *Demonax* and *Xylotrechus*, coloured according to type (2). The tables appended give in graphic form the facts detailed above ; it must be remembered that they have no pretensions to being exhaustive, and further collecting over a wider area would undoubtedly bring to light numbers of new examples of mimicry. It is earnestly to be desired that some naturalists would pay close attention to this question of mimicry amongst Longicorns in other tropical regions of the world ; it is quite certain that very interesting results would accrue from such a study, and the very wide distribution of the phenomenon of mimicry throughout the insect kingdom would be more firmly established.

I will close this chapter with a few remarks on the Lycoid type of coloration. Müllerian mimicry is displayed in its most favourable aspect by large groups of insects belonging to the most diverse families and orders; the members of such a group bear, as it were, the trade-mark of unpalatability—usually a particular type of coloration. The resemblances between the different members of such a group need not be particularly close; it suffices if they show to their enemies the brand which those enemies have learnt to associate with nauseous properties. Such a group is known as a Müllerian group, but if we include in it Batesian mimics, it is known as a convergent group; convergent because the members of it are regarded as *converging* on a central dominant species, or set of allied species, whose unpalatability has been more or less clearly demonstrated. The *Lycidæ* form the centre of a large convergent group; they are very abundant, their integuments are extremely tough though flexible, and they have been proved by experiment to be unpalatable. All the species exhibit a great similarity of colouring—the anterior part of the body, as seen from above, is red or orange, the posterior part is black; the red colouring may be very extensive, covering nearly all the body, or it may be restricted to a very small anterior part. But in casting one's eye over a collection of *Lycidæ* from any part of the world the arrangement of colours is always as here described. It is obvious that such a uniform and widely distributed colour-pattern must be very familiar to all insectivorous animals, and when other insects, which are not *Lycidæ*, display a similar type of colouring, it requires no great stretch of the imagination to suppose that they enjoy an immunity secured to them by their "trade-mark." Wherever *Lycidæ* occur there are found other insects coloured similarly; they are found alike in Africa, Australia, and South America, and they are so numerous that a collection of insects exhibiting Lycoid colouring, if brought together from all parts of the world, would occupy many cabinets. When in such a group the mimicry between any single member and one of the central dominant species is very close, I am inclined to suppose that the mimicry is Batesian rather than Müllerian ; a very distasteful insect can gain much by acquiring a generalized resemblance to the central dominant species, but it probably has many other independent advantages, and may even exhibit a subsidiary warning coloration of its own. But the palatable Batesian mimic has no advantages outside its mimicry, and therefore the resemblance between it and its model, to be effective, must be close and detailed.

The *Lycidæ* of Borneo are mimicked by the following insects (species in italics Batesian) :—

COLEOPTERA :
  Longicornia
    Lamiidæ
      Saperdinæ
          3 species of *Xyaste*
    Cerambycidæ
      Euryphaginæ
          Eurycephalus lundi
      Lepturinæ
          Ephies dilaticornis
      Pyrestinæ
          2 species of Pyrestes
          4   „   of Erythrus
    Eucnemidæ   1 species *Gen. ?*
    Rhipidoceridæ 1   „   of *Ennomates*
    Elateridæ   2   „   of *Agonischius*
    Cleridæ   1   „   of *Tenerus*
    Hispidæ   2   „   of Gonophora

17

HEMIPTERA :
    Coreidæ   2 species Ectatops rubiaceus
    Reduviidæ   1   „   Serinetha abdominalis

LEPIDOPTERA :
    Zygænidæ   1 species Phauda limbata [1]

Several insects, red, orange, or yellow in colour,
with black spots, exhibit another type of coloration
known as the Coccinelliform pattern, since the Ladybirds, or *Coccinellidæ*, constitute the central dominant
models copied by other insects. The Vespiform pattern, dark with bright yellow bands, is another common type of insect coloration, and attention has already
been drawn to the black, white-tipped colouring of the
group converging on *Melipona*. But enough has been
said to show that those who seek to demolish the
theory of mimicry as due to natural selection have a
very difficult task before them.

[1] This species is underlined in Mr. Shelford's manuscript, but,
I think, accidentally ; for the *Zygænidæ* have all the characteristics
of a distasteful group. Furthermore, Mr. Shelford has indicated
his belief that the species is a Müllerian mimic in *P.Z.S.*, 1902, II.,
p. 369. This memoir, pp. 230–84, and the accompanying coloured
Plates, XIX–XXIII, should be consulted in connection with the
present chapter.—E. B. P.

TABLE I.

LONGICORNS MIMICKING HYMENOPTERA.

Mimics.	Models.
Fam. *Lamiidæ*	
Sub-fam. *Phytœcinæ*	
1. *Scytasis nitida*	
2. *Oberea brevicollis*	Red and black *Braconidæ* of the genus *Myosoma*
3. " n. sp.	
4. " *strigosa*, var.	
5. " *rubetra*	
6. " sp. near *rubetra*	
7. " *insoluta*	
8. " *consentanea*	Reddish-ochreous *Braconidæ* of the genus *Iphiaulax*
9. " ? *consentanea* ♂	
10. " n. sp.	
11. *Nupserha*, n. sp.	
12. *Glenea iresine*	*Hylotoma pruinosa*
Sub-fam. *Cerambycidæ*	
Sub-fam. *Callichrominæ*	
13. *Nothopeus intermedius* ...	*Salius aurosericeus*
14. " *fasciatipennis* ...	*Mygnimia aviculus*
15. " sp. near *hemipterus*	" *anthracinus*
Sub-fam. *Necydalinæ*	
16. *Psebena brevipennis* ...	*Myosoma* sp.
17. *Epania singaporensis* ...	*Melipona vidua*
18. " *sarawakensis* ...	Ants
Sub-fam. *Tillomorphinæ*	
19. *Halme cleriformis* ...	"
20. *Clytellus westwoodi* ...	"

TABLE II.

LONGICORNS MIMICKING OTHER COLEOPTERA.

Mimics.		Models.
Fam. Lamiidæ		
Sub-fam. Mesosina	1. Elelea concinna ...	Arthenodes sp. Fam. Brenthidæ
	2. Zelota spathomelina...	Spathomeles near turritus. Fam. Endomychidæ
Sub-fam. Dorcadioninæ	3. Trachystola granulata	Sipalus granulatus. Fam. Curculionidæ
Sub-fam. Hippopsina	4. Atibora sp. ...	Baryrrhynchus dehiscens
	5. Ægobrepis insignis...	Diurus sylvanus
	6. Ectatosia moorei	„ shelfordi
	7. Dymascus porosus ...	„ forcipatus } Fam. Brenthidæ
Sub-fam. Agniinæ	8. Stegenus dactylon ...	„ sylvanus
Sub-fam. Saperdinæ	9. Entelopes glauca ...	Coccinellid, e.g. Caria dilatata. Fam. Coccinellidæ
	10. „ n. sp.	Metriodea apicalis var.
	11. „ ioptera	Caritheca sp. near monhoti
	12. „ amœna	Aulacophora boisduvalii } Fam. Galerucidæ
	13. Serixia aurulenta	Ænidia sp.
	14. „ prolata	
	15. Xyaste invrida	Melambyrus acutangulus
	16. Xyaste torrida	Ditomces sp. } Fam. Lycidæ
	17. Xyaste fumosa	Same model as 15

Fam.	Sub-fam.	Species	Mimicked form	Mimic family
Fam. Lamiidæ	Sub-fam. Astatheina	18. Astathes unicolor	Antipha sp.	Fam. Galerucidæ
		19. " posticalis	" nigra var.	
		20. " flaviventris	" abdominalis	
		21. " splendida	Caritheca mouhoti	
		22. " caloptera	Haplosonyx albicornis	
		23. Tropimetopa simulata	Metrioidea apicalis	
		24. Ochrocesis evanida	Hoplasoma unicolor var.	
		25. Chreonoma n. sp.	Ænidia sp.	
		26. " tabida	Aulacophora luteicornis	
	Sub-fam. Phytoeciina	27. Daphisia pulchella	Callimerus bellus	Fam. Cleridæ
			" catenatus	
	Sub-fam. Lepturina	28. Ephies dilaticornis	Metriorrhynchus kirschi	Fam. Lycidæ
	Sub-fam. Pyrestina	29. Erythrus apiculatus var. rotundicollis	Lycostomus gestroi	
		30. " sternalis		
		31. " biapicatus	Metriorrhynchus kirschi	
		32. Pyrestes eximius	" dispar	
		33.		
		34. Erythrus viridipennis	Prionocerus caeruleipennis	Fam. Melyridæ
	Sub-fam. Sestyrina	35. Collyrodes lacordairei	Collyris sp.	Fam. Cicindelidæ
	Sub-fam. Clytina	36. Sclethrus amœnus	Tricondyla gibba var. cyanipes	

Fam. Cerambycidæ

TABLE III.

LONGICORNS MIMICKING LONGICORNS.

	Mimics.	Models.	
Fam. Lamiidæ			
Sub-fam. Acanthocininæ	1. Driopea clytina ...	Clytanthus sp.	Sub-fam. Clytinæ
Sub-fam. Lamiinæ	2. Cylindrepomus peregrinus	Xylotrechus pedestris	
	3. ,, sp. near comis	Chlorophorus (Clytanthus) annularis	
Sub-fam. Saperdinæ	4. Gen.? sp.? ...	Chloridolum thomsoni	Sub-fam. Callichrominæ
Sub-fam. Phytœcinæ	5. Daphisia sp. ...	Chlorophorus annularis	
	6. ,, ,, ...	Demonax viverra	
	7. Ossonis clytonina ...	Clytanthus sumatrensis	Sub-fam. Clytinæ
	8. Cryllis clytoides ...	,, ,,	
	9. Chlorisanis viridis ...	Chloridolum thomsoni	
Fam. Cerambycidæ			
Sub-fam. Œmiinæ	10. Xystrocera alcyonea	,, ,,	
Sub-fam. Disteniinæ	11. Psalanta chalybeata ...	,, sp.	Sub-fam. Callichrominæ
Sub-fam. Lepturinæ	12. Leptura sp.	,, cinnyris	
	13. ,, sp. near histrionica	Xylotrechus decoratus	
	14. ,, ,, ,, ...	Demonax mustela	Sub-fam. Clytinæ
Sub-fam. Glaucytinæ	15. Polyphida clytoides ...	,, viverra	Sub-fam. Clytinæ

CHAPTER IX

AN EXPEDITION TO PENRISEN

As curator of the Sarawak Museum it was my welcome duty at times to leave the civilization of the capital (Kuching) and visit other parts of the State for the purpose of acquiring new specimens for the Museum collections. I cannot truthfully say that I ever met with any stirring adventures during these collecting expeditions, and the following chapters describing them are written merely in the hope that they may convey some idea to stay-at-home nature-lovers of the delights and difficulties that await a naturalist in the tropics.

Since the Museum collections were very poor in specimens of the mountain fauna of Borneo I decided to spend a month in visiting and collecting on Penrisen, a mountain some 4,000 feet in height standing at the head-waters of the Sarawak River, just on the boundary between Sarawak and Dutch Borneo. My friend Mr. E. A. W. Cox, then district magistrate of Upper Sarawak, decided to accompany me, and since he was both keenly interested in natural history and a good *shikari* his partnership in the enterprise was most welcome.

We left Kuching on half-flood one morning [1] in three boats of the usual up-river type, long low canoes hewn out of tree-trunks with the side-planking attached by rattan lashings, and covering in the craft a low roof of palm-leaf thatch. Besides ourselves and a Malay crew, our party consisted of four Dayak hunters, a Malay, and two Chinese servants. The boats were loaded down to the gunwale with bags of rice containing a month's supply for all of us, provisions of other sorts for Cox and myself, collecting gear, clothes, and other necessaries. Our crews were not large enough, and we made such slow progress that we did not get very far before the tide turned, and we spent some weary hours at a small riverside bungalow until the middle of the night, when we started on again. By dawn we had reached the point of junction of the left-hand and right-hand branches of the Sarawak River; a halt was called for breakfast on a gravel-bed, and for a bath in the sparkling waters of the river. Then on again, and for the rest of that day our undermanned and heavily laden boats struggled up the rapids and shallows of the narrowing river, so that it was six o'clock before we reached the Government bungalow at Segu and received a warm welcome from the gentleman in charge of the Government coffee-plantations at that place.

Next day, after much parleying, we exchanged two of our boats for four lighter craft more suitable for travel in shallow and rapid waters, and engaged some Land-Dayaks to take the place of some of our Malays who now wished to return to Kuching. This day was a

[1] Mr. H. N. Ridley has a note that the date was May 5, 1899. Author's Preface, pp. xxv–xxvii, should be read here.

repetition of the preceding, except that we made better progress; the river was so rapid that paddling the boats was out of the question, and they were poled along at a fair pace against the strong stream. The air grew cooler for every mile that we advanced, and the scenery more beautiful; we had left behind us the mud-flats of the lowlands with their monotonous vegetation of Nipa-palm, and the succeeding zone of scrub and secondary jungle, and were now fairly in the upper waters of the river. Great cliffs of lime-stone, sculptured and grooved by weathering agents, and clothed in a bewildering variety of vegetation, towered above us on either hand. Every reach of the river that we entered on appeared more lovely than the last, and contained some fresh wonder on which the eye could feast. At one spot the river-gorge nar-rowed considerably, and the rush of the water between the huge boulders that here bestrewed the river-bed was so great that we were compelled to disembark, partially unload the boats, and haul them by their rattan painters through the torrents. Dusk found us still some miles from the village that we had hoped to reach that night, but as we had now left behind us the chief river-gorges and had emerged into a region where the stream flowed more placidly between low and gravelly banks we had no difficulty in selecting a spot suitable for a bivouac. There was a brilliant moon, and for long after we had eaten our supper we sat listening to the rush of the stream and to the shrilling of countless insects that made the tropical night clamorous.

On the opposite bank was a small tree growing close by the water's edge, which was covered with thousands of Fire-Flies, small beetles of the family *Lam-pyridæ*; and I observed that the light emitted by these little creatures pulsated in a regular synchronous rhythm, so that at one moment the tree would be one blaze of light, whilst at another the light would be dim and uncertain.[1] This concerted action of thousands of insects is very remarkable and not easy of explanation. Another instance of it was mentioned by Cox; certain ants that are found very frequently proceeding in columns along the floor of the jungle, when alarmed, knock their heads against the leaves or dead sticks which they happen to be traversing; every member of the community makes the necessary move-ment at the same time, and as the movements are rapid a distinct loud rattling sound is produced. In this case the action is probably a danger-signal, and we can understand—theoretically at any rate—how it was brought about. But the value to the species of the rhythmic-light pulsation of the Fire-Flies is not obvious, and as it is doubtful if the emission of phos-phorescent light is under the control of the insects, or is merely a simple automatic process of metabolism its synchronism is a most puzzling fact [2] [Note 19, p. 316].

An early start was made next morning, and we had not proceeded very far on our way when we were overtaken by a light canoe poled along at a rare pace

---

[1] Also observed by Dr. N. Annandale at Kuala Patani (*P.Z.S.*, 1900, p. 865). Dr. Annandale states that the larger bluer lights of three individuals seated together pulsated with a rhythm dif-ferent from that of the hundreds of others, with smaller lights, upon the same large tree by the river-bank.—E. B. P.

[2] There can be no doubt that the light is under the control of the nervous system. See the examples under "Fire-flies" and "Luminous beetles" in Longstaff's *Butterfly-hunting.*—E. B. P,

by five or six women and a man. These Land-Dayak women wore dark blue petticoats, a coil of rattan strips stained red or black round the waist, and brass rings in long series on the arms and round the calves of the legs, with two to three shell rings interspersed amongst the brass armlets. Their canoe was very crank, and I do not suppose that a white man would have poled it very far without capsizing. But these women were experts in the art; the picturesque garb and flashing ornaments setting off their glossy brown skins to best advantage, and the rhythmical swing of their bodies as they drove and lifted the long punt-poles made a beautiful picture which lives vividly in my memory even now. They exchanged some chaff with our boatmen laboriously forcing our heavier boats up the shallows, but they were evidently in a hurry, and soon were lost to view round a distant curve.

We stopped for a while at Brang, a village built on a bluff commanding a fine view of the river, as Cox wished to forewarn the chief that in a month or three weeks he would return to collect the annual poll-tax levied by the Sarawak Government. A messenger was sent up the steep and slippery paths that led to the village, and he returned shortly with the chief and his daughter. The latter was a somewhat forbidding-looking female with a very pronounced squint, but she was a great character, and a few minutes' conversation sufficed to show that the real head of the village was the chief's daughter. The Sarawak Government in this year had found it necessary to demonetize the Japanese yen or dollar, which for some time had been part of the legal currency of the country; the reasons for this course of action and its consequence, that the coins could not be accepted in payment of the poll-tax except at a 10 per cent. reduction of value, were carefully explained to the chief. But he, poor man, was soon hopelessly befogged, and referred us to his daughter for her opinions on the matter; she, after asking a few intelligent questions, grasped the situation at once, and pacified her parent with a few soothing words. Our boatmen subsequently told us that this woman was a spinster, truly a *rara avis* in a Bornean village, who scorned matrimony, that she did none of the women's work in the village or on the farm, that she insisted on making her voice heard at village councils, and that at the harvest-feasts she not only donned male attire, but also took part in the men's dances. In fact she was a Dayak " new woman."

Shortly after midday we reached Pankalan Ampat, and, as henceforth our way lay by land and not by water, we paid off our boatmen and sent messengers to the neighbouring village of Sennah, requesting the presence of the headmen. There is a Government bungalow at Pankalan Ampat, built of wood and Nipa-palm leaves; it had not been occupied for many months, and solitary wasps of the family *Eumenidæ*, which build little clay nests, storing the cells with spiders as food for their young, had taken advantage of the vacant house to construct scores of their nests, which adhered to the palm-leaf walls of every room. Wasps are good collectors, and many a curious spider did I find in their stores. Some were dried up, others had lost their legs, but occasionally I disinterred admirable specimens, which were hailed with joy as the first-fruits of our collecting expedition.

The start of a Head-hunting Expedition. (See Note 20, p. 316). (From the author's photograph, taken at Kapit.)

Plate XVII.

To face p. 253

The Pengara, or native magistrate, of Sennah turned up in the evening with his son, a lad of about fourteen years of age, who, it was plain to see, was the very apple of his father's eye, and endowed with all the petulant airs and graces shown by spoilt children in every clime. To the Pengara we explained our plans, namely, that we intended to live for three weeks on Mt. Penrisen, that therefore it was necessary for a small hut to be constructed for us there, and for all our baggage to be transported to our mountain camp; to every carrier we would give a present of tobacco, but he could expect no pay, for this was a Government expedition, and free service for a couple of days was his due to Government officials. The Pengara raised no objections to our proposals, but said that all details could be arranged more expeditiously in Sennah, and he offered us an invitation to the chief's house for the following day. Next day, then, we transferred ourselves and belongings to Sennah, where we received a cordial welcome. A Land-Dayak village does not consist of one immensely long house as do the villages of the Sea-Dayaks, Kenyahs, and Kayans, but of several houses, all, of course, raised on piles, and all more or less joined to one another in an irregular manner. I have visited several Land-Dayak villages, but I never could find any definite or constant plan in their structure; · they may generally be described as a loose jumble of houses very roughly arranged in a hollow square, one side of which is open. The centre of the square is occupied by a raffle of timber and bamboo, with a few connecting bridges, and the holy of holies, the Head-House, stands in the middle. At Lanchang village, in the Upper Sadong, the Head-House is used as a guest-house, and I spent two days there once [see pp. 286–90]; but at Sennah we were not permitted to go inside it, but took up our quarters in the chief's house—a long building looking on to the river, and occupied not only by the chief and his family but by other families as well.

A European when he enters a Land-Dayak house must give up all idea of privacy; he is an object of intense interest to the inhabitants. His clothes and the way in which he puts them off and on, his food and his manner of eating, his method of lighting a cigarette or pipe, of striking a match, his every trivial action, affords cause for interest and food for comment; the entire population of the village, old and young, male and female, congregate around him and gaze in a bovine manner at him for hours together. After a time this becomes very irksome, but as our stay at Sennah was short, we submitted with as good a grace as possible to the ordeal of being the cynosure of every eye.

With the chief we discussed again our plan of campaign, and he promised to collect the necessary carriers for us before nightfall. The men certainly did turn up, but after sitting in solemn conclave in the outer verandah, they sent in word to us that they could not carry our goods to the mountain as their farms required all their labour and attention. The success of our expedition trembled in the balance, but Cox proved equal to the occasion; he went out to the verandah and addressed the men for a good quarter of an hour by my watch. He spoke to them of the past, recalling to their minds the days when no white Rajah ruled in Sarawak, the days when no Land-Dayak could regard

his soul as his own, when he groaned under the in-
tolerable burden of taxation heaped on him by corrupt
and avaricious Malay princelings. He painted in vivid
colours the uncertainty of life in Upper Sarawak in the
early days of its history, when the country was cease-
lessly harried by Malays and Sea-Dayaks, when no Land-
Dayak could go forth to his labour and be confident
that on his return his home would be intact, his wife
and children ready to welcome him. Then he contrasted
all this misery and wretchedness with the present state
of peace and security, and as a proof of their apprecia-
tion of these blessings he asked the men to give two
days of their labour to forwarding the business of two
officials of the Government to which they owed their
well-being.

This most eloquent and well-timed speech had an
immediate effect; it was punctuated with approving
grunts, and concluded amidst a chorus of acquiescence.
The main difficulty of our journey being thus successfully surmounted—and only those who have travelled
in uncivilized lands know what a constant source of
anxiety and worry transport can be—we distributed
some handfuls of tobacco and two bottles of gin, and
retired with light hearts inside our mosquito curtains.

The crowing of cocks, the grunting of pigs, and the
snarling of dogs under the house render late morning
slumbers impossible in a Dayak house, and the day
was yet young when we began the business of dividing our baggage into suitable loads for the carriers.
Everything had to be made up into one-man loads,
for these people object to carrying anything between
two. All goods are carried in a sort of creel on the
back, the creel being supported by a band of strong

bark cloth, which passes round the forehead, and is
held in the hands to relieve the strain.   Land-Dayaks
are good weight-carriers, and can go for hours at a
stretch up hill and down dale with from five to six
stone on their backs.   The sun was high in the heavens
before we had seen the last of our 120 carriers on his
way, and then we with our servants, three guides, and
the Pengara's son bade farewell to our kind hosts, and
set off.   The path lay for a few miles over the foot-
hills of Penrisen, clothed in scrub and tall grass ; it
was steep, slippery with mud, and very narrow, for
Dayaks always walk in single file, and in walking place
one foot exactly in front of the other.   At times we
came on little brooks and gullies, crossed by crazy
bridges of bamboo or half-rotten timber, which we
ventured on gingerly.   There was no shade, and the
sun beat down on the narrow path cleft through the
matted vegetation with untempered heat ; I do not
think that I have ever perspired so much in my life
before or since ; before long my clothes refused to
absorb any more moisture, and the perspiration dripped
off my coat-sleeves and trickled down the breast and
back of my tunic.   At one o'clock we called a halt,
and rested for three-quarters of an hour ; food would
have choked me, and though I could have drunk a
gallon, I did not dare to drink very much, as I knew
that I should feel the effects directly I began to walk
again.   By 3 p.m. we were on the lower slopes of the
mountain, and for about an hour climbed through a
zone of bamboo forest ; the shade and the more or less
open nature of the ground was a most welcome relief,
and it was no longer necessary to fix the gaze rigidly
on the ground to avoid snags, creepers, and other
traps for the unwary.

Bamboo is the only forest-tree in the tropics which I have observed to grow profusely in a circumscribed area. There is nothing in the tropics to correspond with the oak-, beech-, or pine-forests of more temperate zones. The jungle is a gigantic and bewildering chaos of scores upon scores of different species of trees, most of them swathed in a luxuriant tangle of creepers and parasitic growths all struggling up to the life-giving sunlight ; it is a paradise for the botanist, but I believe that on the whole finer effects of scenery are produced by great numbers of one or two kinds of tree than by an inextricable confusion of varied plant-life.

The bamboo-forest passed, we came into secondary jungle, and from this entered the primeval forest of the mountain. The slope was very steep, but as it was cool enough now we took things in a more leisurely manner and halted for frequent breathers. Land-Dayaks are inveterate smokers, and at every halt our carriers produced short lengths of bamboo which, with a few strokes of their small, angled knives, were quickly converted into pipes. The bamboo was half filled with water, and a small pinch of tobacco was placed on the top of a slender piece of bamboo inserted at an angle in a hole in the side of the main piece. A man having lighted the tobacco would draw into his lungs a great mouthful of the smoke, and then pass the pipe on to his neighbour who would repeat the process. A pipeful would suffice for no more than three or perhaps four men. The tobacco which these people smoke is of Chinese manufacture, and when burning it has a horrid acrid odour, quite unlike the Javanese tobacco which Malays and Sea-Dayaks smoke ; I tried one whiff of the Chinese stuff

18

and regretted it for half an hour afterwards. All the natives of Borneo use these angled knives for cutting and carving small objects; the blade is held between the fingers and thumb of the left hand, the handle lying along the fore-arm, whilst the article that is to be carved is held in the right hand and is turned and pressed against the knife-blade; a left-handed man would hold the knife in his right hand and the object to be carved in his left.

Between five and six o'clock we reached the point where we had decided to camp for the night. There was here an enormous boulder known to the natives as Batu Tinong; it jutted out from the side of the mountain, and overhung so far that a sort of open cave was formed. Close by there was a mountain stream dashing down a rocky ravine; and quickly divesting ourselves of our clothes, supersaturated with sweat, we flung our weary bodies into the foaming torrent. The chill of the water fresh from the mountain-top acted as a splendid tonic and stimulant, and we emerged cool and refreshed. Our followers meanwhile had constructed beneath the overhanging boulder a floor of branches raised about a foot from the ground; on this our waterproof sheets and boat-mattresses were spread, and we were soon discussing a savoury supper such as a Chinese cook can, with the most limited appliances, turn out under the most adverse circumstances.

We then composed ourselves for well-earned slumbers, but sleep was not for me; to begin with I was over-tired, every bone in my body seemed to ache, my bed seemed uncommonly hard, and the knots of the branches composing the floor could be felt through the thin mattress. But above all, it was my first night in the jungle, and the mystery and the majesty of the great primeval forest awed and possessed my soul. I do not think that this feeling of weird mystery ever quite wears off a mind that is at all impressionable; speaking for myself, I can truthfully say that the impression was renewed again and again whenever it was my lot to pass nights in the jungle, and I can even conjure it up now by dwelling on those past experiences. In the daytime the forest is less eerie; you are conscious that there is glowing and active life all around : much of it you cannot see, but the not infrequent glimpses of Nature's great pageant of animal life are enthralling and reassuring, and the interest of collecting keeps the mind constantly on the alert. But at night you can see nothing; an almost impenetrable darkness descends on the forest. Teeming life is still all around, for you can hear it; the air is full of the noise made by millions of insects, a noise that, like the roar of traffic in a great city or like the sound of the sea, so permeates everything that in time the ear becomes dulled, and a special effort has to be made to listen to it. There are, too, strange rustlings in the trees, and occasionally the stillness is rent by some strange cry or weird shriek, at the sound of which, half-scared, you ask your followers its meaning, only to be told that it is some ghost or lost spirit. It may be the despairing yell of some monkey seized by a snake, or the triumphant scream of some night-bird clutching its hapless victim; who can tell ? If you step out of the radius of your camp-fires you feel that you are brought face to face with forces over which you have no sort of control ; you are surrounded on all sides by handiwork that is not man's, by swarming millions of creatures that live out their little lives without the faintest reference to you. If a man die in a city, he knows at least that he leaves behind him a blank—perhaps a small one, a memory—maybe but short-lived ; at any rate, if it be only in the smallest way, his death *does* affect his fellow-man, for none of us lives to himself alone. But if he die here in the great forest, what is his death ? It is but one out of thousands that occur perpetually—uncared for, indifferent, without effect.

With the dawn we were astir again, and, breakfast over, we continued our climb ; by noon we had reached what had once been a clearing, for it was now covered by saplings and undergrowth. Our guides told us that here was the place where a previous visitor to the mountain, my predecessor the late Dr. G. D. Haviland, had camped. It did not look a very promising spot, for the slope of the ground was steep and there was but one small and trickling brook to furnish our water-supply, but we were told that higher up there was still less water, so we had to acquiesce in our guide's choice. The men with us began to cut down the saplings and clear the brush-wood, and in doing so disturbed quantities of insects. Life in the jungle is thickest in the trees, and there is comparatively little on the floor itself ; the felling of a tree always reveals a little world of living creatures. The bearers with the collecting gear, killing-bottles, spirit-jars, and so on, had not yet made their appearance, so I was hard put to it to keep hold of the specimens that I caught and that were brought to me ; my hat and pockets soon were full, and I was driven to tying insects secured by threads of fibre on to the buttons of my coat, until Cox said I presented the appearance of a Christmas-tree hung with living animals. The Dayaks were much tickled with my difficulties and vied with each other in presenting me with more and more specimens, each addition being greeted with roars of laughter. Fortunately I had my butterfly-net with me, and managed to secure a specimen of a rare mountain butterfly, *Cyrestis seminigra*, that flitted across the clearing; another creature that I secured was one of those queer Land-Planarians, or flat-worms, coloured brilliant sealing-wax red with black and white cross-bands.

The appearance of the rest of our train of coolies put an end to my difficulties, and soon all my captures were reposing in boxes or were pickled in spirit. The Land-Dayaks now began to construct us a long lean-to, or *lankau*, but we told them that that was of no sort of use; as our stay was to be one of three weeks, we wanted a proper hut, one good enough, as Cox phrased it, to serve as a Padi barn. So the men set to work and in the space of three hours built us a hut about 8 feet square, raised 2 feet off the ground, open in front but with the sides, back, and roof of well-made palm thatch. A species of *Caryota* palm with pinnate leaves grew in abundance close by us, and the thatch was made from these in a very simple but ingenious way. Two bunks, two shelves, both made of the palm-stems, and a three-stepped ladder completed the house, and I may say here that so efficiently was it constructed that, in spite of some heavy rains, the roof did not leak till the day before we left the mountain, and then the leak

A NATURALIST IN BORNEO

was repaired in a couple of minutes. The rest of
the day was spent in unpacking our gear, in building a *lankau* for our hunters and a kitchen for our
servants, and in damming the brook to make a
bathing-pool.

Towards evening the rain came on, and very shortly
all round our hut numbers of enormous earth-worms,
1½ to 2 feet long and very thick, made their appearance; the Dayaks showed the utmost horror of these
creatures and could not be induced to touch them
with their fingers; we collected a good many
specimens but found that considerable care had to
be taken in preserving them, as many specimens
divided up into short segments when immersed in
spirit. After dinner we sat listening to the din of
insects around us, and rigged a reflecting lamp with
a sheet behind it in the hopes of attracting moths, but
without much success. Dr. Wallace has expressed the
opinion that moths do not come to light in jungle
stations until the light has been shown for many
nights, and this I can fully confirm. I never reaped
such harvests of moths on Penrisen as I did many
times on Mt. Matang when I used to stay with a
friend in charge of the Government coffee estate
there; two or even three hundred specimens was no
unusual haul in four hours; on suitable nights the
moths simply streamed into the house, attracted by
the bright lights which, of course, were visible every
night.

On the following day we dismissed our train of
coolies after giving them the promised guerdon of
tobacco, and retained with us, in addition to our own
servants and hunters, three of the Sennah men who

for a small wage consented to share our fortunes for
the next week or two. One of these men, Latip by
name, was a fine specimen of humanity, clean-run,
stalwart, and as active as a cat; another, whom we
christened the "lion," on account of his flowing mane
of black hair, was inclined to corpulency, and before
very long we discovered that he had a rooted objection to hard work, and a very large appetite; however,
he was of an amiable and good-natured disposition,
and was a source of constant amusement to our
hunters. The Pengara's son also stayed with us, as he
was anxious to display his prowess with a new muzzle-
loading gun that his indulgent father had given him.
After breakfast we decided to explore our surroundings,
and dispersed in all directions; for my own part I
did not go far, the immediate vicinity of our camp
contained enough interesting material to keep a
naturalist happy for a month, and I soon had a fine
series of insects of all sorts, including such insignificant-
looking creatures as escape the notice of collectors on
the hunt for more striking animals. About midday
we re-united and the results were not very promising;
none of the birds obtained were different from low-
country forms and none of the butterflies were new
to me. Cox reported that in his wanderings he had
come on a magnificent plateau at a slightly higher
elevation than our present camp, it was well supplied
with water and commanded a splendid view; it
was evident that our guide had not taken us to the
best place, and cross-examining him we found at
length that his chief reason for not leading us to this
ideal spot was that the Caryota-palm with which our
hut was thatched did not grow there in sufficient

abundance, and so to save himself and his fellows the labour of carrying up loads of the palm-leaves he had obliged us to camp in a less suitable place. We were very annoyed, but it was too late to change our quarters as all the bearers had gone, but we gave the guide *un mauvais quart d'heure*. The afternoon was fully occupied in skinning the birds, in pinning the insects into collecting-boxes, folding up butterflies in sheets of paper, pressing plants, and the other occupations of collecting naturalists. After dark we set our moth-trap, but again without much result. As we were waiting, nets in hand, for our victims, we heard from many points around us a sharp bird-like chirp ; it seemed impossible that a small bird should be moving about at that time of night, and we were prepared to give up the puzzle as hopeless, when suddenly a small frog leapt out of the darkness on to the chimney of our lamp, clung there for a brief second, then uttered a sharp chirp and dropped with singed toes to the floor of the hut. We quickly captured it, and found it to be a handsome reddish-brown species of the genus *Rhacophorus*, showing by its fully webbed feet that it was a near relation of the celebrated Wallace's Flying Frog. On our return to Kuching I found that this was a new species, afterwards described and named *Rh. shelfordi* by Mr. Boulenger.

Since collecting on the lower levels of the mountain had yielded poor results, Cox started next morning with some of the hunters and Latip for the summit ; in the afternoon he sent down word that he intended to stay near the summit for three days, since the locality seemed to promise well. As proof he sent down by the bearer a specimen of the Mountain Trogon, *Harpactes dulitensis*, the first example of which had been shot by Dr. Charles Hose at a high elevation on Mt. Dulit; a handsome spotted Toad with very long legs, *Bufo jerboa*; a crab of the genus *Potamon*, and a new species of Stick-Insect. I despatched the bearer with a supply of rice and provisions, and spent an hour or two trying to make a satisfactory skin of the Trogon. Trogons have skins which may aptly be compared to wet tissue paper, and as I am not a skilled taxidermist the result of my labours was horrible to behold, and I threw it away in disgust.

The next few days I spent pretty well by myself, for Cox extended his stay near the summit of the mountain, and I sent up to him all the hunters as he was doing well in the collecting of vertebrates and needed men to help him skin them. One Land-Dayak—the "lion"—stayed with me and the two Chinese servants, one of whom shortly fell ill with fever and lay like a log in the lean-to that served as a kitchen. There was a good deal of rain and butterflies became scarce, but I shall not readily forget one glorious afternoon; the sun was shining brilliantly in a perfect blue sky flecked with a few clouds, and presently I heard the peculiar rushing noise made by Hornbills as they fly (a noise due, I believe, to the air rushing through the quills of the wings, for the wings on the under side are only very thinly protected by coverts), and from various directions I could see numbers of these birds winging their way to a huge *Ficus* tree that was in fruit close to the camp. The birds began to feed greedily and, fetching a pair of field-glasses, I lay on my back and gazed for long at their curious antics. There were two or three species, one of which, *Anorhinus galeatus*, as it fed uttered a strange, mewing noise; the others had more raucous cries; sometimes a bird would pluck off a fruit, throw it in the air and catch it, throw it up again, and again catch it and swallow it; sometimes one would stand on a branch and solemnly jump up and down on it in the most ludicrous manner. One could not help being convinced that the birds were filled with the *joie de vivre*, and I felt fortunate in being able to get a good view behind the veil that is nearly always stretched between the naturalist and bird-life in the tropical forest.

Cox eventually climbed on to the summit of the mountain, but it was a bleak wilderness covered with Pandanus and very poor in animal life, so he descended and moved his quarters to a lower peak known as Mt. Prang. He sent down some interesting insect larvæ, and I made up my mind to join him on the peak of Mt. Prang and investigate the habits of these creatures for myself. The second Chinese servant had now fallen ill with fever, and it was only with a great effort that he was able to cook for me, so I left them both with a supply of quinine tabloids and a Dayak to look after them, and joined my companion. I found that he had prepared a fine camp by making a large clearing and erecting a long lean-to; we commanded a magnificent view right down to the sea, and could distinguish Kuching very clearly in the distance. The felled trees in the clearing had attracted crowds of Longicorns and Weevils and I soon added very largely to my insect collections. One day was very like another, and it would be tedious to describe each in detail : we were generally up shortly after sunrise, and wandered about near the camp till 7, then every one went off on the day's hunt and did not return till after midday ; the afternoon was busily employed in skinning and preserving our captures, while as soon as dusk set in we were occupied with catching moths and other insects attracted by our lights. When we were discussing the plans of our expedition in Kuching, we had visions of an abundance of game on Mt. Penrisen, and one of the most cherished articles of our baggage was a large cooking-pot which we fondly intended to keep ever full with a savoury stew. But game on the mountain was conspicuous by its absence, there were neither deer nor pig, nor Fire-Back Pheasants, not even Button-Quail,[1] and we were driven to feed on the pickled beef which we had brought with us, and on the fowls which we bought from the Dayaks. The trees round Mt. Prang swarmed with Barbets, but they were poor eating, and Hornbills with their dark red flesh were not very appetizing.

Our supply of fowls having given out, and being tired of the endless diet of rice and bully-beef, I decided one day to eat a monkey, *Semnopithecus rubicundus*, that one of the hunters had shot, and having overcome a slight feeling of repugnance at eating an animal not so very distantly removed from the genus

[1] Deer and pig do not ascend the mountains of Borneo above 2,000 feet, except perhaps on very rare occasions when in search of food. Fire-Back Pheasants are found in the bamboo area, and on the spurs of the mountains, but not above 1,000 feet. The Argus and Bulwer's Pheasant (*Lobiophasis*) are found up to 2,000 feet. Button-Quail do not inhabit the old jungle ; they are common on any cleared spot in the low country.—C. H.

Homo, I enjoyed my meal very much, but I could not induce Cox to join me. After the meal our Sea-Dayak hunters and our Land-Dayak guides engaged in a long discussion on what animals were good to eat and what were not; the former were nearly sick when they heard that our guides ate bear when they could get it, and did not believe us when we told them that in Canada bear's feet were considered a delicacy. Land-Dayaks will not eat deer, because they fancy that in doing so they acquire the timorousness of that animal; but also it is amongst these people tabu to eat beef or butter or to drink milk, and as their name of the Supreme Being is Tŭpa [Note 21, p. 318] some authorities have sought to trace a connection between these Borneans and the beef-eschewing, cow-worshipping Brahmins of India. Ethnological speculations are almost proverbially wild, but wilder shots have been made than this, for it is certain that the Land-Dayaks are amongst the more primitive people of Borneo, and are of the same stock as certain tribes of Java, where Hinduism was once the national religion. The Land-Dayaks have a tradition that they came from Java, and it may well be that they migrated from that island before its Hindu conquerors were driven out by the Mohammedan invaders.

Both Sea-Dayaks and Land-Dayaks found common ground in descanting on the merits of pickled pork. Whenever these people prepare for a future feast, they fill great jars with lumps of pork to which is added a modicum of salt; the jars are sealed up and are not opened till the feast days arrive, and then the putrid, stinking masses of greenish-coloured meat are devoured with gusto by young and old. That wholesale death does not ensue from ptomaine poisoning seems little short of miraculous.[1]

After some days we moved down to our old quarters, and stayed there till our allotted time had expired, when we sent down word to Sennah for the bearers to transport our baggage. The carriers made their appearance next afternoon, and amongst them were some men from a neighbouring village, Tebia ; they were the ugliest and most unprepossessing-looking lot of natives that I have ever seen, and they were held in some contempt by the Sennahs, but they were certainly great people at getting about in jungle. Some of them asked me why I was at such pains to put together these collections of insects and reptiles : it was the usual question almost always asked by natives, and to it I made the usual answer that they were of use for medical purposes ; no view but the strictly utilitarian one appeals to a native, and this reply always put an end to further inquiries. The Tebia people on this occasion immediately volunteered to get specimens, and I handed some of them killing-bottles and tubes of spirit ; in a short time they were back again with every receptacle choke-full of every variety of animal from reptile to worm ; others joined in, and before long I had the whole gang busily employed, with the result that in about an hour I got more specimens than the rest of us had been able to get in a couple of days. We spent the afternoon in packing up our gear, and Latip asked if he might have some

---

[1] The pickled pork is well cooked before it is eaten, and when cooked, a good deal of the offensive smell passes off—the cooking may have something to do with its harmless effect on the people. —C. H.

old clothes which we were about to throw away as they were pretty well worn out. We gave them to him and he bashfully retired into the jungle to put them on ; in a few minutes he returned in a high state of glee, clad in an ancient pair of trousers, a canvas shirt, and an ill-fitting coat: from a fine, active athlete he had been transformed into a disreputable-looking tramp, and we implored him to doff his newly acquired garments and resume the red loin-cloth or chawat that set off his muscular limbs to such advantage—but he was like a child with a new toy, and was so fascinated with his appearance in a white man's clothes that he could not be persuaded.

Next morning we bade a reluctant farewell to our camp. I proposed to burn down our hut, but my proposal was met with outcries by the natives, who said that it was *mali*, or tabu, to do so ; all sorts of evil would recoil on our heads if we were so wicked as to destroy a hut in which we had lived—so it was left to rot. On the way down we suddenly encountered two bears that were slumbering on a fallen tree-trunk ; as soon as they caught sight of us they rushed off barking almost like dogs, and we had not a chance to get a shot at them. Lower down the mountain one of the bearers suddenly uttered an exclamation, and, dropping his load, began to hack down with his chopping-sword or "latok" a small tree that stood a little way off our path. His fellows came to help him, and before long the tree was down and the trunk split up ; it was riddled with burrows, and from them the Dayaks extracted a pinkish grub with a faint but delicious scent—these were the larvæ of a Longicorn beetle, and the Dayaks explained that they were excellent eating when boiled.

In the low-country I was all but bitten by a green Tree-Viper; it was curled up round the branch of a bush by the side of the path, and in walking by it I tripped and nearly fell into the bush against the snake, but was saved from actually doing so by a man just behind me.   The snake appeared ready to bite, and showed no intention of gliding away, and I was struck by the sluggishness of the creature, for many of our train had passed close by, and doubtless on account of its green colour had failed to notice it. We did not stop at Sennah, but pushed right on to Pankalan Ampat, which we reached about 5 o'clock. We had to stay here a day or two, for Cox had to collect the poll-tax of $2 per adult male.   The method of collecting the tax was amusingly archaic.   Cox sat at a table with the account-books before him; the chief of some village would then present himself, the pockets of his coat full of copper coins: taking one coin out of his pocket he would lay it on the table and give the name of a man in his village; the name was checked by Cox, and then another coin was produced and another name given, and so on till the tale was complete, when the money was handed over.   The headman of a small village, with one or two followers accompanying him, turned up one day at noon; though he had walked nearly ten miles in the blazing sun he was perfectly cool and collected, but directly he began to recount the names of the men in his village who had to pay tax his face became flushed, the perspiration began to form on his forehead, and he became so confused that one of his followers, in his impatience, seized hold of all the copper coins and began in his turn to recite the names; ere long he was in similar case to his chief. I could not help being astonished to see that whilst prolonged physical exertion had little effect on these men, a mental effort produced the effects described. The tax being all paid up we packed the money in stout wooden boxes, and leaving the collectors behind us to hunt for a few more days, we embarked on our homeward way. Travelling down-stream was a very different thing to travelling up-stream, and we went at a great pace; at one spot where the stream was very rapid and some care had to be exercised in steering between rocks, one of our Chinese servants, in a sudden access of nervousness, leapt to his feet and endeavoured to thrust the boat off from a rock with a pole; I thought that we were over that time, but by a miracle we righted, and we took care to restrain our nervous cook from repeating his offence. At Segu we rested again for half a day to collect the tax from the large village there. The chief by a perfect *tour de force* of memory successfully recited without a break the names of nearly two hundred men, and we set off for Kuching at about 4 o'clock, our boats loaded down to their gunwales with bullion. There was plenty of water in the river, and before dusk we had passed all the rapids, which on our upward journey it had taken us a whole day to conquer; by 11 o'clock we were once more in Kuching.

Except that Penrisen was disappointingly poor in mammals and birds, we had had a thoroughly success-ful trip, and our collections in all other orders were very rich, whilst I, for one, had enjoyed an experience of life in the jungle which is amongst the most precious of my memories. If now, settled quietly at home, I ever hear the "East a-calling," it is not the life in the towns that calls me, not the freedom of social intercourse, not the boundless hospitality of friends and neighbours, nor the luxuries of a tropical home, but the dark, mysterious forest with its teeming life, the nights on the river-bank with the rushing stream beside me, the starry sky above, the camp-fire with the natives huddled round telling tales in murmuring tones, the shrill clamour of the insects filling the whole air—these are the things that call. Forgotten are the discomforts of poor food, Mosquitoes, hard sleeping-places, the weariness of travel. One was in closest contact with Nature then—Nature almost savagely triumphant, riotously luxuriant ; and whosoever has learnt to know her in this mood can never altogether forget his lesson.

CHAPTER X

OTHER EXPEDITIONS

THE Penrisen trip, described in the last chapter, was the first of a series of collecting expeditions made with the object of filling blanks in the zoological and ethnographical collections of the Museum. Mt. Matang, which is only a few miles from Kuching, and on which there are two bungalows, was often visited, as also Santubong at the mouth of the Sarawak River. In 1902 I went up to the northern end of Sarawak to stay with my friend Cox, who had now been transferred to the Trusan district. The scenery in this part of Borneo is distinctly weird. Opposite the island of Labuan is a large bay, at the western horn of which is situated the Sarawak Government station of Brooketon, in Brunei territory; the eastern horn is the territory of the British North Borneo Company. Into the bay discharge the three rivers going from west to east, Limbang, Trusan, and Lawas, the latter only recently acquired by the Sarawak Government. The bay is very shallow, and the Trusan River is slowly pushing out a spit of land into the sea; the bay is dotted in all directions with large fish-weirs, or "kelong," and the channel leading to the mouth of the Trusan is marked with stakes which are not covered even at high-water mark. So shallow are the waters of this bay that it is possible to walk across it from Trusan mouth to British North Borneo territory and never to be much more than waist-deep.

I have never seen such curious mirage effects as in this part of the world ; from a small boat the horizon appears to be in the immediate foreground, and it is broken by the little wavelets lipping over sand-banks ; the true horizon is simply invisible, and it would be impossible to have the faintest idea of its position did one not see in the distance islands which appear to be suspended in mid-air. This disappearance of the horizon has an extremely distorting effect on one's vision, and it becomes a matter of great difficulty to judge distance or size accurately : a small steam-launch at a distance of 300 yards looks like a great mail-steamer a mile away, and a man wading through the water towards the boat seems a great distance off, and you are astonished that he should reach you so soon. One November morning the Government steam-launch *Gazelle* dropped me at about a mile from the Trusan mouth, for the tides were neap and it was not possible on a half-tide to get any further inshore. As it was, the small boat which was waiting to transport me and my belongings over the intervening space drew rather too much water, and we had to stop just outside the mouth waiting for the tide to rise and carry us over the bar. The muddy banks were thickly covered with hundreds of Egrets and Little Herons, and they made a very pretty picture in the morning sun, stalking over the mud-flats picking up their daily food. Egrets, I am glad to say, are very strictly preserved in Sarawak, on account of the benefits they confer on cattle by clearing them of ticks. As we sat waiting for the rising tide a man passed us wading through the water and leading two buffaloes with their calves; he had walked through the water from a small river between Trusan and Lawas. The Brunei Malays often bring consignments of buffaloes across to Trusan. The method of transport inflicts needless suffering on the poor animals; a raft is constructed, and to this the buffaloes are attached by their noserings; to prevent themselves from drowning they have to swim, and this propels the raft, on which stand the owners, urging their charges to further efforts by goads and shouts; but their heads have to be carried at an awkward angle, and by the time they arrive at their journey's end they are sometimes so exhausted that they can hardly walk ashore.

Those peculiar amphibious fish the *Periopthalmi* were swarming on the mud-flats; one large species with a sail-like dorsal fin, when startled, would dive down into the mud and throw up a great squirt of liquid mud from below. Another very conspicuous form was a Gar-Fish that was leaping about in the shallow waters; they simply shot out of the water and travelled like shimmering waves of light for several yards above the surface. One of my boatmen related that a Malay sitting in a boat fishing with a line had his side pierced by one of these fish which leapt out of the water and shot against him, but I don't know if there is much truth in the story.[1]

[1] During my stay in Singapore there were two cases of fishermen killed in the harbour by this fish. The men were struck in the chest by the pointed snout, which broke off in the thorax. One of these fish weighed two pounds. They run nearly erect for a long distance, striking the tail against the water at intervals.—H. N. R.

The tide at last serving, we entered the river and paddled on at a good pace. Just near the river-mouth the scenery was no different from that to which I was well accustomed : there were the same stretches of black, viscid mud and the same monotonous Nipa-palms on either hand, but before long there opened out quite a different type of view. The banks grew hard and stood out of the water, great expanses of turf dotted with clumps of *Pandanus* were frequent, buffaloes were grazing peacefully or standing in herds knee-deep in the river with Egrets perched on their backs; here and there was a Murut village, and the whole scene was delightfully fresh to eyes jaded with the monotony of tangled .vegetation that shows few variations of tint. Ere long we arrived at Sundar, where is situated a Malay village, and on the opposite bank a small bungalow or shooting-box, where my friend was awaiting me, and where I received the warm welcome that dismisses at a breath the tedium of the previous journey. That evening we dropped down on the tide to the river-mouth to shoot shore-birds, and we took with us the headman of the village, Pangeran Besar, the most delightful and courteous Malay that it would be possible to meet ; on our way down river we saw the Great Fruit-Pigeon *Carpophaga œnea* [1] flying overhead, and Cox was suc-cessful in bringing down one or two; one that fell was only wounded, so it was given to Pangeran Besar, since, being an orthodox Malay, he could only eat animals that had had their throats cut by a Moham-medan. He whipped out a small pocket-knife and

[1] *Carpophaga œnea* is the large pigeon, but *Treron capellei* I should consider the most commonly seen of fruit-pigeons.—C. H.

sawed the head of the pigeon nearly off, but the bird
was already at its last gasp, and verily I believe that
it died before the knife touched it; still, orthodoxy
was satisfied.   As we drew near to the river-mouth
we saw that the receding tide had uncovered a few
isolated sand-spits, and some of these were covered
with flocks of Curlew, Whimbrel, Godwits, Sandpipers,
and other birds of like kind, all busily engaged in
searching for their supper.   The crew were told to
paddle without letting the shafts of the paddles touch
the gunwale of the canoe, for the "chunking" of the
paddles is a loud sound that carries a great distance
over water; we stealthily drew nearer one of the
most densely populated sand-spits until Cox was
enabled to wade on to it; then, doubling his burly
form in a vain endeavour to elude the observation of
the already suspicious birds, he progressed like some
grotesque bear until he was within range, when he
fired a right and left into the flock.   Scores of birds,
so densely had they been packed, fell to the shots, and
the remainder flew screaming in wide curves round
and about us.   Black thunderclouds were rapidly
coming up in the south-east, and as the wheeling
squadrons of birds were seen against the dark background they appeared of a beautiful silvery-white, and
then, as they circled round between us and the sun,
their shining appearance vanished and they became
black silhouettes against the orange and gold of the
sunset sky; it was a beautiful sight that I could have
watched for hours, but the curves of the screaming
squadrons grew larger and larger, and soon they
vanished from sight.   I have few if any sporting in-
stincts myself, and the destruction of animals for the

sake of sport does not appeal to me, but the slaughter
of all these beautiful creatures was not undertaken in
purely a wanton spirit ; we were shooting for the pot,
and it may be mentioned for the benefit of epicures
that a Curlew stewed in claret—with an onion in his
inside to draw out his fishy flavour—is a dish fit for
kings, and we were in search of one of the rarest of
birds — *Macrorhamphus taczanowskii*, the Snipe-Billed
Godwit ; a bird like a Godwit, but with the tip of the
bill soft and flexible like a Snipe. This bird nests in
Eastern Siberia, but winters in China, India, and
Borneo ; very few specimens have ever been obtained,
and the only example in the Sarawak Museum had
been shot at the mouth of the Sarawak River amongst
a whole host of other waders, and our slaughter of
the innocents at Trusan was largely undertaken in the
hope of securing another specimen of this rare visitor
to Bornean shores. But our luck was out, and we
had to be content with materials for a stew. On our
way back the sun sank and it became intensely dark ;
the thunderstorm broke on us in all its force, with
crashing thunder, brilliant lightning, which for one
brief moment lit up the whole country-side, and absolute
torrents of rain. We were drenched to the skin in
no time, and it was almost impossible to see where
we were going ; but our crew rose to the occasion and
seemed thoroughly to enjoy the situation : they shouted
and yelled and fairly roared with laughter whenever
an unsuspected turn in the river took us crashing
into the bank. My experience of boat-journeys in
Borneo under varied conditions has taught me that
Malays and Sea-Dayaks wax most animated and cheerful
whenever discomfort or perhaps danger has to be
faced and overcome,

Next day we went down-river and along the coast for a short distance to a point on the sea-shore where Cox had erected a small two-roomed hut. As our stay was to extend over several days, we took provisions and a large cask of water, for there was no fresh-water spring within several miles of the spot. Pangeran Besar and one or two of his numerous progeny accompanied us, and at the fishing village of Awat-Awat we called for the furniture of the hut, which had been left there; it was very simple, consisting of a table and two chairs. The hut was built right on the sands and was surrounded by Casuarinas and a low scrub, amongst which I found a few insects, a snake, shells, and a curious Land Nemertean worm. The sand was swarming with Hermit-Crabs, *Clibanarius longipes*, dragging their shells about, and there were numbers of little Fossorial Wasps digging their burrows in the sand or clearing the entrances to their burrows whenever they returned with food for their young. These Hymenoptera belong to the *Bembex* tribe of Solitary Wasps, which do not store up food for their larvæ to feed on and then seal the nest up, but constantly keep their larvæ supplied with fresh food—in this case flies—opening up the nest whenever they arrive with their burden and closing it again when they depart in search of more. Our days were spent in fishing with a seine net, in shooting, and in examining the contents of the fish-weirs that dotted the seascape in all directions. It was a pleasant, idyllic life, spent in glorious sunshine or balmy breezes, and I was sorry when the time came for Cox to return to the Government fort. On our way up-river we witnessed a rather interesting spectacle: a flock of Egrets was flying in

Awat Awat, a Malay Fishing Village at the mouth of the Trusan River. (From the author's photograph.)

Plate XVIII.

To face p. 280.

a **V**-formation down-river, and we were lazily watching them, when suddenly the leader "put the brake on hard" and wheeled over at a sharp angle to the right, the whole flock following him with one accord ; we were at a loss to account for this sudden change of direction, when all at once we perceived a huge swarm of bees progressing up-river. They passed us with a prodigious hum, and there is no doubt that if the Egrets had not suddenly altered their course they would have flown straight into the bees, and there would have been trouble. It seems rather remarkable that the Egrets should have realized their danger so readily, as such an encounter could not have been of sufficiently frequent occurrence for the birds to have acquired experience of the danger ahead.[1]

The Malays living in this part of Borneo work sago to a limited extent, and the method is very primitive. A platform is built out over the river and beneath it is placed an old canoe ; by the side of the platform is rigged a lever with counterpoise at one end and a string to which is attached an empty paraffin-oil tin at the other. This is for raising water out of the river and is the "shadoof" of Egypt. The felled sago-tree is split open, and the pith is scraped out by means of

[1] Mr. H. N. Ridley thinks that such encounters would be quite common.—E. B. P.

I agree with Mr. Ridley that such encounters would be quite common. The birds would hear the bees coming some little distance away. These bees sometimes settle on one's boat in journeying along the rivers, and if they are allowed to go where they please for a short time, they crawl all over one without attempting to sting, and depart as quickly as they came. They have nests hanging below the large boughs of the "Tapang" trees, *Abauria*, and sometimes one of these trees will have as many as seventy or eighty nests on it at the same time.—C. H,

planks through which are driven numbers of nails—
in the old days a V-shaped instrument with a thong
of plaited rattan joining the limbs of the V was used
instead.   The triturated pith is spread on a mat on
the platform, and the worker, pouring water on it, dances
on the mat and continually pours more water on it ;
the fine sago flour is washed free from the woody
fibre (which is left on the mat) and suspended in
the water which flows through the mat and floor of
the platform, and falls into the empty canoe below ; it
is deposited as a sort of slime in the bottom of the
canoe, and the superfluous water flows off.   The dancing of the sago-workers is sometimes singularly graceful,
and if the worker be a young man, and he knows that
he is observed by some of the opposite sex, he dances
con amore.

My few days at Trusan fort were not very eventful,
and I will spare my reader an account of my daily
wanderings in the neighbouring jungle.   One other
expedition that I made was to Tabekang in the upper
waters of the Sadong River, in August 1903, and the
following extracts from my diary may be of some little
interest :—

22nd.—Left Sadong at midday in the Government
boat, with five prisoners from the Sadong gaol and a
policeman as crew ; at 4.30 we reached Gedong, a
small Malay village with one Chinese shop ; had
dinner in the shop and slept in the boat.

23rd.—Was waked at 4 a.m. by the roar of the bore
rushing up-river.   As we were lying in a tributary of
the main-river we were in no danger of being swamped,
but the boat rocked considerably ; the bore was not a
big one, owing to recent heavy rains, and the tide was

Plate XIX.

Upper Sadong River at Tabekang. (From the author's photograph.)

a long time in reaching Gedong. The bore having passed, it was now safe to proceed up-river, and at 5 a.m. I woke all the men and we paddled on till 8, when we stopped to bathe and breakfast; we stopped again at 1 for a short time, but nearly all day the men were paddling against a strong stream and it was 4.30 before we reached Empongau, a considerable Land-Dayak village. I slept in the boat.

24th.—By virtue of the Sarawak flag which we flew at the stern of our boat I was able to impress the services of six Dayaks to help us on our way to Tabekang, and with this addition to our crew we made good progress; the Malay prisoners were in great fettle and put their backs into the work. The scenery was not particularly interesting, the banks being covered with tall grass or secondary jungle, and there was not much animal life about; I saw, however, several kingfishers and some squirrels. There was an epidemic of swine-fever raging both amongst the wild pigs and the domestic pigs, and we passed numbers of carcases floating in the river. At 1.45 p.m. arrived at Tabekang, a very picturesque spot. The banks of the river are high here, and on the right bank stands the Court House, the Government bungalow, Chinese bazaar, and Malay Kampong; on the left bank is a large Land-Dayak village. At 5 o'clock I watched canoe-loads of Dayaks returning from their day's work on their farms, which this year are 2 or 3 miles down-river; the men wore the usual red or dark-blue loin-cloth, the women the dress described on p. 251. On arriving at the landing-place they all bathed, the men stark-naked, the women with all their clothes on; after their bath the men picked up their paddles, and walked up to the village leaving the women to shoulder the heavy loads. As the ground all round the bungalow was much overgrown with grass, I had a contingent of Dayaks over from the other side to clear it.

25th.—Visited the Tabekang village; it consists of three houses of 17, 18, and 20 rooms respectively. In each house there is an outer verandah open to the sky, an inner verandah ("ruai" of the Sea-Dayaks) and rooms opening off from this. The inner verandah is not used much as a general sitting place as in Sea-Dayak houses, but the people sit more in the rooms, which are of very fair size. Attached to each house and opposite to it is the "Bala," [1] or Head-House, a small one-roomed building raised high on piles, and connected with the outer verandah by a primitive staircase composed of one notched log, with or without a hand-rail. The skulls, all very ancient, are slung from a beam across the room, and a fire is generally kept burning beneath them. The young unmarried men of the village sleep in the Head-House, and it is also used as a club-house in which the elders discuss affairs. At the time of head-feasts only old men are allowed to enter the "Bala." The Tabekang Dayaks are a mannerless lot and unusually inhospitable; they strongly objected to being photographed, but I was able to take the head-measurements of a few.

26th.—At midday started for the neighbouring village of Lanchang; it was a terribly long walk through

---

[1] *Bala*, with *Balul*, and *Baluh*, which occur several times in this chapter, are different pronunciations of the word Balai and Bali, meaning sacred. Full account of the use of this word is given in *The Pagan Tribes of Borneo*, London, 1912.—C. H.

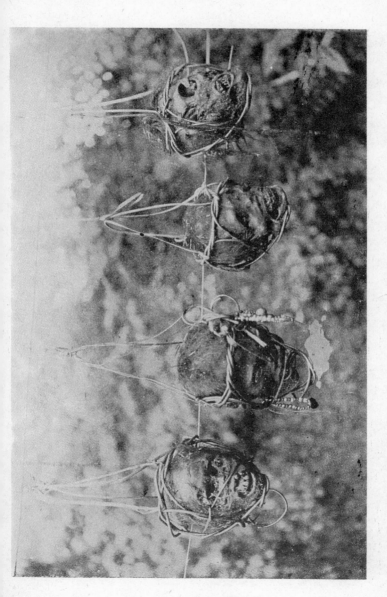

Punan heads, recovered from the murderers whose expedition is described in Note 20, p. 316. (From the author's photograph, taken at Kapit.)

Plate XX.

To face p. 84.

secondary jungle over a very bad path. As I was suffering from rheumatism I was carried part of the way by two men in turns, in a sling-basket (" galaos "), the basket resting on the bearer's back and suspended by bands of bark-cloth from his forehead. The posture in which I was compelled to huddle in this sling was so uncomfortable that I could not endure it very long, and had every now and again to get down and walk. Dayaks, like other savages, are unable to express with any accuracy terms of time or distance. At one point in our march I asked one of the train of Lanchang men how far we then were from his village ; he made the usual vague reply that it was not very far. When I suggested ten minutes' walk as the distance he assented readily, but when after walking for a good half-hour I suggested that the village was still an hour's walk distant, he again agreed that that was probably the distance: as a matter of fact we arrived in a few minutes. As no savages reckon time in minutes or hours, it is not surprising that such an expression as "ten minutes' walk" conveys no sort of idea to their minds ; if pressed to give some measure of the time it takes to traverse a certain distance, they will say that if they start at sun-rise they will arrive when the sun is at a certain height, which they will indicate by pointing to the sky. The following are some of the expressions used by Sea-Dayaks to denote short periods of time : " Enti mandi ditu bok agi basah datai din," if one bathes here one's hair is still wet when one arrives there ; "sakali niawa," one rest ; " sakali niawa ngema," one rest [after] carrying a burden ; "salumpong tenggau," one length of firewood, i.e. the time it takes to burn. Some of the

Sea-Dayak expressions for denoting the different hours of the day are very delightful, e.g.—

"Mansang jimboi," time to dry things in the sun : about 8 a.m.
"Ujong nutok," the end of the padi pounding : about 4 p.m.
"Salah kelala," to see indistinctly : between 6 and 7 p.m.
"Pupus tindok anembiak," when all the children have gone to sleep : about 8 p.m.
"Dini ari dalam," dawn deep down : about 3 a.m.
"Empliau bebunyi," the gibbons calling : this at first streak of dawn.
"Tampak tanah," to see the ground : about 5 a.m.

I found the village of Lanchang gaily decorated with flags in my honour, and I was met at the entrance by the three chief men, the Orang Kaya, the Pengara, and the Penglima. The latter is rather a remarkable character, a talkative, pushful old man, extremely argumentative and litigious ; he is most unpopular in the village, and on this account has never been elected to the office of Orang Kaya, the nominal head of the village, but on account of his distinct ability the Sarawak Government created the special office of Penglima for him, and he runs the entire place, his two superiors in office being mere nonentities. I was conducted to the chief " Bala " of the village, which for the nonce had been converted into a guest-house, the heads having been removed and some appearance of comfort attained by rugs and a mattress spread on a bench against the wall, with the addition of a European table and chair which looked strangely out of place. I shook hands with innumerable people and distributed some arrack and tobacco ; all the women of birth, both young and old, came in and settled themselves all round me—they were most persistent in their

Plate XXI.

Land-Dayak Head-House, or Bala, of Lanchang Village on Upper Sadong River.

(From the author's photograph.)

To face p. 287.

demands for tobacco, but otherwise were not conver-
sational. I observed in the rafters a number of drums,
and one of huge size known as a *sabang*, about 4½ feet
high and 1½ in diameter ; I tried to buy it for the Museum,
but was told that it was "pemali," or tabu, being used
only at head-feasts. The Penglima told me that at
head-feasts the heads were brought down from the
rafters and put into baskets with little bamboo-tubes
filled with arrack attached to them ; the celebrants
wear fantastic costumes, with head-dresses of grass, and
after offering rice and fowls to the heads, beseech
them to send good luck in harvesting and sowing—
and in former days in war ; a great deal of food and
drink is consumed, and a dance round the heads is
performed. The Penglima's heads he declared were
very antique, and in his opinion had lost their virtue,
so he had given them to his brother, who was very
attentive to them and frequently gave them a fowl
and put rice into their mouths whenever he held a
feast. He (the Penglima), however, wanted some new
heads with skin and hair still adhering to the skulls,
and as the fighting days of the Land-Dayaks have
gone for ever, he proposed to visit the Sea-Dayaks in
the Kalaka and persuade them to give him some ; he
was careful to point out that bought heads would
have no virtue. The installing of new heads in the
Head-House is a great ceremony ; they are first slung
up on a large bamboo erection outside the Head-House
by which is erected a tall and thick bamboo, one
length of which is filled with arrack ; four old men
dance round this for a while, then one of them bores
a hole in the arrack-filled joint, and as they dance they
stop every minute or so to suck the liquor from the

bamboo till it is finished. A large hole is then cut in the bamboo, and by some sleight of hand from it is extracted a canine tooth of the Clouded Leopard, which had been placed there by divine means—this is a powerful charm sufficient to ward off bullets from the possessor. Then rice dyed yellow with turmeric is flung up to the heads, with many prayers to drive off sickness, send good crops, and so forth, the prayers being punctuated by a sort of wailing screams. The women dance in a large circle all round the central figures, and much beating of gongs and firing of guns goes on all the time. There is much feasting, which may last for four or more days, and then the heads are transferred to the Head-House.

27th.—I was waked early by the usual chorus of cock-crowing, pigs grunting and dogs snarling beneath the " Baluh" ; spent the morning in trying to photograph the unwilling natives, in taking measurements, and in buying odds and ends of ethnographical interest for the Museum. At 4 p.m. I descended from the " Baluh " and went into the inner verandah of the Penglima's house : here was arrayed a row of dishes piled up with uncooked rice, and reposing on the rice cooked eggs ; between the dishes were joints of shaved-down bamboo containing cooked " pulut" rice (*Oryza glutinosa*). Nine or ten boys battered unceasingly on a row of gongs, and an old man clad in an English soldier's red tunic and a pair of Chinese trousers sat at one of the doors leading into the verandah and chanted an immensely long prayer, whilst we sat in front of the dishes ; the prayer being at length ended, we fell to on the eggs and "pulut" rice. A man with a bowl of water in one hand, a bead-necklace in the other, sprinkled us all

Plate XXII.

Murut Head-Feast. (From the author's photograph.)

To face p. 288.

with water, dipping the necklace in the water and shaking it over us. After the meal the uncooked rice was put into baskets and presented to me, and the gongs struck up again ; the women of the village now appeared on the scene, and a gangway down the length of the verandah was cleared. A young Dayak then donned the soldier's tunic and a skirt, which was bulged out round the hips by means of a coil of plaited fibre ("tekal"), and after uttering a weird screech he stretched out his arms, assumed a most lackadaisical expression and went through a variety of postures ; the feet were not moved very much : as a rule the whole of the sole rested on the ground, and the heels were shifted occasionally. Gongs accompanied the dance, and the performer broke off several times as he was not satisfied with the rhythm in which they were beaten. The dance, which was supposed to represent the soaring of the Brahminy Kite, lasted about twenty minutes, and long before that time had elapsed the man was pouring with perspiration. He was succeeded by three women, whose dance was a very simple affair : they put small shawls round their necks, stretched out their arms, placed the feet together, and just bent up and down at the knees so as to scrape their brass leglets together, producing a clicking noise. Then two men danced a Malay sword-dance, a sort of sham-fight, very artistic and with a good deal of life-like action in it. At 8 I went up to the "Baluh" for dinner, and was amused by a very drunk old man who showed me how he could dance. I tasted some of the spirit brewed by Land-Dayaks from fermented rice, and found it far more palatable than the Chinese-made arrack, which, however, they much prefer, on account, I expect, of its higher percentage of alcohol. At 8.30

my presence in the Penglima's house was requested, and, on going down, I found the verandah packed with people and lit by smoky lamps and flaming torches ; many of the people had come from a good distance, and some young men who were celebrated as songsters, from the village of Slabi ; during the intervals of dancing these men droned at their lugubrious " pantuns," as they call their songs. The Penglima circulated amongst the crowd doling out infinitesimally small doses of arrack and pinches of tobacco, so that my limited supply of these commodities sufficed for the lot. At 10.30 I retired for the night to the Head-House and most of the people went off home, but the gayer spirits kept up the pantun-singing and gong-beating till dawn, so that I got little sleep.

28th.—As soon as I could collect enough coolies, I started back for Tabekang and arrived there at 11 a.m. Found that Jiloom, my Sea-Dayak collector, had returned from Piching, where I had sent him, and that he had brought back a number of Land-Dayak things. Amongst others he had brought a " Ton-Ton," or zither, cut out of bamboo ; the body of the instrument is one joint of bamboo and the strings are strips of bamboo cut out of the joint, left attached at their ends, and bridged up with strips of wood.[1] The performer sits cross-legged, rests the zither against one leg, beats the strings with a short

[1] This method of making stringed instruments, by raising and bridging up strips or fibres of the bamboo or reed of which the instrument is made, has a very wide geographical distribution, the range extending from India through Burma and the Malayan Archipelago eastwards to the Philippines and New Guinea. It also occurs in Madagascar, Egypt, West Africa, and parts of South America.—H. B.

stick, and beats on one end of the bamboo-joint with
his open hand ; he is accompanied by a man who beats
his hand on the top of a short length of bamboo,
making a noise like water coming out of a bottle.
Some Dayaks brought in two Tarsiers, *Tarsius spectrum*,
which appears to be not uncommon here.

29*th.*—Spent the day photographing and developing.
Bought a Flying-Squirrel, *Sciuropterus*.

30*th.*—Some natives came over to the bungalow and
I took head-measurements of a good many ; some of
the Lanchang women appeared and, to my surprise,
expressed a desire to be photographed—I was not long
in gratifying their request. An Engkro man attracted
my attention, as he presented a very different appearance
from the usual type of Land-Dayak ; he wore his hair
long at the back and with a deep fringe in front, whereas
the Land-Dayaks always shave the hair in front; he
had on a bead necklace, armlets of bark with ground-
down sections of cowries stuck in them, and plaited
fibre bracelets : altogether, he looked more like a Sea-
Dayak ; these people and the Milikin are worth investigation, as I do not believe that they ought to be classed
amongst the Land-Dayaks. Most of these people when
their head-measurements are being taken stand quite still
and unmoved like old cows, but a handsome young
Kuran Dayak with an aquiline nose and swaggering
manner fidgeted and giggled all the time that I was
measuring him, saying that he was ticklish.

31*st.*—Walked over to Piching and got a very good
reception from the people, who are singularly kind and
hospitable. The usual feast was prepared for me, but
there was no beating of gongs at it, and I was asked if
I would excuse this want of orchestral accompaniment

to the feast, as a child had died the day before in one
of the houses of the village.

September 1st.—Started at 7.30 from Tabekang with
a full crew; reached a point about a mile below Gedong
at nightfall in pouring rain; tied up to a Malay house
for the night. The river is very wide here, and the bore
on reaching these wide spaces flattens out; canoes
always make for these spots when they know that the
bore—" bena "—is due. Had a wretched night, owing to
countless mosquitoes and a leaky covering to the boat.

September 2nd.—Started at daybreak, the rain still
pouring down; at 9 a heavy storm overtook us, and
the wind was so violent that I thought we should be
blown over; the gusts, getting under the palm-leaf shelter
of the boat, caused us to heel over perilously near to the
capsizing limit : we made for one of the banks and
tied up till the worst was over. Reached Sadong at
midday.

CHAPTER XI

ANIMAL LIFE OF THE SHORES: VISIT TO A TURTLE ISLAND

BESIDES the last described expeditions, a number of others to different parts of Sarawak were made for collecting purposes, among which were trips to the mountains Matang and Santubong.

Mt. Matang, which is only a few miles from Kuching and easily accessible, was visited on several occasions; there are two comfortable bungalows on the mountain, so that collecting could be carried on with all the comforts that civilization affords. Mt. Santubong, situated at one of the two mouths of the Sarawak River, was also a favourite hunting-ground of mine, but I never succeeded in getting to the top of this mountain, as it was very steep towards the summit—in fact, almost sheer. The fauna of these two mountains, in spite of their proximity, presented well-marked and constant differences; thus some species occurring commonly on one mountain would not be found on the other. There are many analogies between insular and mountain faunas, for tracts of low-lying land intervening between isolated mountains are almost as effective barriers to the free interchange of species as are the seas which separate islands. Most of the species common to both Matang and Santubong were widely distributed lowland forms, analogous with those widely distributed mainland forms which spread on to adjacent islands.

The sea that washes the Sarawak coast affords a comparatively poor harvest to the naturalist, for it is shallow and the bottom is of fine mud, discharged by the great rivers, which, in a country where the annual rainfall averages about 130 inches, are always swollen and turbid. As I considered it of more importance to collect land animals than marine, I never devoted a great deal of attention to the latter. The marine fauna of the tropics stands in no danger of decrease on account of the depredations of man, whereas even in Sarawak, that peaceful backwater of civilization, there have been notable alterations in the land fauna in the neighbourhood of towns and Government stations within the last twenty-five years, whilst the natives themselves, by their extravagant system of cultivation, whereby tracts of jungle are annually destroyed, must be responsible in the long run for the extermination of many species. Still, it was not possible to live any length of time at Santubong without taking at least a passing interest in the animals which were to be found on the river-banks and seashore.

I had a great ambition at one time to investigate thoroughly the fauna of the mangrove-swamps, and determined to make a beginning by excavating the burrows of that aberrant Crustacean, *Thalassina anomala*, a sort of Crayfish. These creatures burrow deeply in the mud, throwing up a large cone of the material that they have excavated. One roasting hot morning

a Malay and I attacked with large mattocks one of
these cones; at the end of an hour the Malay was
knee-deep in water in a long trench that he had cut
along the track of the Crayfish's burrow, and I could
hardly see the man's back for the crowd of mosquitoes
on it, while my own hands were too busily employed
in brushing mosquitoes off my person to permit me to
dig at all. As the end of the burrow seemed as far
off as ever, we retired defeated from the field. The
investigation of a mangrove-swamp fauna I decided
henceforth to leave to some other naturalist endowed
either with the skin of a rhinoceros or with an
enthusiasm that could rise superior to acute physical
discomfort. The stems of the Nipa-palms that grew
in this swamp were closely studded with peculiar flat
shells that presented a sufficiently near resemblance
to shells of *Lingula*, a Brachiopod that has persisted
from the most ancient geological times to the present
day, to lead me at first to think that I had made a
great find. A closer examination, however, showed
that these were the shells of a true Mollusc belonging to the *Anomiacea*, a sub-order that includes the
common *Anomia ephippium* (Linn.) of Europe and is
related, though distantly, to the Oysters. The name of
this mollusc, *Ænigma ænigmatica*, shows that it had
puzzled naturalists before me. The shell is a bivalve;
the left valve, which is the only one that the observer
can see before the animal is removed from the palm-
stem to which it is attached, is elongate-oval, dark
purplish-red in colour, very thin and more or less
translucent; the right valve is much smaller, white,
transparent, and very delicate; it is perforated in
the middle, and through the hole passes a structure

called the *byssus*, which attaches the animal firmly to
the surface on which it is found.   The shells are
attached to the palm stems well above low-water mark,
and in many cases above the high-water mark of neap-
tides ; consequently for the greater part of their lives
they are exposed to the full glare and heat of a
tropical sun.   The shells, when above water, fit so
closely to the palm stems that they can hardly be
removed with the blade of a sharp knife.   Having
grown in one position, they are perfectly adapted to
all the slight irregularities and inequalities of curvature
of the palm stems, and the space under the left valve,
in which of course the animal lies, must be well-nigh
air-tight.   When the shells are immersed in water the
byssus relaxes slightly, and as this organ is attached
at one end to the inside of the left valve, and, passing
through the animal and through the right valve, at the
other to the palm stem, the effect of its relaxation is
the loosening of the left valve so that water can flow
under it and bathe the tissues of the Mollusc.   It is
only during these periods of immersion that the animal
can feed, and it is probable that it lives on small particles
that are swept into its mouth along some ciliated grooves
that traverse the foot.   Professor G. C. Bourne has made
a careful anatomical study of this animal,[1] and has
discovered some interesting features adapted to protect
it from desiccation.   In bivalve Molluscs there is a
fold of the body wall immediately underlying each valve
of the shell and enveloping the body of the Mollusc
between them; these folds are termed the mantle-lobes,
and the space between each lobe and the actual body
is the mantle-cavity.   In *Ænigma ænigmatica* the lower

[1] *Quart. Journ. Microsc. Sci.* (*N. Ser.*), LI. (1907), p. 253.

parts of the mantle-lobes, i.e. the parts near the edge of the shell, are much thickened and corrugated ; the thickenings help to seal up the mantle-cavity and the corrugations probably contain a certain amount of water, so that the mantle-cavity is always moist, and evaporation is reduced to a minimum. In fact, the tightly fitting junction between the upper or left valve and the palm stem is supplemented by an internal thick cushion which acts like the indiarubber washer of a watertight joint in a metal pipe. The mantle-cavity is also produced here and there into sinuses which run into the body, and they can be cut off from the main cavity by ridged folds with interlocking hairs. Professor Bourne considers these extensions of the mantle-cavity to be water reservoirs. One other feature of this Mollusc's anatomy is worthy of attention. There occurs on the left or upper mantle-lobe a ring of pigmented spots ; these are rudimentary eyes with cornea, lens, and retina, or at least primitive representatives of these structures. As they are situated at some distance from the edge of the mantle-lobe, it is obvious that light can only reach them through the upper valve of the shell, and since this shell is translucent, but by no means perfectly transparent, the light that reaches the eye-spots must be very dim. The structure of the eye-spots is so simple that probably the utmost extent of their powers is to discriminate between dark-ness and light, and Professor Bourne suggests that they are of use in giving warning to the animal to keep the valves of the shell closely pressed to the palm stem during the heat of the day.

Another denizen of the mangrove-swamps at Santu-bong was a little crab of the genus *Sesarma*, bright blue in colour. At low tide it could be seen running about on the mud or on the mangrove-roots, but as the tide rose the crabs retired to their burrows, bearing in their claws a lump of mud. This mud was used to plug the mouth of the burrow, the crab backing into its burrow and manipulating the mud from inside until the opening was hermetically sealed. When the tide fell again the mud plugs were pushed out and the crabs emerged into the open once more.

The great stretches of sand exposed at low tide just beyond the mouths of the Sarawak River had a characteristic fauna of their own. On one occasion, after a heavy blow in the North-East Monsoon, I found the shore strewn for at least two miles with thousands of a peculiar gelatinous Holothurian with a smooth white skin. Shoals of those queer little amphibious fish, the *Periophthalmi*, were a very characteristic element in this shore fauna. At low tide they were seen sunning themselves in shallow pools, and at the least disturbance would rush towards the sea, the flapping of their bodies and tails against the wet sand making a noise like the squattering of ducks in mud. As the eyes of these fish are situated high on the top of the head they can detect the approach of an enemy from any side very readily, and as they are easily alarmed and can move at a surprising pace, it is a matter of difficulty to catch them. The only practicable way of getting large numbers of specimens is to fire into the brown of a shoal with small dust-shot. A species of *Periophthalmus* closely allied to the shore-frequenting form is found on river banks as far inland as the influence of the tides is felt; it occurred also at Kuching in ditches, and lived in burrows well above low-water mark ; the natives assert that this species is viviparous, but I was never able to confirm the statement. It would take a long time to detail all the creatures which frequent these shallow seas and sandy shores, and as the habits of many of them have been charmingly described in Colonel A. Alcock's *A Naturalist in Indian Seas*, I will pass on to give the briefest possible account of two interesting little crabs that were found, one in the sand off Santubong, the other at Buntal, on the opposite side of the big bay.

The Santubong crab is named *Dorippe facchino*, and, as in all the species of the genus, the two hinder pairs of walking legs are reduced in size, turned upwards, and terminated by prehensile claws. In this particular species the legs hold in their claws an oval gelatinous plate on which grows a little Sea-Anemone ; the crab rests with the hinder part of the body buried in the soft mud or sand, the front part of the body and the big claws being exposed, but the former partially sheltered by the sea-anemone growing on the plate that is borne aloft by the peculiarly modified hind-legs of the crab. This is a very interesting case of symbiosis, and no doubt the crab derives much advantage from the association, for the Sea-Anemone is furnished with stinging powers that render it an unsavoury morsel to fish and other enemies of the crab. Whether the Sea-Anemone is also benefited is not so certain, but at least it is provided with a *pied-à-terre* in an environment where these creatures cannot usually flourish owing to the shifting, unstable nature of the sea-bottom. The little plate on which the Sea-Anemone grows is secreted by the crab itself, it is always of the same outline and size as the base of the Sea-Anemone, and it is marked by concentric lines of growth, showing that it has increased in size as the associated animal has grown in girth. If a crab be deprived of its burden, it manifests every sign of disturbance, and hunts about the vessel in which it is confined until it finds the object of its search, which is then hoisted up in the two hinder legs into the old position, the crab then backing down into the mud until almost concealed from view. It is difficult to imagine how the association of the two creatures commences ; how does the newly formed crab succeed in getting hold of a young unattached Sea-Anemone ? That is a very pretty problem for some one to settle.

Opposite to Santubong the character of the sea-bottom was different. Here no large river poured out its load of mud, but instead were several smaller streams draining through mangrove swamps and carrying with them waterlogged leaves and sticks. The sea-bottom was of a harder sand, and here lived another *Dorippe*, *D. astuta*, which did not bury itself in the sand, but moved about freely. It was protected from observation by a large leaf, which it invariably bore aloft in the two hinder pair of legs, and with which it covered the body completely. So close was the resemblance between one of these leaf-covered crabs and a waterlogged leaf washing to and fro in the gentle bottom-currents, that the closest scrutiny was needed to detect the presence of the crab. I think no more remarkable instance can be found of a wide difference in the habits of two closely allied species—differences evolved in response to differences of environment.

Lying some distance out at sea, off Santubong, are three coral islets, the only examples of coral formation within easy reach. The reefs were fringing reefs, but the extent of the coral was not very great ; still, it was coral, and therefore worthy of examination. The islands were much resorted to by turtles, which at night came up on the sandy foreshore and deposited their eggs in large numbers in pits which they dug in the sand and then covered over. As turtles' eggs are held in high esteem as a delicacy in the Far East, the owner-ship of these turtle islands was a valuable possession, and to prevent jealousies the Sarawak Government permitted the principal Malay chiefs to hold the islands in annual rotation. The commencement of the egg-laying season is attended with all sorts of ceremonies, known as " nyama " and " tabus." The spirits of the turtles have to be propitiated with sacrifices, and no one is allowed to land on the islands for three days after the ceremonies have begun. Most unfortunately, it was on one of these days that a friend and I elected to visit one of the islands, Satang by name, for the purpose of collecting reef-dwelling organisms. As our launch approached the island we saw some Malays gesticulating and haranguing three Chinamen in a dug-out canoe belonging to a large junk anchored about twice a stone's throw from the shore. It soon became evident that the Malays were preventing the Chinamen from landing for the purpose of getting the wood and water which they required. On our arrival we were saluted by a Malay, who courteously informed us that it was " pemali " or " tabu " for strangers to land on the island during that or the next two days. Fortunately, my friend had an unrivalled knowledge of Malays and the Malay character, and instead of precipitating a quarrel by brutally forcing his way ashore, he set to work to argue the matter in a friendly way. The magic word " prenta," i.e. Government, played a great part in the argument, and finally it was agreed that we should land on the other side of the island as far from the turtle-shrines as possible. The day was spent in reef-collecting, and in the course of it I made a discovery concerning the habits of an abundant and widely distributed Crustacean which appears worthy of record, since to the best of my knowledge the observation is new. Whilst turning over lumps of weathered coral in search of creatures harbouring below them, I noticed in one lump a cylindrical hole, evidently made by a reef-boring worm ; incautiously I put my finger into this hole, and instantly received on its tip a blow of such force as to cause a sharp pain. I quickly removed my finger from this mysterious hole and thrust down into it the end of a walking-stick. I could then feel by the jarring sensation that a rapid succession of blows was being rained on the ferrule of the stick. On withdrawing the stick, an elongate, olive-green animal that looked rather like a fish leapt out of the hole, swam with great rapidity across the pool in which I was standing, and took shelter under a large boulder. It was the work of a few moments only to upheave the boulder and grab the animal, which was then seen to be a Crustacean belonging to the group Stomatopoda and named *Gonodactylus chiragra*. As I held it in my hands it continued to deliver with its large front-legs, or chelipeds, the most persistent and painful blows on my fingers and hands, until at last I was glad to immerse it in a glass tube full of spirit. But, hey presto ! one blow of these redoubtable chelipeds and the stout glass tube was shattered, the animal dropped into the water and was swimming for dear life to the nearest shelter. Eventually it was secured and plunged into a stone jar filled with alcohol, and the animal could be heard delivering its postman's knocks against the wall of its prison until it expired. The Stomatopoda include the well-known genus *Squilla*, those elongate, almost crayfish-like Crustacea with huge raptorial claws or chelipeds, that call to mind the raptorial claws of the *Mantidæ* amongst insects. The function of these chelipeds is obvious : they are admirably adapted for grasping and holding the creatures on which the *Squilla* feeds. But in *Gonodactylus chiragra* the chelipeds are not in the least adapted for grasping purposes ; the basal joint is long and very robust—its apex carries a smaller dumb-bell shaped joint, a small quadrangular joint intervening ; this "dumb-bell" joint shuts down on the lower side of the basal joint, and its apex bears the terminal joint, which is so hinged that it shuts back on the upper face of the "dumb-bell" joint. The terminal joint is produced to form a spine, but its base forms a more or less rounded and smooth knob—the percussive part of the whole apparatus. The animal rests near the top of its burrow or hole with the chelipeds drawn up in front of it in exactly the attitude which a Mantis adopts when at rest ; on the approach of an intruder the "dumb-bell" joint, with the terminal joint closely applied to its upper surface, is violently pushed or flung out by the action of the strong muscles inside the robust basal joint. The action is as rapid as that of a strong spring, and the force of the blow has to be felt to be appreciated, and I am quite certain that it is sufficient to stun any small fish or other Crustacea.

I cannot say whether the *Gonodactylus* uses its chelipeds in defence only, but it is conceivable that a stunned animal could be held between the basal and " dumb-bell " joints and quietly devoured ; while the *Squilla*, not stunning its prey first, has need of a more efficient grasping apparatus.

CHAPTER XII

NATIVES OF BORNEO

BEFORE the ethnography of Borneo had been studied
the inhabitants of that great island were termed
collectively Dayaks, and the term is still applied by many
continental ethnologists to tribes that have few affinities
with Dayaks in the strictest sense of the word. This
loose application of the term Dayak leads to immense
confusion, for to say that the Dayaks are the inhabitants
of Borneo is as far from a complete statement of fact as
it would be to say that Yorkshiremen or Welshmen are
the inhabitants of the British Isles. Sir James Brooke,
first Rajah of Sarawak, was one of the earliest to attempt
a classification of the Sarawak tribes. In his day the
people inhabiting the upper waters of the Sarawak and
Sadong Rivers were continually subjected to raids by
Malays and their mercenaries, the men of the Saribas
and Batang Lupar Rivers. Sir James Brooke recognized
that the raided and the raiders belonged to two distinct
stocks; to the first, inasmuch as they lived inland in
hilly country, he applied the name Land- or Hill-Dayaks;
to the second, since they came across the sea from their
own headquarters to those of their victims, he applied
the name Sea-Dayaks. The names have stuck in spite

of being rather cumbersome, and in the case of the
Sea-Dayaks very inappropriate. Explorations in Sarawak,
British North Borneo, and Dutch Borneo have revealed
the presence of a whole host of tribes, each with a
distinctive name and a well-defined area of distribution,
but it is only within recent years that it has become
possible to sort these tribes out into a few main cate-
gories. I will not try to give a complete list of all the
tribes of Borneo, but will try rather to sketch the bare
outlines of a scheme of classification which has been
compiled from the writings of the leading authorities on
the subject. Most ethnologists now agree that in the
islands of the Malay Archipelago there exists, in addition
to the coastal, round-headed Malayan stock, an older,
narrow-headed race to which the term Indonesian has
been applied; such, to take a few examples, are the
Tenggerese of Java, the Battaks of Sumatra, the Muruts
and Land-Dayaks of Borneo. The main feature of the
ethnography of the Malay Archipelago then is, that
the centres of the islands are occupied by a narrow-
headed, or at any rate only moderately broad-headed,
race, while the coasts are inhabited by a broad-headed
people. Any further subdivision in the present state
of our knowledge can only be tentative. Concerning
Borneo the most recently published views are those of
Dr. Charles Hose[1] and myself. We distinguish a typical
Indonesian stock that we regard as the oldest stock
extant in the island, and we suppose that it slowly filtered
into Borneo in far distant times from various sources,
but mainly from Further India. To these Indonesians,

[1] Hose and Shelford, *Journ. Anthrop. Inst.*, XXXVI. (*N. Ser.*), IX.
(1906), pp. 60–3. See also the fuller statement in *Pagan Tribes of
Borneo*, Hose and McDougall.

divisible into many different tribes, the generic name of Kalamantan has been applied, to distinguish them from the Indonesians in other islands of the Archipelago. Pulo Kalamantan is the name applied by Malays to the island of Borneo, and is possibly derived from the word *lemanta* (raw sago), sago having been one of the principal exports of Borneo for many generations. When the country was thinly covered with Kalamantans there followed successive immigrations of Kenyahs, a race characterized in the main by a moderate brachycephaly; these mixed with their Kalamantan predecessors, so that at the present day there are found tribes difficult to place in either category. At some period, the length of which is quite uncertain, there followed up the principal rivers of eastern and southeastern Borneo the Kayans, a powerful race, that drove before them the weaker Kalamantan and Kenyah tribes; some of the Kenyah tribes amalgamated more or less with the Kayans, and at the present day are superficially very like them. The wave of immigration still continuing to flow, the Kayans, and those Kenyahs who had not amalgamated with the Kalamantans, swept over the great watershed dividing Sarawak from Dutch Borneo, and occupied the Baram and Rejang Rivers in Sarawak. Last of all came the Sea-Dayak, a brachycephalic Malayan; advancing up the Kapuas from the southwest, he drove all before him and overflowed into the Batang Lupar and adjacent rivers in Sarawak, where to this day he remains in great force. In recent years the Sea-Dayak has migrated in numbers to the Baram and Rejang Rivers, and advancing up these he is slowly but surely driving before him the Kenyahs and Kayans who in ancient times moved down these rivers from their sources. The Malays, a maritime, trading people, are found on the coasts and cannot be regarded as an indigenous race ; they have spread all over the Malay Archipelago and Malay Peninsula from a centre which has been fixed by universal consent at Menangkabau, in Sumatra. Their civilization is of a much higher order than that of any of the savage tribes, and at one time they exercised a nominal sway over the whole island of Borneo. If we plot out roughly on a map of Borneo the distribution of the various tribes at the present day, we get a sort of epitome of the changes that have taken place in the past. We see that the Kalamantans are congregated in some force in two parts of the island, the north-east and the west ; we see furthermore that there are no large rivers in these parts, and this gives us the clue. The great rivers of a densely forested land are its highways, and up these rivers have poured the waves of immigration, not up the small rivers ; the lands watered by small rivers are then the last refuges of the Kalamantans, now weakly and decadent ; either they have been driven here by Kenyahs, Kayans, and Sea-Dayaks, or they have lived here ever since the time when in the heyday of their vigour they spread all over Borneo. Other Kalamantan tribes, as, for example, the Kalabits, Ot-Danum, and Kahayan, linger on in the interior highlands, mere flotsam and jetsam thrown high and dry by the rushing tide that submerged so many others, such as the Long Utan, now only a memory. Some of these people, living far from great rivers, are ignorant of the way in which to handle a canoe, and are struck dumb with awe and fear when at the instance of the white man they have been brought down from their mountain homes and have viewed for the first time great expanses of water. In the Batang-Lupar low-country linger on the last remnants of the Srus, in the Rejang the Kanowits and Tanjongs, decadent tribes tottering on the verge of extinction, their ancient habits and customs forgotten, melancholy evidence of the severity of the struggle for existence amongst savage communities. On the coast at Matu, Oya, and Muka are found the Milanos, a Kalamantan tribe that has to a great extent adopted the Mohammedan religion and Malay customs : they are great fishermen, and are perhaps in less danger of extinction than related tribes ; whether they were driven down to the coast by the immigration of Kayans and Kenyahs, sweeping over the watershed of Borneo, or whether they, like the Land-Dayaks in the west, and the Muruts and Dusuns in the north-east, are " outliers "—to use a geological expression—of a former continuous stratum, is quite uncertain. Concerning one tribe, the Punans, there is considerable doubt : they are a nomadic people, with no fixed abode ; they wander through the jungle in search of the wild sago-palm, which is their staple diet, and of jungle produce such as rattans, camphor, and gutta-percha, which they barter with more settled tribes and with such enterprising Chinese and Malay traders as penetrate to the interior. Dr. Haddon of Cambridge and Dr. Nieuwenhuis of Leyden, than whom there are none better qualified to pass an opinion on the matter, regard the Punans as a race apart ; the former because head-measurements show them to be moderately broad-headed, the latter because of their singular habits of life. Dr. Hose, however—and I am inclined to agree with him—considers them to be of Kalamantan stock.

Dr. Haddon [1] would abolish the term Dayak altogether on account of the confusion that has been
caused by its inaccurate use ; and to the Sea-Dayaks
he applies the term Iban, a corruption of the Kayan
"ivan," [2] a man, and a term applied to themselves by
the Sea-Dayaks.   For the Land-Dayaks he would prefer
to use another term, or would as an alternative call
them the Dayaks.   Dayak is a word that cannot now
be eradicated, and as the Sea-Dayaks are to-day the
dominant tribe in Borneo and are destined, I fear,
eventually to oust from Sarawak, at any rate, nearly all
the other tribes, I would apply the word Dayak to them
alone.   Like Dr. Haddon, I still search for a satisfactory
name for the Land-Dayaks.[3]

The following table will show in a succinct manner
the ideas of classification discussed above :—

[The author had written below his concluding paragraph " Repro-
duce Table from Tatu Paper," referring to his own and Dr. C. Hose's
" Materials for a Study of Tatu in Borneo." [4]   The greater part of
this memoir is reproduced in Hose and McDougall's *Pagan Tribes of
Borneo*, vol. I. p. 245, and, as Dr. A. C. Haddon's Appendix to vol. II.
of the same work includes on p. 320 a more recent classification
drawn up by Dr. Hose, I have with his kind consent reprinted this
rather than the earlier one.   Dr. Haddon in adopting this classification states (p. 319, *n.* 1) that "it will be found to agree very closely
with the anthropometric data," and that " we may regard it as
expressing the present state of our knowledge of the affinities of the
several tribes."—E. B. P.]

---

[1] In his memoir, " A Sketch of the Ethnography of Sarawak,"
Archivio per l'Antropologia e l'Etnologia, XXXI. (1901), pp. 341–55.

[2] Ivan is a Kayan word meaning a person who moves from his
home to that of some one else—as in the case of marriage.—C. H.

[3] It would probably be simpler to retain the term Dayak for the
" Land-Dayaks" and to call the " Sea-Dayaks " Iban.—H. B.

[4] *Journ. Anthrop. Inst.*, XXXVI. (*N. Ser.*), IX. (1906), pp. 60–91.

NATIVES OF BORNEO 311

A Classification of the Peoples of Sarawak.

I. Murut Group :
Murut, Pandaruan, Tagal, Dusun ;
Kalabit, Lepu Potong ;
Adang, Tring.
II. Klemantan Group :
1. South-western Group :
Land-Dayaks ;
[Certain tribes of Netherlands Borneo] ;
Maloh.
2. Central Group :
a. Baram sub-group : Bisaya, Tabun, Orang Bukit, Kadayan, Pliet, Long Pata, Long Akar.
b. Barawan sub-group : Murik, Long Julan, Long Ulai, Batu Blah, Long Kiput, Lelak, Barawan, Sakapan, Kajaman.
c. Bakatan sub-group : Seping, Tanjong, Kanawit, Bakatan, Lugat.
3. Sebop Group :
Malang, Tabalo, Long Pokun, Sebop, Lerong ;
Milanau (including Narom and Miri).
III. Punan Group :
Punan, Ukit, Siduan, Sigalang.
IV. Kenyah Group :
Madang, Long Dallo, Apoh, Long Sinong, Long Lika Bulu, Long Tikan.
V. Kayan Group.
VI. Iban Group :
Iban (Sea Dayaks) and Sibuyau.

NOTES

NOTE 1, p. xxiv.—*Annual Cost of Sarawak Museum.* The author had not filled in the amount, which has been calculated from the following statement of expenditure for 1905 in *The Sarawak Gazette*, XXXV. (1905), p. 117 :—

Sarawak Museum—				$	c.
Establishment	...	...	...	4,836	43
Furniture and Stores	...	...	...	155	06
Purchase of Specimens ...		...	...	405	45
Miscellaneous	...	...	...	964	47
Total	...	...	...	6,361	41

Dr. Hose has kindly given me the following information as to the Sarawak currency : " We use the Straits dollar, the value of which is 2s. 4d. There are, however, Sarawak half-dollars, 20-cent and 10-cent silver pieces ; and also copper coins, 1 cent and ½ cent. 100 cents go to 1 dollar. 1 cent is worth just over a farthing, its exact value being ·28d." The value of 6,361.41 dollars is therefore approximately £742 5s.—E. B. P.

NOTE 2, p. 12.—The " Soursop," *Anona muricata*, may have been first introduced by the Dutch.—C. H.

NOTE 3, p. 13.—A pair of *Nasalis* which I tried to bring to England suffered so severely from sea-sickness that both died before reaching Colombo.—C. H.

NOTE 4, p. 29, n. 1.—*Kink-tailed Siamese Cats.* Dr. H. O. Forbes kindly writes :—

"It is many a year since I made some remarks at the Liverpool Biological Society—probably four or five if I may venture a date—on that kink-tailed, blue-eyed, Siamese Cat. My memory is vague as to their publication or not. My remarks referred to the interest I had in exhibiting the creature's skin from the occurrence in the East of what I had noted as extremely common, if not universal, in the cats of Portugal when I lived there about 1876. The kink, I was told, was there believed to have become hereditary from a custom long practised by the Portuguese of pinching or breaking the tails of the new-born kittens, and it would be of special interest if the fact could be established that the kink in Malayan cats' tails had been communicated to them through those imported by the early Portuguese into the East. My recollection is that I exhibited the *skin*—presented to the Liverpool Museum—of the cat in question only, and that the body—presented to Herdman after removal by my taxidermist from the skin—was dissected and the anatomical data discussed by him at the same meeting. If I can trust my memory, the tail of this particular cat, though short and kinked, had its full number of vertebræ, some of them reduced in size and wedge-shaped (*bones* not *cartilage*), which produced the kink. These were really deformed vertebræ, which, together with the undeformed vertebræ, completed the full number found in normal tails of *Felis domestica*."

Professor W. A. Herdman, F.R.S., has written, saying that his memory agreed with that of Dr. Forbes. He also kindly enclosed the following copy of all that was published on the subject :—

From *Proceedings of the Liverpool Biological Soc.*, vol. IX. (1895), p. xi.

"At the 4th meeting of the session, on Jan. 11, 1895, Prof. Gotch, President, in the chair.

" I. . . .

" 2. Dr. H. O. Forbes and Prof. Herdman, F.R.S., described some of the anatomical peculiarities of the tail of a Siamese Cat belonging to Mr. Richard D. Holt. Mr. Ridley, of the Botanic Gardens, Singapore, added some further remarks on the habits of the animals. The skeleton and stuffed specimen were exhibited."

The subject seems to be well worthy of detailed investigation, and breeding experiments on Mendelian lines may be expected to yield interesting results.—E. B. P.

NOTE 5, p. 32.—*Prehensile-tailed Mammals in Old World.* A. R. Wallace states in his *Malay Archipelago*, 1869, vol. I., p. 211, that the tail of Galeopithecus " is prehensile, and is probably made use of as an additional support while feeding." Mr. Oldfield Thomas, F.R.S., "doubts whether the tail of *Galeopithecus* is prehensile, as it is included to the tip in the interfemoral membrane, and its under side is hairy to the end. Probably, as with Bats, it is used to retain insect captures of sorts, its general build being very much as in many Bats. It is, however, curled downwards at the end, and the hook so made can hardly help sometimes finding itself round branches, even if not deliberately used for the purpose."—E. B. P.

NOTE 6, p. 53.—*Egg of the Frog-Mouth.* So far as we know, eggs are turned over periodically during incubation, and adhesion to the nest would render this difficult. Specially directed observation is required.—H. B.

NOTE 7, p. 53.—The nests of *Collocalia lowi* are bought by the Chinese at from $80 to $100 a *pikul* (133⅓ lbs.), those of *C. fuciphaga* at from $10 to $20 a *kati* (1⅓ lbs.).—C. H.

NOTE 8, p. 84.—*Change of Colour on Immersion in Formalin.* The author's experience with the snake may be compared with Dr. G. B. Longstaff's Chameleon, *C. dilepis*, which assumed its palest colora-tion—"a uniform pale yellowish colour"—when chloroformed. *Butterfly-hunting*, etc., 1912, p. 216.—E. B. P.

NOTE 9, Plate XIII, facing p. 105.—*The Flying Frog.* The author had intended, but was unable, to include Frogs in Chapter IV. Among his drawings, however, were found the two figures on this Plate. Mr. Boulenger, F.R.S., informs me that the upper figure is the Bornean Flying Frog, *Rhacophorus nigropalmatus*, and that it is well worth publishing. A description of the Flying Frog is given by Wallace (with a figure) in his *Malay Archipelago* (pp. 59–61, vol. I., 1869 edition), and by M. Siedlecki, of Krakau, in *Bull. Acad. des Sci. de Cracovie*, 1908, pp. 682–89, and in *Biol. Centralblatt*, Leipzig, XXIX. (1909), No. 22, pp. 704–14 ; No. 23, pp. 715–37. In flying, or rather gliding, the limbs are held so close to the body that the feet make one continuous surface with it, while the lungs are strongly inflated. The frog can alter its direction in the air by powerful strokes with its hind legs.

Mr. Boulenger cannot decide whether the lower figure represents the tadpoles of the same species, but it certainly shows the de-velopment of some tree-haunting species which, like *Rhacophorus*, surrounds its eggs with a mass of froth enclosed between leaves.—E. B. P.

NOTE 10, p. 115 *n.*—*The Common Cockroach found wild in Russia.* Mr. North has kindly looked up the reference. The full title of the paper is " Adelung (N. von) Beiträge zur orthopteren fauna der südlichen Krim, pp. 388–413." The section referred to deals with *Stylopyga orientalis*, L., pp. 401–2. The author remarks that of nineteen specimens examined *all* were taken in the open under dead leaves and sticks.—E. B. P.

NOTE 11, p. 149.—*Stick-Insects* (*Phasmidæ*). These insects are very abundant any time during the day when trees are being felled, numbers being disturbed by the fall of each tall forest tree.—C. H.

NOTE 12, p. 150.—*Heteropteryx grayi*. Usually met with on the ground. The native name is "Senantun."—C. H.

NOTE 13, p. 156 *n.*—*Dr. Koningsberger on Collyris Larvæ*. Mr. North, who has kindly looked up the reference quoted by the author, finds that it is only the general title of the Bulletins of various Botanic gardens in the Dutch E. Indies, and unless the *place* is given the reference is useless. It is *not* Buitenzorg, for there are no papers by Koningsberger in the issue of 1901 or 1910 or any other between these dates. The reference is probably to the following paper : "Koningsberger (J. C.) en Zimmerman (A). De dierlijke Vijanden der Koffie cultur op Java [the animal pests of coffee culture in Java], Part II, Med.'s Landen Plantentuin, Batavia, 1901." Part I was published in 1897.—E. B. P.

NOTE 14, p. 173 *n.* 2.—*The Light of Lampyridæ, etc.* When in Jamaica this winter (1915–16) several large fawn-coloured Lampyrids flew to the lamp on the verandah and settled on the wall, where they were attacked by a rather small spider which had its habitation in holes in the wall. I rescued one from a spider, and it recovered, but immediately flew back to the same spot and was attacked again. The Lampyrid kept flashing its light the whole time, but it did not keep off the spider by this defence. Of course the wall was brightly lighted, so possibly the flashlight was not in that case conspicuous enough. But the real use of the light, if not for defence, I do not understand.—H. N. R.

NOTE 15, p. 174.—*Malacoderm Larvæ*. Mr. C. J. Gahan informs me that he does not know of any observations similar to that recorded by Mr. E. J. Bles, "but it is known that Lampyrid larvæ use the terminal sucker to clean their head and limbs from the slime of the snail after having fed on the latter." It is probable that Mr. Bles's observation points to the use of a secretion which prevents the slime from adhering closely to the larva, thus making its removal easy.—E. B. P.

NOTE 16, p. 181.—*Laccoptera sp.* Dr. D. Sharp fears that there is no means of determining the species, of which the specific name had been left blank in the author's manuscript. It does not appear to be a species mentioned in the papers quoted.—E. B. P,

NOTE 17, p. 221.—*Migrating Swarm of Cirrochroa bajadeta.* I have seen this taking place in July at Miri in the Baram district, Sarawak.—C. H.

NOTE 18, p. 235.—*A. R. Wallace and Mimicry of a Brenthid.* The statement was apparently not published by Wallace himself, and I had some difficulty in verifying it. It is quoted by F. P. Pascoe, evidently from information supplied to him by Wallace or noted on a Wallace specimen (*Trans. Ent. Soc.*, 3 Ser., III. [1864–9], p. 113). —E. B. P.

NOTE 19, p. 250.—*Synchronous Flashing by Fire-Flies.* See also Edward S. Morse on " Fire-flies flashing in unison," in *Science* (N.S., vol. XLIII., No. 1101, pp. 169–170, Feb. 4, 1916), and K. G. Blair on " Luminous Insects" in *Nature* (1915–16, XCVI., p. 411). It is strange that the phenomenon should be so rare. Prof. Morse saw it once fifty years ago in Gorham, Maine, but although he has been on the look-out for it ever since, has never seen it again.—E. B. P.

NOTE 20, bearing on Plate XVII, facing p. 253, and XX, facing p. 284.—*A Head-hunting Expedition in Recent Years.* The following account of " The Recent Troubles in the Rejang River" was contributed by R. Shelford to *The Sarawak Gazette*, XXXIV. (1904), p. 211.

"In the beginning of September [1904] information was laid at Sibu to the effect that a party of forty-three Ulu Ai Dayaks from the Yong, Chermin, Sut, Kapit and Palagus rivers had started off to attack the Punans in the Mujong River. Dr. C. Hose followed up the party at once and succeeded in overtaking one boat containing eight men who were brought back to Kapit ; a small force was sent after the remaining thirty-five with instructions to arrest or to attack them, the force however failing in its objective returned to Kapit. Later in the month news was brought that the thirty-five Ulu Ai had killed twelve Punans on the 15th, the slaughter being attended with circumstances of revolting brutality. The Punans had entertained the Dayaks overnight with their customary hospitality, but in the morning the Dayaks fell on their hosts and killed all, men and women indiscriminately ; one girl clung to her lover of the previous night in the hope that he would spare her at least but she was pushed off and struck down without mercy. On the 22nd Dr. C. Hose again arrived at Kapit, this time determined to mete out punishment with no sparing hand ; he found that one of the leaders of the murderous gang had already been arrested in Kapit bazaar by the orders of Mr. F. de Rozario, and small parties of loyal Dayaks were at once dispatched to the various homes of the other murderers with strict injunctions to bring back the guilty or, persuasion and threats failing, to attack them. With one exception these parties were successful in their missions and the Pengulus of the various houses for the most part brought down themselves those implicated in the Punan massacre. On the 29th news was brought that four of the worst characters, men from the Lamanak River, were intending to evade justice by crossing over to the Empran district, there to join the notorious Bantin ; on hearing this thirty men under Pengulu Dalam Munan were dispatched with orders to bring back the recalcitrant four, dead or alive ; instructions were issued to the small but well-armed force at 5 p.m. and by 5.30 p.m. the boats had started up-river ; at nightfall it came on its quarry lodging in the house of Umbi in the Wong River ; three of the ruffians were at once sent down to Kapit under escort, but Munan for judicious reasons of his own stayed with the other till next day when he too was brought down and incarcerated in company with his fellow-murderers. Eleven in all of the leaders and worst characters were imprisoned and a fine of $5,200 in old jars and gongs was levied on the remaining thirty-two of the gang ; of this sum $1,200 is to be paid to the Punans as compensation (*pati nyawa*), the property looted from them is to be restored and the heads, all of which were recovered, are now buried at Sibu. From the date of issue of Dr. C. Hose's mandate to the close of the proceedings numerous Dayaks might be seen daily wending their way to Kapit fort, some bearing on their backs the precious jars and gongs in which they had been mulcted ; each jar as it was brought in was carefully examined and its value assessed, whilst the gongs were weighed and their worth readily calculated ; in a week's time a goodly array of these forms of Dayak currency stood in the fort. Care was exercised in every individual case to fix the fine in proportion to the gravity of the offence, thus, the eight men who were overtaken by Dr. C. Hose whilst on their way to attack the Punans were fined only $20 apiece ; on the other hand, one evil character failing to pay the requisite amount had his parang, ivory armlets and coat stripped from him to make the full tale complete. During the week of trouble the supply of salt was entirely cut off from innocent and guilty alike and this severe action far from exciting any animosity against the Government amongst the loyal Dayaks stimulated them to fresh efforts to secure all the guilty men as they realized that the embargo would not be removed till that object was achieved.

" A loyal Dayak, Balin by name, has been entrusted with the task of bearing to the Punans their stolen property and some presents ; lest the Punans should echo the well-known saying of the suspicious Trojan, " Timeo Danaos et dona ferentes," Balin takes with him as a token of genuine peace a white tunic of Dr. Hose's ; needless to say there is no chance of the Punans mistaking a garment of such Gargantuan proportions for the property of anyone, other than the original owner. On the 30th the entire party of ruffians having been secured and the fine paid up almost to the uttermost farthing Dr. Hose returned to Sibu with his prisoners and spoil ; the eleven desperate characters were lodged in gaol and the remainder with some of their relations have been placed across river within range of the fort guns and Munan will be responsible for their good behaviour in the future. To employ a term in use amongst gold miners, the whole "clean-up" occupied eight days or to be more exact, fifteen days from the date of the murder to the return to Sibu of the punitive party. It would hardly be seemly for one who holds no executive office in the Government of Sarawak to criticise or even comment on the conduct of the whole affair, but it is difficult to refrain from remarking that the decision and rapid action of Dr. Hose created an enormous impression amongst the Dayaks at and around Kapit ; the disaffected and lukewarm were convinced that the arms of law and order in Sarawak were far from paralysed, whilst the loyal cordially approved of every step taken and zealously lent their aid in bringing the guilty to justice, Pengulus Munan and Mroum with all their followers being especially prominent."

No information concerning Plates XVII. and XX. was found among Mr. Shelford's notes except that conveyed in the respective titles—"The start of a Head-hunting Expedition" and " Punan heads," but Dr. Hose's recollection, together with the above article from *The Sarawak Gazette*, makes it clear that the heads were those recovered from the murderers and photographed before they were buried. Dr. Hose believes that the expedition was one sent out from Kapit by him to arrest the murderers. If this be so, it was a Head-recovering rather than a Head-hunting Expedition. Mr. Shelford took these photographs when he was staying with Dr. Hose at Kapit.—E. B. P.

NOTE 21, p. 268.—The word for the Supreme Being had been left blank by the author. Dr. A. C. Haddon, F.R.S., has kindly sent me the following statement from *The Natives of Sarawak and British North Borneo*. H. Ling Roth, I. (1896), p. 165. " Tŭpa is so called from *tŭpa* the Dyak form of the Malay word *tŭmpa*, to forge as a blacksmith—because he created mankind and everything that draws the breath of life, and daily preserves them by his power and goodness.

"Tenŭbi made the earth and all that grows upon it, and, by his unceasing care, causes it to flourish and to give seed to the sower and bread to the eater.

"Some Land-Dyaks say that Tŭpa and Tenŭbi are but different names for the same great being—the creator and preserver of all things both visible and invisible—a view which the Rev. W. Chalmers inclines to as the original and true one."

Neither Mr. Balfour, Dr. Haddon, Dr. Hose, Dr. McDougall, nor Mr. Ling Roth can say what the author had in his mind in the passage on p. 268 here referred to. It is possible that Mr. Shelford was thinking not of Tŭpa but some other word which would give the clue.

Concerning the refusal to eat deer, Dr. Hose tells me that several Bornean tribes refuse to eat any horned cattle, and that some Land-Dayaks consider themselves to be related to deer, into which they believe certain of their people have changed.—E. B. P.

The Sarawak Museum, Kuching. (From the author's photograph.)

Plate XXIII.

The Fish Market and other Public Buildings, Kuching, from the Sarawak River. The top of the Mosque is seen in the distance. (From the author's photograph.)

Plate XXIV.

Kuching, across the Sarawak River, from the Astana, or Rajah's Palace. (From the author's photograph.)

Plate XXV.

Plate XXVI.

The Astana, or Rajah's Palace, Kuching. (From the author's photograph.)

The Astana, Kuching, from the Sarawak River. (From the author's photograph.)

Plate XXVII.

The Sarawak River, Kuching, on Regatta Day : the Astana in the distance. (From the author's photograph.)

Plate XXVIII.

The paddock and two views of the racecourse, Kuching. (From the author's photographs.)

Plate XXIX.

The Fort, Kuching, from the Sarawak River. (From the author's photograph.)

Plate XXX.

The Public Offices, Kuching. (From the author's photograph.)

Plate XXXI.

The Square Tower, occupied by the guard, and the Gaol, Kuching. (From the author's photograph.)

Plate XXXII.

INDEX

22

*

INDEX

hatching of, 142–6; larvæ of, 143; parasites of, 143

Marmessoidea quadriguttata, 147

Marshall, Dr. G. A. K., on a terrifying Mantis, 132; on distasteful *Lycidæ*, 165; on birds eating butterflies, 208, 222; on a weevil as model, 235

Matang, Mt., 216, 221, 237, 262, 274, 293–4

McDougall, W., 318 n. 21; "Pagan Tribes," &c., by Hose and, 284 n., 306 n., 310

Megalocolus notator, 217

Melanism in *Pierinæ*, 225

Melanitis ismene, 220

Melastoma, 138, 139

Melipona, 35; *apicalis*, 216–17; *lacteifasciata*, 216–17; evidence of protection, 216–17; mimicry of, 217, 242–3

Menangkabau, 308

Menexenus, 155 n.

Metallyticus semianeus, 142

Metriona trivittata, 180, Pl. XV (facing 181)

Mimetic series of Squirrels and Tree-Shrews, 25; of insects resembling Lycid beetles, 241–2, 244–5; of Longicorn beetles, 241, 243–6

Mimicry, xx; between Squirrels and Tree-Shrews, 24–7; aggressive, 25, 56–7; in Musteline Carnivora, 29–31; of Drongo by Cuckoo, 56; in snakes, 101–3; of and by Hemiptera (bugs), 137, 224, 242; by young Mantis, 137; Batesian and Müllerian, 206 *et seqq.*; by moths of *Pierinæ*, 209, of *Euplœinæ* 223, of Hemiptera and *Lycidæ* 224, 242; of Tiger-Beetles, 210, 238, 245; of Danaine butterflies by *Elymnias*, 211–14; in *Pierinæ*, 222; of *Melipona* bees, 217, 242–3; of Lycid beetles, 228, 239–45; of snakes by caterpillars, 229; of ants by caterpillar, 230 (Pl. XVI), by spider, 231 (Pl. XVI),

by beetles, 233, 243; *see also* Longicorns

Minchin, Prof., adventure with cobra, 100

Mitchell, Dr. P. Chalmers, experiments with snakes on Primates, 75–6; on Python swallowing prey, 88–9

Mongoose, 32

Monomorium pharaonis, 185

Mormolyce phyllodes, 162; habits of larva, 163–4

Morse, E. S., on Fire-flies, 316 n. 19

Moths, mimicry by, 209, 223–4, 242; attracted to light at Mt. Penrisen, 262

Moulton, J. C., 52 (Pl. IX from photograph of), 54; "Trilobite-Larvæ" brought to England by, Pl. XIV (facing 169)

Mouse-deer, 44, 45

Mud-turtles, 113

Muir, F., on *Collyris*, 159, 160; on egg-laying of *Cassididæ*,175–8,181 n., 182

Müller, Fritz, on mimicry, 206–7

"Munsang" (Musang), 33; coffee-berries eaten by, 33, 34

Murray, on *Prisopus*, 127 n.

Murut, 306, 309, 311; Head Feast of, Pl. XXII (facing 288)

Mus ephippum, 37; *neglectus, rattus, sabanus*, 38

Museum, Sarawak, at Kuching, xxiv–v; annual cost of, 312; Pl. XXIII (end of vol.)

Mydaus javanicus, meliceps, 30

Mygnimia, 232

Myosoma, 228

Myotis, 20

Myrmecodia, 160, 186–92, 199, 204; *tuberosa*, 187–8

Myrmecophilous plants, 185–205; table of, 187

Naia tripudians, 91, 92; *bungarus*, 92

A NATURALIST IN BORNEO

50p

7/12